Braided Lives

Thank you for all you
do for the Mercy Mission
Sr Katherine

Braided Lives

The Sisters of Mercy in Sacramento, 1857–2008

Mary Katherine Doyle RSM

AMERICA
THROUGH TIME®
ADDING COLOR TO AMERICAN HISTORY

America Through Time is an imprint of Fonthill Media LLC
www.through-time.com
office@through-time.com

Published by Arcadia Publishing by arrangement with Fonthill Media LLC
For all general information, please contact Arcadia Publishing:
Telephone: 843-853-2070
Fax: 843-853-0044
E-mail: sales@arcadiapublishing.com
For customer service and orders:
Toll-Free 1-888-313-2665

www.arcadiapublishing.com

First published 2022

ISBN 978-1-63499-376-0

Typeset in 10.5pt on 13pt Sabon
Printed and bound in England

Preface

As you begin this story, know that it springs from two roots—one of longing, the other of wondering. It is a story about both past and present for it is about Sacramento's Sisters of Mercy. The Sisters of Mercy came to Sacramento over 160 years ago, yet they remain a vital part of its life today. This circle of women helped to build the infrastructure of the town, offered women a path of autonomy, and provided healing both in times of crisis and in the day to day. Knowing their accomplishments stirred in me a longing. I wanted to know more about these women and discover what they say to us now. I wondered how a small group of women could have made such an impact upon both individuals and a whole city. What kind of vision and practice, love and challenge made that possible? I realized that the history of Sacramento and the story of the sisters were braided together, each separate but intricately linked.

Sacramento is part of my soul marrow. I was born here and absorbed its stories and spirit throughout my whole life. Bernice, my mother, was a woman of the foothills, a gold miner's daughter to be exact. Hers was a family with deep roots in the American story. Her ancestors, Joseph and Henry Merriam, came to Massachusetts in the 1600s, fought in the Revolutionary War, and finally moved to Philadelphia. My dad, James, was the son of Irish immigrants. They arrived in Sacramento on the same day that our Sacramento soldiers were leaving for the Spanish–American War. My paternal grandparents were farmers and they worked a farm near the Elkhorn ferry on the Sacramento River. My grandmother, born just as the American Civil War ended in 1865, left the poverty of post-famine Ireland as a young teen. She ventured to England and worked in an English high house. There she learned to be a great cook and, after arriving in Sacramento, opened a riverside restaurant for steamers going up and down the Sacramento River.

As a child, I heard their stories of the early days of the city and got caught up in its history and its mystery. I wanted to know more about the story of which I was a part. Sacramento's story is my story, too. Yet there is another story braided into that narrative. It is the story of a circle of women who made a significant difference in the life of the city—the story of the Sisters of Mercy.

Mercy women have always intersected with my life. My grandparents traveled to California with the Redmonds, close friends from their village in Wexford, Ireland. While my grandparents headed for the fertile farmlands around Sacramento, the Redmonds settled in San Francisco. During the summer, the Redmond girls, Mary and Catherine, would come upriver and stay with my grandparents. Both entered the Sisters of Mercy in Sacramento and were my first link to the Sisters of Mercy for I was their namesake. I was born in Mercy Hospital and had Mercy sisters for teachers. In due time, I became part of that circle of women myself, for I am a Sister of Mercy. I am part of both the Mercy story as well as the Sacramento story.

As I explored the story of the sisters in Sacramento, I found that they left a vision that still is true today. They believed that you can do more together; that the only essential prerequisite required to serve need is a love that has no boundaries; that you achieve most when you empower people to be their best selves. These beliefs shaped their response to the world around them. I cannot help but wonder: "If they could do what they did, can we do the same for our times? Can churches, small faith communities, and individuals be that same light and witness?" If you also would like to find the answer to that question, and are ready to be challenged, inspired, or moved to wonder, risk entering their story—the story of Sacramento's Sisters of Mercy.

Acknowledgments

Gathering and telling a story as vast as that of the Sisters of Mercy in Sacramento could never be done alone. It is a task that took many, many participants. I owe a great debt of gratitude to my religious community who supported this project, especially Sister Patricia McDermott, president of the Sisters of Mercy of the Americas, and Sister Susan Sanders, former president of the West Midwest Community, who allowed me the time and resources to discover the richness of our heritage. I also owe a debt of thanks to the Louisville Institute for providing a generous pastoral study grant to help underwrite the expenses of the undertaking. Their assistance and support were great blessings. My deepest appreciation and thanks go to all the Fonthill Media staff who have embraced this work as their own, especially Alan Sutton and Kena Longabaugh; you have allowed this legacy to be shared for years to come.

The story of the sisters constantly showed the power and importance of a circle of supportive collaborators in any project. I was gifted to have a wise, talented, and honest circle of readers and reflectors who walked through this story with me. Without them, the work would be impoverished. Sisters Anne Chester, Marie Michele Donnelly, and Michelle Gorman, thank you for your suggested revisions, for all your questions and edits, and for the hours you invested in making this a better publication. Thanks to Sisters Susan Sanders, Sister Margaret Mitchell, and to Mark and Liz Schiele for your feedback and encouragement. Thank you, Barbara Pauly, my archival research assistant, for your hours of research, clarifying discoveries, and partnership. This work could not have been finished without your help.

No historical work can be written without the assistance of dedicated archivists. A special word of thanks and appreciation goes to the staff of Mercy Archives and Heritage Center in Belmont, N.C., especially Elizabeth Johnson who provided mountains of scanned documents for me during my "pandemic research days." I am forever grateful. Last, I would like to thank all the sisters and partners who generously gave their time for interviews, story sharing, and listening. Your contributions make this story come to life.

Every story leaves some things left to say. So it is with this history. I ask forgiveness for my shortcomings as the storyteller, for any mistakes I have made, and for leaving behind so many untold tales. May reading this work stir up in you the same desire and wonder that prompted me to tell this remarkable story.

Contents

First You Have to Get There

There are stories as warm and familiar as a long-treasured sweater. There are other tales that beg to be discovered and brought into the light. This story is a bit of both. For generations of Sacramentans, Mercy is a familiar name, associated with hospitals and schools. Behind these institutions, however, is a circle of women, the Sisters of Mercy, dedicated to the care of the sick, poor, and uneducated. The extent of their contributions to Sacramento is memorialized throughout the city. They are found on Sacramento's Pioneer Wall, on a memorial stain glass window in the Cathedral of the Blessed Sacrament, and on historical plagues at the sites of their first school and first hospital. They are in the California Women's Museum, have a special room at Stanford Home and, most notably, a memorial statue at the entrance to the State Capitol Building honoring their contributions to the people of California. The scope of these memorials leaves one wanting to know more. What makes these women so much a part of California history? It is perplexing but true that these Mercy women are known but unknown.

To understand the story of the Sisters of Mercy in Sacramento, one has to travel back in time to 1850, seven years before their arrival in the city. That year was a year of enormous significance. California transitioned from being Mexican territory to becoming the thirty-first state of the United States. At the onset of the Gold Rush years, California found itself with little real organization and even fewer resources, especially in the areas of education, healthcare and social services.

The discovery of gold changed all that. The California of 1857 was nothing like its 1847 predecessor. One example of this radical transition is seen in the growth of San Francisco. As a port of entry, San Francisco welcomed a steady stream of persons from all over the world. Gold seekers came from every state in the union and from other countries like Chile, Australia, China, Ireland, and all parts in-between. The city had to deal with overwhelming, unplanned expansion. It went from a population of 2,000 at the beginning of February 1849 to a town of 20,000 by the end of that year. The whole of the state saw similar growth going from a population of 15,000 at the beginning of the Gold Rush period to 250,000 at its end.[1] Just trying to develop adequate infrastructure was challenging and oftentimes efforts failed due to lack of resources and changing circumstances. Even today, such growth would be seen as unmanageable.

The period of upheaval, excitement and lawlessness engendered by Gold Rush conditions raised grave concerns on many levels. The realities of the gold fields removed folks from the lifestyles that they formerly experienced. A Methodist minister, Isaac Owen, put it this way:

> With shame and confusion we are constrained to say that many that left their friends and home acceptable members of the church and doubtless made fair promises to maintain their Christian character have not only failed to report themselves here as members of the church, but have fallen into the common vices of the country.[2]

Catholic Church leaders shared that concern.

Many new Californians were Catholic immigrants needing sacramental and pastoral services but found both lacking. California lacked sufficient priests, churches, and religious institutions. Bishop Francisco Garcia Diego y Moreno, O.F.M., the only bishop in California, had died prematurely in 1846. Letters during the intervening years (1846–1850) concerning the state of Catholic religious life in California were unanimous in theme. In the opinion of the writers, the Catholic Church in California was on the verge of extinction.[3]

It took four years for church leaders to finally respond to the call for a new bishop in California. The delay was not caused by a lack of concern, but by the difficulty of finding someone who was healthy enough for the task, had the proper talents and, most of all, was willing to say yes to such a formidable mission. Finally, in 1850, Rome found its man and responded to the critical need in California by appointing Joseph Sadoc Alemany, O.P., as California's first archbishop.

Bishop Alemany initially took up his duties as the archbishop of Monterey, a diocese that covered all of California. By 1853, it was clear more was needed. California was divided into two dioceses with Alemany becoming the archbishop of San Francisco. His first order of business was finding clergy and vowed religious to serve his vast diocese of which

San Francisco was the largest town. California church historian John B. McGloin, S.J., notes:

> Bishop Joseph Alemany must have found his new responsibility for the Catholic community in Northern California daunting. He lacked personnel, especially clergy and religious; possessed scant resources and had a territory that expanded north to the Oregon border, eastward to the Nevada border and all the territory north of Monterey that bordered the Pacific Ocean. In his first report to the Society for the Propagation of the Faith [July 19, 1851] he estimated the Catholics under his care to number about 40,000 for whom there were forty-one priests.[4]

Alemany saw two things necessary to address the sad state of his diocese—he needed more priests and, in particular, he wanted women religious to establish schools.

That was easier said than done. Those who accepted the missionary call in the 1800s had to possess not only a strong faith and zealous spirit, but they also had to be strong in body. They would face hardships never imagined. In addition, the missionaries had to possess a wholehearted generosity. Returning home for visits or family occasions simply was not possible. This was the reality for the women leaving Ireland to embrace life in America as missionaries. Recognizing the finality of emigration from Ireland, families sometimes had what they called an "American wake" during which the families ritualized that they would never see their loved ones again. For those leaving and those remaining behind, going to America was a type of living death. In addition to the pain of separation, the trip itself was replete with dangers. In fact, some never survived the journey.[5]

The trip to California began with a two-week voyage across the Atlantic. Thomas Gallagher gives contemporary readers a vivid description of the hardships encountered on the journey. He tells us that emigrants took with them food for the passage, bedding, what few clothes they had, and animals when they could. Those with little money were booked in steerage where they were limited to a small patch of space without dividers. Everything had to fit in their allotted space. Privacy was not a consideration.

Lack of sanitation facilities was another surprise, especially on English ships where the only bathroom provided was located above deck, yet during storms, the steerage passengers were locked below deck.[6] Without any sanitation facilities, passengers had to deal with increasing stench. The steerage compartment became a breeding ground for disease. If fever hit, death followed quickly. Ships' logs show that on some passages as many as one quarter of the passengers making the trip did not arrive. They were buried at sea. It is no wonder that some of the ships were later called "coffin ships."[7] Sad but true, the poorer and more desperate one was, the costlier the journey.

Perhaps because of the time and hardships of an ocean passage, Bishop Alemany first looked to the Sisters of Charity of Emmitsburg, MD, to take up the California mission. Even though they avoided the two-month Atlantic journey, the sisters endured horrific conditions as they crossed the Isthmus of Panama and ventured up the California coast. The sisters first went by sea from New York to the Isthmus of Panama. Then they walked through ankle-deep water and mud for three-quarters of a mile to reach a resting place. Upon their arrival, they were lodged in a "hotel," actually a small shelter previously used as a stable for mules. The accommodations included no mattresses and only a few pillows.[8]

It seems their travails kept getting worse. First, the boat that was to carry them on the next leg of the journey was too small, and another had to be found. When they did find another vessel, the captain would not take them all the way to their destination. The indigenous men, conscripted into service by ship owners, were overheard planning to drown them in the rapids. Things were just not going their way. In the end, the sisters made the trip across the Isthmus by horseback, exposing them to torrential rains. Two of the sister pioneers, Sister Honorine and Sister Mary Ignatia, died before the company reached the Pacific coast, where the sisters then took the ship *Golden Gate* to San Francisco.[9] They arrived in there in 1852.

Like these pioneer sisters, the Sisters of Mercy coming to California would experience a similar journey, not only crossing the Atlantic but also making their way across the Isthmus of Nicaragua and then up the Pacific coast to San Francisco. The trip was not the only hardship they would face. By 1854, the excitement of the Gold Rush dimmed and its promised wealth proved elusive for most Californians, including pioneer clergy. The church in California was very poor, depending upon donations from the Society of the Propagation of the Faith for support. Accommodations were rarely what they were purported to be. While Mother Mary Baptist Russell, when writing the story of the trip in an official record called the *Mercy Annals*, did not leave us a description of their first convent, we can get a hint from the experience of the Sisters of Charity two years before in the convent provided by Father John Maginnis.

Father Maginnis, pastor of the parish in which the Sisters of Charity would serve, did his best to provide housing for his new teachers, but the sisters discovered the convent was barely more than a shanty. Living lives of poverty took on a vivid reality. Their new pastor assured them that many tears would water the works they were beginning. When the sisters entered their new home, they encountered a picture of pure desolation. There were no chairs and only one rough stool. A wine barrel substituted for a table and seven cots with straw mattresses and goats' hair pillows were their beds. Unfortunately, the cots lacked sheets or blankets.[10] The Sisters of Charity were not the only community of sisters to have such an experience. All across the west, the same story emerged for women religious.

Sisters coming to America from monastic settings were suddenly faced with situations and experiences that challenged their normal customs and understandings. The monastery life from which these sisters came was characterized by stability, regularity, and cloister.[11] Their lives were structured around their common prayer. Anne M. Butler, who has chronicled the impact of the west on women religious, points out:

> Moving into and about many western spaces immersed the sisters in multifaceted situations that countermanded their lifestyle, which had evolved in European monastic regimens grounded in class distinctions and constricted female decorum.[12]

For these nuns, everything was upside down, including social interactions, personal dangers, and being in the middle of the people rather than enclosed. Bishop Alemany knew that, instead of cloistered nuns, he needed women religious who would move out beyond the walls of their convents. The Sisters of Charity did that and so did the Sisters of Mercy, so much so that they were known in Ireland as the "walking nuns."

Flexibility was a vital virtue for all the early sisters. The pioneer sisters of the West had to respond to unpredictable changes around them. When gold strikes were publicized, whole towns could be emptied of their residents. Building a permanent monastery outside of a major city was risky business. School populations could triple in the course of a week, and sisters were expected to be ready to begin their ministries within days of their arrival. For those raised in today's age of long range and strategic planning, such realities seem daunting.

By 1854, travel and living conditions common in 1852 had improved somewhat, and the stage was set for new companies of women religious to come to San Francisco in response to expanding need. Archbishop Alemany sent Father Hugh Gallagher to Ireland for the purpose of recruiting new workers for his growing community. Alemany specifically wanted to bring the Sisters of Mercy to his diocese because he felt they were well-suited to meet western needs. Their freedom from the constraints of cloister allowed them to be sent to the most distant of parishes, travel when needed, and make do with whatever accommodations were available.

The Sisters of Mercy had come to the Pittsburgh, Pennsylvania, in 1843, established a foundation in Chicago in 1846, and had shown their flexibility and skills in adapting to the culture and needs of the country. Father Gallagher, familiar with the work of Sisters of Mercy in Pittsburgh, argued for applying to that foundation for recruits. Bishop Alemany did not agree. He thought that the young Pittsburgh group would not be able to grant such a request. Instead, Alemany wanted sisters from Baggot Street, Dublin, Catherine McAuley's first foundation.

The "fountainhead" at Baggot Street was where Mercy began and where the pattern of their lives and works first emerged. The archbishop was familiar with the works there and believed that sisters near the original center of the Mercy Order would be most steeped in Mercy tradition. However, things do not always work out as planned.

When Father Gallagher sought volunteers for the California mission at Baggot Street, Mother Mary Vincent Whitty, the superior of the community, declined the request due to a shortage of sisters. She referred Gallagher to the Mercy community at Kinsale, known for its rigor in serving the poor. The providential aspect of this change is hard to underestimate for the Kinsale community had skills that would be greatly needed in the new mission. They were experienced in responding to a wide range of need, everything from education to nursing, from social services to religious formation. They developed innovative ways to help women to develop sufficient skills to earn monies for their survival. The sisters sent teachers to learn the art of lace making as well as how to create fishing nets so they could pass these skills on to their students. They were quick to adapt their work in response to urgent need.

All did not go smoothly in Kinsale, and Father Gallagher's mission almost met defeat. First, he presumed that Mother Mary Vincent had made known to the Kinsale community his request and that plans had begun to hasten departure, but that was not the case. Mother Mary Francis Bridgeman, Kinsale's superior, knew nothing about the request when Gallagher came to Kinsale on July 28, 1854. The planned departure was only six weeks away. Recognizing the time urgency, the sisters immediately began to consider the proposal. As there had already been instances in Ireland of misunderstanding about the terms of accepting a mission, it was decided to put their response and conditions of acceptance in writing to avoid confusion. This fortuitous decision gives us insight into the negotiations for the mission.

Between July 28 and August 21, the conversation between Gallaher and Mother Bridgeman continued through letters. Mother Bridgeman could be classified as a strict constructionist when it came to the interpretation of the Mercy Rule. She was adamant that the Mercy charism to care for those who were poor would be honored and wanted written assurance that this would be the case. In a letter dated July 29, 1854, she required of Father Gallagher a guarantee:

[The sisters] will not be required to undertake any duties but those which it [the Mercy Rule] prescribes, or which, if not expressly prescribed, are obviously in accordance with its spirit, for example, tho' an hospital is not prescribed we would gladly devote ourselves to it.[13]

The letter continues:

The Sisters should not be, in any way dependent on their own exertions for support—I believe you are aware that the real duties of our Institute are, the visitation of the Sick, Instruction of the poor, the protection of distressed young women. To these duties we are really devoted, in them we hope to find content and perfection, we could not hope for a blessing on duties (however good for others) to which we are not called by God, if we were to undertake such.[14]

There was some confusion in their correspondence. When Father Gallagher tried to describe their future ministry, Mother Bridgeman felt his comments were calling for the sisters to teach wealthy and middle-class students as a main focus. That was not acceptable in her eyes. She writes on August 11:

Your letter has convinced us that the principal duty that awaits the Sisters in your mission is the education of the higher and middle classes, a holy and meritorious duty that is for those who are called by God to it, but it is not our vocation; no one in our Community has any attraction for it. We have vowed to "serve the Sick, poor & ignorant," and our Sisters would willingly go to the "ends of the earth" to accomplish this vocation. If you know our Rule you must know that the whole spirit of it breathes devotedness to the poor.[15]

Mother Bridgeman later on in the letter even went so far as to suggest other possible teaching orders that would be suitable for such a mission.

For Mother Bridgeman, the discussion was ended, but Father Gallagher was a man of great determination. San Francisco needed sisters. He continued the conversation and assured the sisters that the California mission was consistent with the Mercy Rule. On August 21, a final letter went between Mother Bridgeman and Father Gallagher in which Gallagher states categorically: "We have all the objects of your Institute in our mission—and these shall be the Sisters' primary duties—no duties shall be pressed on the sisters but such as they shall cordially approve."[16] With this assurance, the proposal was accepted. Departure time was less than a month away.

Accepting the proposal did not mean that Mother Bridgeman's fears were completely gone. Her concern for her sisters was deeply tied to her fears that distance and circumstances could result in a weakening of fidelity to the rule. For her, no deviation from practice was permissible. Whatever the rule said had to be carried out exactly. This rigidity of interpretation caused her to find adaptations made by earlier Mercy foundresses in the Americas like Mother Frances Warde and Mother Agnes O'Connor unacceptable. In particular, Mother Bridgeman considered academies as contrary to the rule. In her opinion, Mother Mary Frances Warde, who started many academies, was an innovator acting outside the strict confines of the Mercy Rule. Throughout the early years of the San Francisco community, a steady stream of letters would flow from her about what was and was not to be done.

Mixed feelings must have stirred in Mother Bridgeman's heart as the day of departure neared. She knew that her daughters would face hardship and danger in their new mission. She was not excited about prospect of sending the sisters into the unknown. Sister Mary Howley tells us that Mother Bridgeman had heard some "strange stories" about California and feared the sisters would be killed. The vastness of the geographical distances within the United States caused some confusion for Mother Bridgeman. She worried that her sisters might be caught in the Apache and Sioux uprisings of the period, even though they were occurring in places far distant from California. Only the reassurances of a traveling merchant from California freed her of her apprehensions.[17]

With her fear of physical dangers assuaged, only the selection of the members remained undone. Once Mother Bridgeman was sure that her sisters would be able to be true to their charism and rule, she brought the selection of the sister pioneers to the community. When the request to undertake service in California first came, the Kinsale sisters had begun nine days of prayer asking for openness to God's desire. At the end of the time of prayer, eighteen professed sisters—almost the entire group—offered themselves for the Californian Mission. Even though the time for departure was fast approaching, it was September 3 before the delegate of Bishop Delany, the bishop of the diocese, could preside at the selection of the band for the mission.

The selection was the joint task of Father Kellegher (the bishop's designee) and Mother Bridgeman. Five professed members were to be selected: Sister Mary Francis Benson, Sister Mary Baptist Russell, Sister Mary deSales Reddan, Sister Mary Bernard O'Dwyer, and Sister Mary Howley. Three novices—Sister Mary Gabriel Brown, Sister Mary Paul Beechinor, and Sister Martha McCarthy—begged to be added to the group and their request was granted.

The depth of generosity involved in releasing eight sisters for the California mission was profound, for among those selected was Joanna Reddan, called in religion Sister Mary deSales. Joanna was the aunt of Mother Bridgeman, who she raised her after the death of Mother Francis's parents. She put on hold her own desire for religious life. Joanna devoted her life to abused women, opening a refuge for them in her hometown of Limerick. When Catherine McAuley came to open a Mercy foundation in Limerick, the two women met and became good friends. In the only surviving letter of their correspondence, Catherine writes:

> I have not known many whose esteem and friendship I should be more desirous to possess ... I have great reason to rejoice in our visit to Limerick. Every report is animating and delightful. The institution will be very valuable to the afflicted poor, and very edifying to all. I trust you will soon be added to their number—more than in spirit. And I shall never be surprised to hear that you are an obedient humble sister.[18]

When the call to California came, Sister Mary deSales was fifty-four years old. It is hard to imagine how difficult it was for Mother Bridgeman to give Mary deSales to the California mission. She was saying "yes" to a decision to send a woman who was a mother to her into a world of hardship knowing she would never see her again. What would cause such a choice? Given all the challenges of the new foundation, the hardships and the unknowns, it seems that Mother Bridgeman wanted the young community to have an anchor and comfort to sustain them. Seasoned by time, Mother Mary deSales would be that community anchor and a strong support for its twenty-five-year-old superior, Mother Mary Baptist Russell.

The sisters from Kinsale were not the only religious sisters recruited by Father Gallagher. Among other convents receiving a visit from this ardent advocate for the Church of California was the Convent of the Presentation Sisters at George's Hill in Dublin. Here, a contingent of sisters was given for the Sacramento mission. Both groups lost little time in preparing for a commitment that would ask everything of them—loss of home, family, country, and, for some, their lives. The poignancy and gravity of their sacrifice is captured in the events of their departure. Father Gallagher had gathered so large a party that all could not be accommodated on the *Arctic*, the original ship of passage. Plans had to be delayed and bookings on a later ship, the *Canada* departing from Liverpool, were obtained. When the party arrived in New York, they discovered that the *Arctic*, colliding with an iceberg, had perished at sea. All aboard were lost.

The change in plans not only saved their lives, but it provided the Mercy sisters with two other unexpected blessings. First, they were able to visit the Mercy foundation in Derby, England, where their sisters had experience in serving in a mixed faith community frequently hostile to Catholics. The Derby community shared with the California contingent, how they managed that transition and some of the challenges that were involved. Secondly, Mother Mary Agnes O'Connor, superior of the New York Mercy Community, was returning home from Ireland on the *Canada* after receiving medical treatment for an eye condition.

Mother Mary Agnes and her sisters had arrived in New York in 1846 and experienced the hardships of adapting to the American context. The New York ministries had many similarities to the conditions the sisters would encounter in San Francisco. Both were port cities, both had many young women in need of protection and shelter, and both called for flexibility in meeting emergent needs. Mother Mary Agnes extended to the pioneers the hospitality of her community. Since Father Gallagher was to be delayed in New York due to business, the sisters accepted the invitation. Unaccustomed to travel and feeling more confident with Father Gallagher as guide, the sisters remained in New York until he was able to travel with them.

It is in New York that the fortunes of the Sacramento mission were shaped. While Father Gallagher conducted other official business, the eight Sisters of Mercy studied the works and learnings of their sisters in New York. The Presentation Sisters, however, immediately started the journey to Sacramento with the assistant pastor Father James Cassin. Prior to their departure from Ireland, the Presentation Sisters maintained a type of cloistered life that they anticipated continuing in California. For some of the members, leaving behind their convent in Middleton, Ireland, for California was the first time they had left the convent since they had entered. In the minds of some, leaving for California was seen as going to the other side of the world.[19]

During their journey to San Francisco, the Presentation Sisters began to hear rumors of life in Sacramento. It is likely that they learned on the trip that Sacramento was a town with lots of churches but not a lot of Catholics. It was a city built on capitalism and commerce. Its location made the city a gateway to the mines, a last stop to load up on needed supplies. Prices were inflated and monies were tight. It was less developed than San Francisco, possessed a difficult climate and was subject to much disease. Stories of Sacramento's great floods of 1850 and '52 must have added to apprehensions about Sacramento's unhealthy climate, its heat, swampy conditions, and rigor. They discovered that given the shortage of priests and the vastness of their diocese, daily mass would not be a possibility. On the whole, the prospects were not promising.

Given these considerations, the sisters decided that Sacramento was wholly unsuited for cloistered religious. If the bishop required them to fulfill their original mission to Sacramento, they would return home instead.[20] This was not a turn of affairs expected by Archbishop Alemany, but after calming the sisters' fears, he allowed them to stay in San Francisco and open a school. The city would provide a better chance of success for the school since it was a larger urban setting with a larger Catholic population. It also could provide greater spiritual resources including the desired daily Eucharist. Sacramento would have to wait.

Meanwhile, the Sisters of Mercy were making their way to San Francisco with Father Gallagher as their guide. They did not take the same route, but did meet with some of the same challenges. Father Gallagher had gathered a formidable group of missionaries. In addition to the eight Sisters of Mercy, there were some Jesuits and Sisters of Notre Dame. All traveled together on the *Star of the West* destined for San Juan del Norte, Nicaragua. Mary Baptist notes in the *Mercy Annals* that it took ten days to arrive at their destination and prepare for the next leg of the journey. This time, they would journey across the Isthmus of Nicaragua.[21] Mother Austin Carroll, Mercy historian and annalist, describes the trip in *Leaves from the Annals of the Sisters of Mercy*:

> At Greytown the Sisters were transferred to riverboats and packed so close that no one thought of lying down, so great were the crowds going out in search of gold ... In the middle of the night they reached a point on the river that was impassable. All had to go ashore, and after walking some distance north they embarked in another boat.[22]

Accommodations were rugged. The "hotel" where they were to stay before crossing Lake Nicaragua lacked both chairs and beds. It did provide a single tallow candle and table. Fortunately, they did not need the beds for they were soon summoned to board the riverboat taking them to yet another boat—the steamer that would cross Lake Nicaragua. The group boarded the steamer, the *Virgen Maria*, at 5 a.m. on November 24. It would take a full day to cross the lake.

Unlike the torrents of rain that greeted earlier travelers, the weather was most auspicious. Space on the boat was at a premium, though, so the exhausted travelers leaned on their bundles and dozed when they could. The sisters' decision to wait for Father Gallagher proved to be a good one. An experienced traveler, he was aware that food would be scarce and housing would lack basic comforts so he brought with him the provisions needed for the journey. What food they had, they shared with other passengers who lacked sufficient provisions for the crossing.

To women who spent most of their lives in Ireland, the beauty of Nicaragua must have seemed extraordinary and possibly even exotic. The lake itself covered about ninety by forty miles and was dotted by islands of volcanic origin. Although some were still active at the time of their passage, there is no mention of that volcanic activity in the description of the crossing. Mother Austin Carroll, who gathered the stories of early Mercy missions from the pioneers, describes the experience:

> The full moon added to the beauty of the scene but prevented the fireflies from showing off to advantage. When the party reached their destination, they expected to be obliged to mount mules, but to their great delight large, double-seated wagons, each drawn by six beasts, awaited them. From the lake to the seacoast, about fifteen miles, the drive was delightful.[23]

To say that the trip to the seacoast was "delightful" is probably an exaggeration. It was more like "delight short lived." The beauty was accompanied by the dangers of steep and treacherous roads, hard to control animals, and fear of what would happen next. At one point, the mules pulling the wagon carrying the Notre Dame Sisters became unmanageable as the animals pulled the wagon to the edge of the precipice. Only the quick action of Mr. James Kelly, a member of the party, saved the sisters from almost certain death. Summoning up extraordinary strength, he ran alongside the wagon for a full mile while guiding the lead animal away from danger.[24]

Without further mishap, the party reached San Juan del Sur at about 5 p.m. The sisters settled into their second "hotel" to await the next portion of the trip. The accommodations were slightly improved over their first "hotel" as this time, the establishment had cots and sheets. The sisters never got to use the cots, however, as shortly after they arrived, Father Gallagher came to bring them to the *Cortes*, the ship that would carry them up the Pacific coast. For reasons not explained, Gallagher felt it was better for the sisters to stay on the ship instead of at the "hotel." Perhaps he did not want to risk missing the boat's departure since getting to the boat was somewhat of a challenge. It was also quite a surprise for the sisters.

The ship docked in deep waters offshore. Mother Austin Carroll describes the adventure:

> When they came to the beach they were bewildered at the sight that greeted their eyes. Men almost naked were carrying ladies and gentlemen about fifty yards into the sea to a point at which small boats

were stationed to take them to the steamer that stood far out in deep water. There was not the least semblance of a wharf, and in that shallow water not even the smallest *pirogue* could reach the shore.[25] Presently their escort appeared with four "natives," whom he had induced to dress in linen shirts and pantaloons. By these the Sisters were carried in "My Lady to London" style to the skiffs.[26]

This vivid memory, shared with Mother Austin Carroll, almost twenty-five years after the event, gives us an idea of what a deep impression the journey made on these intrepid pioneers. The saga continued once they reached the *Cortes*. The captain and purser were not on the vessel when the passengers arrived. With only one large dinner table for passengers and no organized seating plan, the famished passengers chaotically rushed to the table trying to get to the food first. When Captain Cropper did return, Father Gallagher's party was assigned seats nearest the captain where, by custom, the food would be served first. This small courtesy aroused bad feelings among some of the other passengers. The offended passengers made folks in the Gallagher's group pay a heavy price for the captain's courtesy. Upon arrival in San Francisco, disgruntled passengers spread false stories in the public newspapers accusing the sisters of inappropriate conduct while on the boat. It was a harbinger of what was to follow.

The sisters arrived in San Francisco on December 8, 1854. By the time of their arrival, San Francisco had grown to a city of over 40,000 people, but did not really have the infrastructure to support a community that size. Among other things, it lacked an adequate legal system, medical facilities that were prepared to deal with major health crises, and laws governing public sanitation. There were rival factions from various cultures, in particular Australians fighting with Chilean immigrants, a strong anti-Irish faction. and a Chinese community whose rights were trampled. Trafficking of women was alive and well. This was the San Francisco greeting the sisters on that cold December day as they disembarked from the *Cortes*. They had no idea that realities had changed since they left New York. Their arrival would demand of them a profound act of trust and a vast amount of courage.

Claimed by Two Cities

When Mother Mary Baptist Russell and her sisters arrived in San Francisco on that cold December morning, they had no idea of what lay ahead. They only knew that they came to open a school and serve the needs of San Francisco's sick poor. That was the plan. Still under the impression that they would be opening a school in San Francisco, they did not know that the mission to Sacramento had failed or that the Presentation Sisters had already opened the needed school. That realization was quick in coming. Plans had to change.

It is hard to imagine the thoughts and feelings that must have coursed through the hearts of the newly arrived pioneers. One can only get a sense of it by thinking about our own experiences of being strangers in a different country, unfamiliar with the customs, resources, and dangers of a place while being excited about a new challenge. There is a sense of it being right for us to be there and a spirit of adventure. Excitement and anxiety blend. To this is added the reality that this was a band of women who entered into a context where women had little voice or power. What made it possible for these intrepid pioneer sisters to move forward? While they did not leave written diaries of this moment, we do know that their strength was rooted in three constants: their absolute trust that God was with them; a commitment to the mission that called them forward; and strength found in community. With these three elements, they could face the unknown future. Surprises there would be.

Upon their arrival, the sisters discovered they had no beds to call their own since no convent was yet ready. The Sisters of Charity, having just moved into a new convent, offered them hospitality until their own house could be established. It must have been comforting for the little community to be in a hospitable and safe home, for in less than twenty-four hours, they were under attack. *The Christian Advocate,* a strongly anti-Catholic paper, immediately began to publish a series of articles accusing the sisters of everything from drunkenness to neglect of the Sabbath while on the *Cortes.* The attacks continued for weeks until Thomas B. Cropper, captain of the *Cortes,* returned to San Francisco and publicly defended the honor of the sisters. For women far from home, insecure in their surroundings, and struggling to adapt to an entirely different society, it was a hard beginning.[1]

Being the target of personal attacks was only one challenge. Another challenge was deciding what to do. Realizing that the main reason for their coming—opening a school—no longer existed, the community had to determine what work of mercy was most urgently needed. With a city full of unmet needs, where was the place to begin? Sisters of Mercy were always called to respond to unmet needs, but there were limitations involved. Those limits were outlined in the letter from Mother Francis Bridgeman to *Monsignor* Gallagher on July 29, 1854, in which she asked for a guarantee that the sisters "will not be required to undertake any duties but those which it [the Mercy Rule] prescribes, or which, if not expressly prescribed, are obviously in accordance with its spirit."[2] With this guide and the Mercy mission as her compass, Mother Mary Baptist Russell looked for the most urgent need of the city. That need was healthcare.

San Francisco, with no health regulations, provided little relief to the sick. The indigent were housed in the State Marine Hospital on Stockton Street, where nurses were untrained and sometimes uncaring. Often persons stayed in their homes because they feared being confined in the hospitals of the time. To them, hospitals were places to die. The sisters brought a different approach to healthcare. Mary Sullivan, RSM, Mercy historian and biographer of Catherine McAuley, comments on this philosophy:

The "visitation of the sick poor" was one of three central elements in Catherine McAuley's vision of the merciful work to which she and, later, her companions in the Sisters of Mercy were called. She conceived of this "visitation" as affording to the desperately ill and dying both material comfort and religious consolation. What is especially striking about her service and advocacy of the sick poor is not only her willingness to care for people with extremely dangerous infectious diseases (cholera and typhus, for example), with consequent risk to her own life, but her overwhelming desire to offer these neglected and shunned people the dignity and Christian solace that she felt was rightly theirs, as human beings with whom Jesus Christ himself was intimately identified.[3]

While still in Kinsale, the San Francisco sisters had put this vision into practice. They visited in the hospitals and workhouse as well as the homes of the sick poor.[4] Their nursing skills were finely honed through cholera epidemics and ministry to the dying. In fact, shortly after the California sisters' departure for the United States, Mother Frances Bridgeman would lead a contingent of Irish Mercies to the Crimea, where she worked in battlefield hospitals side by side with Florence Nightingale. The unplanned change of ministry for the sisters unexpectedly brought San Francisco its first visiting nurses. The city had gained a circle of women fully prepared to meet the health crises to come.

Archbishop Alemany lost no time in applying to the county supervisors for permission to have the sisters begin visiting the sick in the State Marine Hospital on Stockton Street. The permission was submitted right before Christmas, on December 20, and the sisters began to visit the hospital on January 1. Meanwhile, other things would take up Mary Baptist's energy. She had to find a house. In surveying the possibilities, the proximity of the house to ministry was an important element and she finally selected a six-room house on Vallejo Street near the County Hospital. Every day, two or more sisters walked to the hospital and ministered to its suffering inmates.[5]

The sisters did not limit their work to visitation of the sick. By the beginning of February, with just eight sisters, they had already opened a House of Mercy for the shelter of young women, added visitation of the sick in homes to their duties, and opened a night school for adults. By March, they were teaching elementary school in the basement of the cathedral located near San Francisco's Chinatown. The experience of those visiting the sick in their homes brought the sisters face to face with people trapped in poverty while the House of Mercy was a constant reminder that young women coming to San Francisco were often easy targets for exploitation. The sisters provided such vulnerable women shelter and support as well as a new start.

Mother Mary de Sales Reddan was most familiar with young women caught in the web of prostitution and exploitation. Limerick, her home, was a garrison town where exploitation of local women was rift. Before her entry into Mercy, she had opened a home for women pushed into prostitution, a Magdalen asylum. Such a woman, Amanda Taylor, showed up on the convent steps one day begging shelter even in a coal hole.[6] Although short on monies and personnel, the sisters offered her refuge and began yet another work of mercy, San Francisco's Magdalen Asylum. Yet more was to come.

By April 1855, Mother Baptist Russell decided that some things needed to change. At the time, San Francisco had a "bidding" process in place for care of the sick. The lowest bidder got the hospital contract even if they did not have a good track record for results. Mother Mary Baptist, after seeing the results of that practice at the State Marine Hospital, bid on the contract to care for the hospital's sick. Throughout April, there was public discussion of her bid, some asserting that it would constitute "support for religion," and others lamenting the fact that missing from the bid was a male signature. If only a man had signed the bid, it would be acceptable.[7] In the end, the sisters were not awarded the contract. Both the nativist perspective and cultural norms around the role of women converged to win the day. That being said, the sisters were undeterred.

To understand Mother Mary Baptist's desire to take responsibility for the State Marine Hospital, it is important to understand the state of medicine in the mid-1850s. One's imagination has to jump to a very different context than modern hospitals. The whole period was part of what is sometimes called the "dark ages' of nursing. Germ theory had not been discovered. Nurses were not well trained. The causes of diseases like typhoid and cholera were unknown. Wards were overcrowded and sanitation scanty.

In 1858, one Methodist minister, William Taylor, described conditions by saying the private rooms were dirty enough to kill any one while wards were offensive to both eyes and nose. Only the most caring could stay. He goes on to tell us that nurses, mainly male, lacked sympathy and were devoid of those characteristic desirable in a caregiver. With pay of $100 per month, there were always an insufficient number to care for the sick.[8] Given the realities of care, it is easy to see why Mother Mary Baptist was eager to provide a more compassionate way of caring for the sick.

The works of mercy were not the only thing that occupied the attention of Mother Mary Baptist. From the time of their arrival in San Francisco until establishing another convent in Sacramento in the fall of 1857, fifteen women joined the community. The new members had to be formed in the spirit of the Institute, oriented to the works of the community, and taught the core values of religious life. The work of forming new members would have fallen to the professed members of the founding group, who had learned the life through living it. Events intervened to make that task even harder. Novices like Mary Gabriel Brown and Mary Paul Beechinor, both of whom would later serve in Sacramento, found their novitiate experience shaped by a major health crisis visited upon San Francisco in September 1855—a cholera epidemic.

San Francisco was not ready to deal with the epidemic. Few people knew how to treat the disease, and many were just unwilling to put their own lives at risk. In the middle of the crisis, Mother Mary Baptist offered the nursing services of the sisters to the city. Cholera was not new to the sisters. They had already nursed its victims during the cholera epidemic that gripped Kinsale in 1849. County supervisors immediately accepted the offer. Four or five sisters worked around the clock at the hospital, rotating groups morning and evening. This service was a significant part of Mary Gabriel Brown and Mary Paul Beechinor's novitiate, a total immersion in compassionate, merciful care. The *Daily Times* brought that service to the attention of the public:

> The Sisters of Mercy (rightly named) whose convent is opposite the hospital, as soon as they learned of the state of matters, hurried to offer their services. They did not stop to inquire whether the poor sufferers were Protestants or Catholics, Americans or foreigners, but applied themselves to their relief ... The idea of danger never seemed to occur to these women. In the performance of the vows of their Order, they heeded nothing of the kind. If any of the stricken are saved, they will in great measure owe their lives to these ladies.[9]

Their witness needed no words. Actions spoke loudly.

The epidemic finally came to an end in October, and with public sentiment now in their favor, Mother Mary Baptist once more applied for the hospital contract. Things had changed, however. Earlier, the State Marine Hospital was a jointly sponsored work of the State of California and San Francisco County. In August 1855, the state ended that partnership and required the county to care for its own sick. To do this, San Francisco County leaders decided to sell the State Marine Hospital and build a new facility.[10] At this point, Mother Mary Baptist made a really audacious decision. She risked going into debt—approximately $14,000—in order to purchase the old hospital on Stockton Street.

The enormity of this decision is hard to fathom. When the sisters came to San Francisco and later to Sacramento, they had no source of income and received no salaries or even small stipends. They only had three sources of income to fund both their community needs and the various charitable ministries they opened: personal dowries; philanthropy, and income derived from such things as music lessons, benefit events, and the sale of handiwork. Even though these monies were theirs, they were not always able to use them as they saw fit. Church norms of the time required women religious to get the permission of the local bishop to spend any monies and all properties had to be held in the bishop's name.

This situation was not limited to San Francisco. It was common across the West. Anne Butler comments:

The wide spread belief circulating among Catholics and non-Catholics that the Vatican-centered European and then American church supported and sustained women's religious orders was not only completely inaccurate but also possibly amusing to strapped congregations and destitute sisters in the field. Religious women never received a regular, automatic infusion of money into convent coffers. Rather than basking in church largesse, a congregation, embracing the motherhouse and all daughter convents, shouldered responsibility to generate the income for its own shelter, food, clothing, education, religious ceremonies, medical care and travel and work initiatives, as well as church-mandated charities, miscellaneous expenses, and long-term debt.[11]

The work of the sisters went on in spite of such constraints and struggles. While Mother Mary Baptist might have had some monies left from the Kinsale endowment given for the foundation, those funds had to stretch to feed and house the residents of the House of Mercy, provide food for the poor, and pay rent and all other expenses of the convent and community. Debt was a constant presence in the life of the community.

Mother Baptist Russell once more submitted her bid to care for the county's sick, and this time, faith and gender did not act as a barrier. The sisters were awarded the contract and toward the end of October, the sisters assumed responsibility for the care of San Francisco's indigent sick. In return, the county was to pay them $400 per month to care for these patients at the old county hospital site.[12]

When the sisters took charge of the facility for the county, they immediately discharged the attendants and ended a pattern of neglect and poor management. They scrubbed the rooms and created three new wards for patients. They also made sure that two hallmarks of Mercy nursing were put in place: cleanliness and fresh air. For the first months, November to March, all went smoothly but trouble was on the horizon.

One harbinger of trouble was the failure of the county to keep up with their fiscal obligations to the sisters. To make matters worse, monthly expenses were not $400 a month but ran up to $5,747 per month since many needed things like blankets and dishes had to be purchased for the hospital. One of the underlying problems was an economic depression that set in during this period. In the fall of 1855, the county of San Francisco had a budget deficit of $850,000. This deficit led to the county repudiating $1.5 million of public indebtedness.[13] Still, the sisters continued to care for the sick poor.

While many held the work of the sisters in high esteem, not all San Franciscans held that opinion. Among them was the editor of the *San Francisco Daily Evening Bulletin,* James King, a stanch nativist with a strong bias against Catholics. When the sisters converted a small hospital room into a chapel, they opened themselves to the ire of nativists.[14] In April, Mr. King began a relentless eight-week attack on the hospital. The first accusations had to do with the establishment of the chapel. He accused the sisters of using public funds for the support of religion. From there, it only got worse. The sisters were accused of abusing their patients, forcing death-bed conversions, starving the patients, and even hitting one troublesome patient over the head with a hammer to make him sleep.[15]

The attacks were not just bad press; they posed a clear danger to the safety of the sisters. The mid-1850s was a time of great nativism in the state; in fact, members of the Know-Nothing Party had swept the statewide elections.[16] In the nativist climate, Catholics, especially Irish Catholics, were suspect and indiscriminately branded as a criminal class. In a city without strong laws or a respected judicial system, vigilantism emerged. The vigilante members chose to march right on the street outside the convent, reminding the sisters of their vulnerability. The sisters had to be nervous due to earlier attacks on convents occurring in the east.

In March 1855, the Mercy Sisters in Providence, Rhode Island, had been threatened with attack by Know-Nothing members. Contending with the daily attacks in the press and the real threat of violence from the nativist extremists must have made fear a constant companion for the sisters.

Undeterred by all the hardships, threats and challenges, on March 6, Mary Gabriel Brown made her final vows. Three months later, Mary Paul Beechinor did likewise, and other young women continued coming to join the pioneer community. At this point, just three weeks after Mary Gabriel's profession, Mr. King's attacks expanded from the hospital to the life of the sisters themselves. Bigots charged that young women were being kept in the convent against their will and pressed the Grand Jury to investigate the work and life of the sisters. Such challenges and trials would cause the strongest women to lose heart, but Mother Russell and her sisters trusted that the integrity of their lives and work would hold firm. She invited the Grand Jury to do their work. The outcome: total exoneration of the sisters and the Grand Jury's designation of the sisters as one of the treasures of the city.[17]

There is no certainty on how long James King would have kept up his attacks on the sisters had fate not intervened. The sisters were not the only persons to fall under his verbal attacks. One target was James Casey, a local politician, who like many others came to California seeking a new life. Mr. Casey had spent time in New York's Sing Sing Correctional Facility and did not take kindly to Mr. King's efforts to publicize his past. He found a radical solution. Mr. Casey killed Mr. King, setting off a wave of vigilantism. Taking the law into their own hands, the Vigilance

Committee jailed Mr. Casey and condemned him to death. Mother Baptist Russell, whose sisters visited prisoners in the jail, asked to visit Mr. Casey before he was hanged. The Vigilance Committee denied that request. In looking back, while visiting the prisoner is a long-standing act of mercy, it was utterly courageous to ask to "visit the prisoner" given the dangerous and hostile political climate of the times.[18]

After the Grand Jury inquiry, the county paid its debts but soon fell into its old pattern of not making the payments owned. Mother Mary Baptist could no longer find ways to meet costs. The county had not paid its bills for nine months. She warned the county supervisors of the situation:

Date: February 28, 1857
To the Board of Supervisors
Gentlemen,

Finding no notice taken by your honorable body of the communication sent you on our behalf by J. S. McGlynn, E. P. Seymour and others respecting the care and maintenance of the County Sick, we are obliged to address you directly.

It is now nine months since we have got any money from the treasury and [you] must be aware of the immense outlay necessary to carry on a Hospital such as this averaging one hundred & forty patients; it cannot, therefore, be a matter of surprise that we should be obliged to give up the contract. We would, indeed, be very anxious to continue the care of the Sick, and would also be anxious to accommodate the Authorities, especially in the present state of the city funds; but it is utterly impossible to hold out longer and we feel every just mind will exonerate us from all blame when they consider what a sum it requires daily to supply food, medicine, attendants, fuel, &c &c for such a number.

We are, therefore, obliged for the reasons given above to decline entering on another month except on the following terms: 1st that the Board engages to cash on the first day of each month two of the audited bills now in our possession beginning with the one for July last. 2nd that the terms of the monthly contract henceforth be $2800.00 in audited bills.

If these terms cannot be granted you will please consider the contract with us at an end on and after the 1st day of April from which date no new patients will be admitted and the City and County will be charged for those remaining at the rate of $1.00 each per day.
February 28th. 1857.[19]

The county failed to pay up and Mother Russell was true to her word. No new county patients were accepted and those well enough to be moved were dismissed on April 1. That same day, what was once the State Marine Hospital, now owned by the sisters, became St. Mary's Hospital, open to all.

Mother Mary Baptist had a full plate of responsibilities and obligations that spring, but Archbishop Alemany brought her one more. Ever since the Presentation Sisters had decided to stay in San Francisco, Sacramento waited for sisters. Writing under the pen name of "*Philos,*" Dr. Nicholas Phelan, a prominent Sacramento physician and contributing correspondent to New York's *Freeman's Journal*, had written in 1854 that Father H. P. Gallagher had just returned from his trip to Europe. He went on to note that Gallagher had brought with him a number of Jesuits and secular priests, five Presentation Sisters, five Notre Dame Sisters, and eight Sisters of Mercy. Dr. Phelan speculated that half of the Mercy Sisters would remain in San Francisco while the others would come to Sacramento to start a school for girls. He even said that the old St. Rose Church would be converted into a convent and school for them.[20]

His comments had been more wishing than reality, but now Archbishop Alemany hoped Sacramento's time had come. He made a visit to Mother Mary Baptist on March 19, 1857, begging her to found a branch house in Sacramento. He tried before, but circumstances and shortage of personnel caused a delay. This time, with almost twenty-one members in the community, Mother Russell promised she would see if such a foundation was feasible. After waiting three years, Sacramento might get its sisters.

Having brought the hospital situation to resolution, Mother Mary Baptist arranged to visit Sacramento in late April. She and her companion, Mother Mary deSales Reddan, left by steamer on April 20. It was not an easy trip. The steamer always left San Francisco for Sacramento at 4 p.m. Once underway, it entered into San Pablo Bay and then through the Carquinez Straits and Suisun Bay, Little Honker Bay, and then through the twists and turns of the Delta. It would finally turn up the Sacramento River near Rio Vista, about 45 miles from its final destination. The trip was always subject to changes in tides and weather. Since the way was uncharted, unexpected obstacles like sand bars and snags could cause disaster. There was a human danger too. Sometimes, imprudent captains would push their steamers too hard by racing up the river.[21] Explosions, fires, and loss of life was the cost. If all went well, however, around 6 a.m. the following morning, the steamer would arrive in Sacramento.

The trip would have been bad enough, but the steamer was jammed with miners and materials for the gold fields. Due to the crowding, both Mother Mary Baptist and Mother Mary deSales elected to spend the night on deck. After surveying the possibilities for a foundation in Sacramento, Mother Baptist and Mary deSales continued their journey to Shasta County. They traveled by stagecoach and must have found the trip strenuous. Even today, it takes around two and a half hours to make the trip from Sacramento to Redding by car. Given the circumstances, Mother Russell declined the Shasta mission but said "yes" to Sacramento.[22] This promise was made despite her realization that the Sacramento sisters would have to struggle with an unhealthy climate, limited accommodations, and a lack of ready access to the spiritual resources accessible in San Francisco. She did not realize that it would also claim the life of her assistant and key support, Mother Mary deSales.

After giving her consent to establishing a Mercy foundation in Sacramento, Mother Mary Baptist returned to San Francisco, again by steamer. Starting any new project or mission is hard work, but for the sisters, it meant juggling two things. They had to both tend to the start-up of a private hospital at St. Mary's and establish a new house in Sacramento that would be more education focused. Monies were not readily available since the hospital had left the community $13,000 in debt. Only the support of Sacramentans would make the new foundation sustainable.

The Sacramento civic community immediately went to work raising funds for the new foundation. The women of the city began with a benefit fair to raise monies and Governor Peter Burnett, a generous benefactor of the church in Sacramento, contributed $500 to the effort.[23] Mother Baptist Russell's return visit in July to finalize arrangements quickened the enthusiasm. Once more, she and Mother deSales Reddan had made the trip by steamer and once again remained on deck throughout the night. This time, the outcome was fatal. Mother deSales caught a severe cold from the night's dampness and chill. She died three days after returning to San Francisco, a martyr to the Sacramento mission.

Losing such a wise and experienced partner at this juncture was a significant loss for Mary Baptist and the small community. Not only did Mother Mary Baptist need to decide which sisters to send to Sacramento, she needed a sister to be their superior and guide. Although the community had almost thirty members, not all were available for leadership. Like other nineteenth-century European communities, the Sisters of Mercy had two levels of membership, choir sisters, and lay sisters. It is hard to understand this dynamic when looking at it through the lens of contemporary times, but it was common in the nineteenth century.

Not all women coming to religious life were educated, and many had no dowry to bring to the community for their support. Such women were allowed to enter as lay sisters. In the U.S., these were plentiful. Mary Baptist wrote to Mother Francis Warde in 1859:

Our community consists of thirty-four, pretty nearly one half of whom are Lay Sisters, in fact we can have any number of them but desirable

Choir Sisters are scarce; as yet we have only twelve professed and in this number I include those from Ireland, so you see we are but a small body yet.[24]

The desire for choir sisters was rooted in the fact that being educated they could manage the responsibilities of leadership. They could read, teach in the schools, and conduct business affairs.

An election was held on August 11 to replace Mother deSales as assistant. Sister Mary Gabriel Brown, less than two years professed, was chosen. A new community distant from the center in San Francisco needed a leader that could act in the place of Mother Russell. Mother Mary Gabriel Brown would be that leader. As mother assistant, she would begin an unbroken period of leadership that extended from 1857 through 1882, fifteen of which she would spend as superior in Sacramento. On the same day of her election, the sisters for the Sacramento foundation were chosen: Mary Gabriel Brown (Superior), Sister Mary Paul Beechinor, Sister Mary Agnes Stokes, Sister Martha McCarthy, and Sister Madeline Murray.[25]

Meanwhile in Sacramento, excitement was growing. On September 30, 1857, *The Sacramento Bee* carried the following announcement concerning the arrival of the sisters and the beginning of their service to the city:

For the present they will occupy the old frame building in the rear of St. Rose's Church, corner of K and 7th, but so soon as the necessary means are obtained, a substantial building will be erected, such as will render them ample room to accommodate day, weekly and quarterly pupils.[26]

Two days later, on the Feast of the Guardian Angels, Sacramento finally welcomed its sisters.

Planting Roots in the City of Trees

When the Sisters of Mercy arrived in Sacramento, they were stepping into a city still young and finding its way. As a city, it was less than ten years old. It started as a loading dock or embarcadero during the Gold Rush times. When John Sutter needed materials going to and from his settlement at what was called Sutter's Fort, they were offloaded from the boats plying the Sacramento River. Sutter discovered that riches came not only from the physically challenging work of digging in the gold fields but also in supplying to miners the resources they needed: shovels, food, ropes, gold pans, and animals. Other pioneers like Sam Brannan, John Bidwell, and Peter Burnett saw the commercial potential of a city that was literally a doorway to the Gold Country. Into Sacramento's spirit were planted the seeds of commerce, capitalism, perseverance in adversity, and hospitality.

Sacramentans have always been intrigued by the legendary gold rush. Even today, fourth grade children come to Sutter's Fort to hear stories of early times and reenact what nineteenth-century life was like at the fort. Not so many folks know the story of how gold brought about John Sutter's ruin. Sutter was widely known for his hospitality but also for his poor financial sense. He spent more than he had, hoping that the next great investment would erase his debts. The discovery of gold aggravated this situation when his workers abandoned their jobs to seek fortunes in the gold country and his fields and fort fell prey to lawless folks taking his cattle and stores.

In 1848, Sutter was surprised by the arrival of his twenty-one-year-old son, John, who immediately recognized his father's dire financial straits. To avoid financial disaster, the senior Sutter turned over the title to his lands to his son. Working in partnership with Sam Brannan, considered a shrewd speculator, and Peter Burnett, a lawyer who would later become governor of California, the younger Sutter hired Captain William Warner to carefully plot out quadrants of land near the riverfront. These were divided into neat lots available for purchase for commercial and residential purposes. The lands near to the embarcadero were conveniently located for newly arrived miners or for those who wished to stay and seek their fortune in this emerging town on the Sacramento River.

The sale of the lots began on January 8, 1849. At the time, there were only two houses near the embarcadero. One was a family house while the other was a saloon.[1] By late summer, the two had multiplied to 300 canvas houses. Land speculation was rife, and prices soared with demand. The proximity of the emerging city to river traffic caused merchants to abandon their shops at Sutter's Fort and find space in the new settlement. Lots could cost anywhere from $600 to $20,000.[2] The lure of ready wealth overshadowed the reality that the new town had no protection from fires or flood. It was a disaster waiting to happen.

Unlike Sutter's Fort, which was built on high land, Sacramento's embarcadero was at river's level. While the embarcadero was alive with the bustle of merchandise and immigrants coming and going, it lacked protective levies. That omission left the settlement vulnerable to the floods that inundated the area in 1850 and again in 1852. As Sacramentans struggled with a town under 4 feet of water, boats were sold for as much as $1,000.[3] The floods were followed by a catastrophic fire. Fire and water were twin demons for Sacramento throughout the decade.

It is at this juncture that the story of Gold Rush Sacramento intersects with that of Catherine McAuley's daughters, the Sisters of Mercy. Alemany saw these pioneer sisters as missionaries, willing to undertake harsh conditions, arduous tasks, and lay down their lives, if needed, for the sake of their brothers and sisters. The women of mercy who came to Sacramento were a match for those expectations.

Into the world created by a spirit of capitalism and commercial undertakings came Sisters of Mercy shaped by a very different spirit—the spirit of their founder Mother Catherine McAuley. They had only been in California for three years, but in that time, they had experienced public hostility, a grave cholera epidemic, the potential of civil authorities to renege on their obligations, and the harsh reality of life for those who were poor. When Mother Mary Baptist Russell came to explore the possibility of sending a foundation of sisters to Sacramento, she realized it would not be easy, but saw the great need crying out for relief.

Sisters of Mercy were particularly suited to meeting the needs of the West. They were quick adapters doing what they could do rather than following a set pattern of response. Catherine McAuley, founder of the

Mercy Order, envisioned a circle of women that would go out among the people, wherever there was suffering. She never wished to be a vowed religious because religious of her times were primarily cloistered, meaning they did not go outside their convents. Catherine wanted to go among the poor, reach out to anyone in need, and provide safe haven and a path to the future for women who were otherwise vulnerable and at risk.

Another strong conviction held by Catherine was that when you had sufficient sisters, you had too many. You needed to give of your scarcity. Mother Mary Baptist Russell followed in that path when she gave sisters to Sacramento. For the next thirty years, sisters moved back and forth between the Sacramento and San Francisco foundations as need demanded. The fact that the Sacramento foundation was going to focus on education and the needs of orphans must have given Mary Baptist a special joy. She was a born teacher and, like Catherine McAuley, believed that education was vital for the upbuilding of communities and the betterment of persons.

Mary Baptist knew from her own experience the consequences of educational deprivation: poverty, oppression, and lack of social opportunities. She had grown up in what is called post-penal Ireland where withholding educations, depriving persons of voting privileges, denying them the right to own land, and imposing oppressive practices had all converged to reduce the poor to lives of desperation and hopelessness. To break that cycle, education was essential and not just any education, but one which would lead to self-sufficiency and a sense of dignity.

Catherine McAuley believed that you never gave those in need less than the best. Excellence in service was a value she passed on to her sisters. Holding the conviction that education was the doorway to self-sufficiency, Catherine was committed to providing schools for the children who lack such education. It was this vision that guided the sisters in establishing their first work in Sacramento, St. Joseph School, but it did not happen instantly.

When the steamer arrived in Sacramento on the morning of October 2, 1857, it brought Mary Baptist and four of the sisters that would make up the community. The next day, Sister Mary Francis Benson and one of the two novices that would come to Sacramento arrived. It would be great to know more details like how the sisters traveled the short distance between the dock and 7th and K Streets where they would make their home. Did they walk? Were they picked up in a carriage? We most likely will never know for there are only the skimpiest of records detailing these early years. Most references are found in the *Annals* of the San Francisco community. They were written by Mary Baptist herself and only hint at some of the hardships and challenges faced by the sisters.

We do know that Father John Quinn, pastor of the only Catholic Church in Sacramento, gave up his small house so the sisters would have a place to live. Many of the houses built in the early city were made of wood and were quickly assembled. Father's Quinn's house was just that and not in the best condition. In fact, the early *Annals* of the sisters noted in 1860 that Mary Baptist was coming to Sacramento to move the sisters from the "Shanty" to their new home at 9th and G Streets.[4]

The sisters really didn't have much time to think about their accommodations. The news of the school they would start was publicized in *The Sacramento Bee* on October 9:

A few days since, several "Sisters of Mercy" arrived in our city with the determination of making it their future home. It is determined to purchase a lot in a central locality, and erect, speedily as possible, an Orphan Asylum, provided the necessary funds can be obtained: consequently, those of our citizens who would like to see such an institution in Sacramento, must step forward immediately and subscribe liberally. It is proposed to erect a building sufficiently commodious to accommodate about one hundred orphans, as well as a large number of day scholars who will be taught, for a small consideration, the higher branches such as are not taught in the Public schools, including French, music, painting, needlework, etc. As orphans whose parents are Protestants, as well as Catholics are to be cared for alike, the project is one of Christian Charity in the largest and truest sense, and should appeal in the most efficacious manner, to all classes who may be able to contribute towards the accomplishment of the end in view.[5]

The need for new accommodations was easy to see. When school opened on October 5, there were sixty-five students in attendance. By the end of the term, that had ballooned up to 115. The classroom was a bit crowded. Space was not the only challenge. The original plan had been to hold school in the basement of St. Rose Church. Long time Sacramentans know the folly of that plan. The church basement could not be a long-term home for a school because of Sacramento's water table.

During heavy rains, the water table tends to push water up through the soil. Its force can break through concrete. Walking through the downtown area today, one can see that most of the old Victorian houses have elevated basements and long stairways leading to the first floor. This was not only for design purposes but necessary to avoid flooding. The full impact of that dynamic was felt even in the 1980s, when the sisters moved their novitiate to a home on 15th and T Streets. Not realizing that sump pumps were a downtown necessity during periods of heavy rain, the sisters soon discovered their basement was filled with water.

The children attending the first school came from a variety of backgrounds. While some might have been from economically solid families, others were too poor to contribute anything toward their education. Mother Baptist explained the shape of mercy education in a letter to Bishop Eugene O'Connell in 1862:

> We do not charge the children who attend our schools, but we take from their parents any voluntary offerings they make us. Our primary duties are the instruction of poor Girls, the protection of unemployed Women of good character, and the visitation of the sick. We do not exclude the Rich from our Schools. We endeavor to give all a thorough education, but we do not teach Music, Drawing, or any of those accomplishments that consume time, and are unsuited to the class to which we principally devote ourselves. We are willing to conduct a school for Infant Boys.[6]

In some ways, Mother Mary Baptist's letter is confusing. She clearly tells Bishop O'Connell, who was seeking a community of sisters for Grass Valley, that the fine arts were not part of the curriculum in a Mercy school. That was not actually the case. The description given in *The Sacramento Bee* was really more accurate. So why the difference? What caused Mary Baptist to change her stance? In the same letter to Bishop O'Connell, Mother Mary Baptist says: "but we never undertake any duty however meritorious in itself for the purpose of supporting the Community."[7] Within the context of life in Sacramento, that was not always possible.

While philosophically teaching only the poor might have been primary, in practice the importance of sustaining the ministry took first place. It was a case of using the resources of the wealthy to provide for the needs of those who were poor. The sisters quickly adapted when such undertakings were necessary to support the ministry itself. Since parents paid for them separately, music lessons quickly became a prime source of income to support the school when the monies coming in failed to do so. This was common among sisters in the American West. Anne Butler tells us:

> Among teaching congregations, no Sister on the faculty was of greater importance for adding to the financial accounts than the music teacher. Accomplishment on an instrument or in voice meshed with convent rituals of prayer and song, making nuns attentive to music in many forms.[8]

The limitation on available money was partially explained in the beginning of Mother Baptist's letter: "We do not charge the children who attend our schools, but we take from their parents any voluntary offerings they make us."[9] While these letters seem to be decisive, there was an important debate going on in the background: "Who were the sisters meant to serve?" Sisters coming from Kinsale were steeped in the belief that the sisters should only teach those who were poor. Other Mercy communities across the United States understood it differently. Mary Baptist, coming from Kinsale, had to struggle with the gap between the real-life situation found in Sacramento and the Kinsalian ideal. In a letter to Mother Francis Warde, the first Mercy foundress in the United States, she wrote:

> I have always been taught to consider Boarding Schools as entirely contrary to the Spirit of our Holy Rule every line of which breathes devotedness to the Poor and which even expressly forbids our receiving Boarders. Even day Academies for the children of the wealthier classes seems to me not in accordance with its Spirit ... Our Schools are entirely free, no child has, up to this, paid us one cent. A great deal will be done for Religious by good free Schools taught by Religious. I hope you will never have any other but for the Poor.[10]

The exchange of letters continued as the two Mercy pioneers sought to reconcile two different interpretations of Catherine McAuley's vision and response to the needs in front of her. They had to take that model and adapt it to their own cultural context and situation. In this conversation, Mother Warde brought new insight to Mary Baptist Russell concerning Catherine McAuley's own educational vision. Mary Baptist tells Mother Francis: "Many things you say are rather startling to me. I was quite unprepared to find our holy Foundress quoted in support of Boarding Schools which I was always led to consider a sort of innovation."[11] Unfortunately, the letter from Mother Frances Warde has been lost over time, but it evidently gave Mary Baptist lots to ponder.

In addition to her conviction that Sisters of Mercy were primarily called to serve those who are poor, another stumbling block remained. Mother Mary Baptist worried that the huge demands of running a boarding school/academy would diminish the time needed to reach out to those most in need. She thought that the sisters would lose their identity as servants of the poor and oppressed. Fortunately for Sacramento, Mary Baptist was always open to persuasion and to what was the common interpretation of Mercy leaders. She realized that other Mercy foundations in the United States did not consider such schools against the Mercy spirit and, in fact, Mercy boarding schools and academies were flourishing.

The question kept surfacing among the various Mercy communities until it was resolved in 1868 at a gathering of Mercy leaders in Ireland. Boarding schools won the day. Despite Mary Baptist's initial resistance, she embraced the idea of an academy. Once this fundamental issue was resolved in favor of teaching wealthy and poor alike, the future of Mercy education in Sacramento was assured.

Overcoming divergent understandings of the mission of Mercy education was not the only challenge the Sacramento community had to face. The popularity of the school forced the sisters to look for a new site. When *The Sacramento Bee* published its announcement about the new school, it included an important prerequisite: "provided the necessary funds can be obtained." Such funds were somewhat slow in coming, however, but by the end of 1857 sufficient monies were raised to purchase a half block on M Street between Tenth and Eleventh Streets. It was prime property, somewhat elevated, protecting it from flooding. The sisters paid $4,850 for the land, a significant investment, but paying for the land did not leave enough to cover the cost for the construction of a new school. The sisters simply had to wait until enough money could be found. Meanwhile, they continued teaching in the basement of the church.

Two years later, Mary Baptist describes the situation to Francis Warde:

In Sac. City their labors are confined to a day School averaging One Hundred & twenty, and the Visitation; in time they expect to have a Half Orphanage, but it is pretty hard to raise the necessary funds even in this so-called Golden Country ... In Sac. also they have a building lot secured but not the wherewithal to go further, however we console ourselves with the reflection that as a general thing great bodies move slowly.[12]

The letter from Mary Baptist is dated December 28, 1859. Less than three months later, in March 1860, the legislature passed the "Capitol Bill" claiming for the state a four-block area, which included the sisters' property. While the sisters had seen the property as ideal for a school, the State of California had other ideas in mind for the location. It was fortunate that the sisters did not begin construction of the new convent and school. It would have caused them great heartache as well as lost monies, since the state condemned the property and forced them to relinquish it.

Over the years, Sacramento had been in competition with other cities for the site of the state capital. Although designated as California's capital, members of the legislature had threatened to move the government center to another city if Sacramento did not do something to address the flooding issue. Sacramento was not about to let that happen. The parcel of land purchased by the sisters seemed ideal when joined with the rest of the block. Seeking to forestall any attempt to move the capital and attempting to find the best site in the city to locate the new capitol building, California claimed the sisters' property through eminent domain. The sisters were left with no land and, in spite of the increase in land prices, were reimbursed only the amount originally paid. Once more, they would have to search for a new site.

The urgency of finding a new home must have been fueled by the condition of the first convent. Mother Mary Gabriel Brown, Sacramento's first superior, had written to Mother Bridgeman in the spring of 1858 describing the house. While we do not have a copy of her letter, we do have Mother Bridgeman's response:

> M.M. G's gave us more real information than we had for a long time and it is better, for one knows the worst then be in doubt—We had no idea that your present dwelling is so unhealthy & in such bad repair—This of course make the building more necessary—May God enable you to get on with it.[13]

The *Annals* tell us that Mother Bridgeman's letter was partly prompted by hearing that five or six of the rooms were wet due to a leaky roof. The dampness of Sacramento's winter was beginning to take a toll on the health of the sisters.[14]

The search continued from March through July with many real estate agents bringing offers of the "ideal" new location. Finally, a hopeful option came up. The property of Colonel Ferris Foreman at 9th and G Streets was up for sale. The Foreman property was a half-block site that is described in the histories of the sisters as "a residence surrounded by a tasteful garden and fine orchard."[15] To this property was added the adjoining half-block. The purchase cost was given in the *Sacramento Daily Union* as about $4,000. The newspaper was greatly mistaken. The sisters had to pay double that for the Foreman residence and another $5,000 for the adjoining lot. Like its sister community in San Francisco, going forward the little community had to deal not only with the daily expenses of life and school but also with paying back the new indebtedness.

Again, trusting in Providence, the sisters set themselves to the task of building the long-awaited school. Mary Baptist traveled to Sacramento to help the Sisters move from the original shanty to the Foreman home. They named it St. Joseph's Convent. Other buildings were quickly constructed so that there would be room to accommodate the 120 students who returned in the fall. It was a huge undertaking. The feel of relief and excitement must have been palpable. The sisters would finally have a home large enough to accommodate more sisters and the space needed for daily convent activities. Students need not be squeezed into a "make-do" classroom. All the last-minute details that make a school welcoming had to be addressed, supplies counted, decorations in classrooms made and hung. When school started that fall, both students and sisters felt the joy of a new beginning. They had a permanent home. No one expected that another disaster would visit before the turning of the year.

Since its founding in 1849, Sacramento has been a city of very hot summers and a rainy season that begins in late November running into March. Early citizens remembered the great floods of 1850 and 1852 but never expected the major flooding that was just around the corner. The sisters had never experienced anything like it. It seemed like an ordinary school day on the morning of December 9, 1860, when around 10 a.m., a father came running into the school to claim his daughter before the flood waters reached the city. The Sacramento sisters shared the memory of that event with Mother Austin Carroll, Mercy historian, who visited Sacramento in 1888 to collect stories of the early foundations. This is how they remembered the day.

The day gave no hint of impending danger. In fact, it was clear and bright. When the first father arrived, they were surprised but soon others followed until diminished attendance warranted all the students being sent home. The sisters were still not particularly worried, not understanding the way of Sacramento floods. As they looked to the horizon, there was no evidence of raging water on the way. Then it happened. The sister on watch sounded the alarm as she saw the water rolling over the roads to the north east of the city. Quickly, the sisters tried to save their supplies stored in the basement, but the waters rapidly rose and whatever remained was lost. By this time, the one-story buildings in the neighborhood were underwater. Desperately, the sisters tried to save the pianos, but the waters came too fast. Soon, 3 feet of water inundated the convent.[16]

Mrs. Manning, a neighbor with two children, saw her home sink below the flood waters and her eight cows struggle to find refuge. Mother Austin summed up her hopelessness saying: "The poor woman, a Mrs. Manning, spent hours on the balcony, gazing vacantly on the surging waters, and bewailing the loss of her hard-earned home."[17] The little community was now trapped on the second floor of the residence. They welcomed the Manning family into the convent and did what they could to comfort them. Sacramentans struggled in the deluge, losing homes, livestock, and businesses. Biblical echoes of the story of Noah must have come to mind.[18]

One of the unsung heroines of the flood was Sister Genevieve McCue. She entered the community just before the opening of the Sacramento foundation and was professed in 1859. She was the convent cook for over twenty-three years. Since the flood had covered all the dry land, chickens in the area found safety on the convent roof. You can just imagine the scene Mary Austin describes:

> Their faithful servant, Pat McCormick, was helping everyone. As he had no way of feeding the fowls, he killed some every day, and boiled chicken was dished in the garret for breakfast, dinner and supper.[19]

Sister Genevieve had only a small grate on which to cook so she had to start lunch right after breakfast and supper right after dinner. It was quite a feat of perseverance and devotion.

After the first flood waters came, four of the sisters left the city and returned to San Francisco. Later that December, Father James Cassin, pastor of St. Rose, asked that the remaining sisters withdraw as well. With the flood waters still filling the city, lack of sanitation facilities, limited food supplies, and the city virtually digging out, father felt it was not safe for the sisters to stay and saw no way in which they could be of assistance. The sisters did return to San Francisco joining their sisters for an annual year-end retreat, but they had no intention of staying away. Sacramento was hurting and that is where they wanted to be. They begged permission from the archbishop to return and return they did in early January. Five sisters arrived back only a few days before there was a second major wave of flooding, one which did not completely dry out until May—a full five months later.

The sisters were right when they felt they could be of help to Sacramentans. Again, we turn to Mary Austin's account of events:

> The Sisters went daily in a large boat to the Pavilion, an immense building thrown open to the poor. Naturally, there was a good deal of sickness, and several deaths occurred. Families that had upper lofts withdrew to them; those who had not, took possession of deserted houses; the Sisters had ample scope for their zeal. As late as May, half the city was still under water. To minister to the sick and dying, the Sisters had to turn their prow towards windows on the second or third floor, and mount planks to enter. All the streets of Sacramento are lined with trees, and rowing between their tops in spring, when they are in full bloom, was like moving through a fairy scene.[20]

Moving through a wonderland of blossoms in a canoe might sound romantic, but reality was quite different. When we think of the great floods of modern time, we realize that floods leave behind contamination, disease, mold and devastation. People who grew up in Sacramento in the 1950s may remember the big floods of 1956 and 1957 prior to the building of Folsom Dam. Looking out over the levy by what is now the California State University, Sacramento, all that could be seen for miles was water.

Those floods always came at Christmas. Farmers like Daniel Doyle arrived in town from his farm in Nicolas with stories of his barn being swept away by the water, landing three fields over, his animals stranded. There was always concern that the levies would not hold or protect the city from its next great flood. That was in the 1950s when there were levies and flood gates protecting the city. In 1861, those were yet to come.

While the sisters waited to reopen the school, they carried on another work of mercy, which they had initiated when they arrived in the city—the visitation of sick in their homes. This was a treasured work of mercy described in the Rule of the Order. The sisters took on this ministry regardless of the conditions. Sacramento streets were not paved, often mired in dirt and mud, the homes of the sick were petri dishes growing disease.

Dr. Roy Jones in his book, *Memories, Men and Medicine: A History of Medicine in Sacramento, California,* calls the sisters the first visiting nurses in Sacramento. He tells us that Catherine's "walking nuns" made their way around the city on the weekends and after school, usually on foot. This was no small task since there were few sidewalks and Sacramento's rainy season made for muddy streets.[21] It is not surprising that the Annals of the sisters are dotted with notations about sisters who were unable to bear the hardships of Sacramento's climate, hardships, and level of disease. Sister Mary Francis Benson, one of the early Sacramento sisters, was forced to return to San Francisco due to the heat while others contracted malaria and consumption due to the environment.

The floods impacted the sisters in three ways. The immediate need was to find shelter for children who were either orphaned by the flood or whose families were left destitute and unable to provide for them. While it had been the desire of the sisters since the beginning of the Sacramento foundation to open an orphanage, it was now imperative and the sisters opened the convent to the children. The children were a combination of orphans and "half-orphans," children whose parents who were unable to care for them due to death of one parent, financial necessity, or necessary absence. At first, the effort was impromptu, but by 1863, the sisters were caring for twenty-nine orphans and half-orphans. The following year, that number doubled.

Another impact was the damage done to the convent by the flood waters. The house that provided welcome relief from the dampness and leaks of the original convent now became damp and leaky itself. Even before the flood, drainage had been a problem. *The Sacramento Bee* of July 26, 1860, had noted:

> The Sisters of Mercy complain that the water thrown from the stable on Seventh Street, between J and K, runs down under their school room and stagnates there, endangering the health and life of the scholars. It is to be hoped that the nuisance will not be continued.[22]

While that problem was resolved, this time relief from the damage caused by the flood waters would be much longer in coming.

Finally, the third impact was one which changed the St. Joseph's property from being a prime location to one which was less than desirable. When the sisters purchased the property, it was higher than the core city and less prone to flooding. After the floods of 1860–61, Sacramento had to do something to stop the destruction. Not only could they not endure repeated loss of lives and property, they were once again threatened with the removal of the state capitol. In fact, work on the state capitol itself was suspended. The result was the decision of city leaders to raise the core city. It is hard to guess what folks thought when that idea was surfaced. It was not a totally new idea having first been put forward in the 1850s, but how do you raise a whole core section of a town?

Sacramento historian Cheryl Anne Stapp gives a vivid snapshot of what the project must have been like. She tells us that a street grading program was launched by 1863 and property owners in the core city "were required to provide brick bulkheads to contain the fill, raise the fourteen-foot-wide sidewalks, and raise or modify their own buildings."[23]

The plan had lots of problems. You had to wait for the fill to settle. Then, not everyone was moving to the same clock. Sections of a street might be at various phases of the process, leaving pedestrians to navigate as best they could. Crude ramps and stairways were used to maneuver moving from one level to the next. In modern times, we grow impatient when a freeway construction project takes more than a year. For Sacramento, the raising of the downtown streets took ten years to complete.

The raising of the streets was great for Sacramento but bad for the sisters. The newly elevated city meant that the St. Joseph's property was no longer higher than the downtown property. Now the waters were draining into the 9th and G Street area. *The Sacramento Daily Union* of February 1866 gives us an idea of the problems:

> For several days past, the water which percolates through the ground from Sutter slough, as well as that which is accumulated by drainage,

has done considerable damage to the gardens and yards located in the vicinity of Eighth and Ninth and G and H Streets. This water collects, as heretofore, at Lake Hedenberg at Eighth and G Streets. The lake has been full to overflowing for two or three days and has found an outlet across Eighth Street which overflows the grounds of the Sister of Mercy.[24]

The article goes on to describe the route of the waters and the way in which the city was addressing the problem. They wanted it to be a quick resolution so forty men were employed to dig a ditch from 8th and R Streets. Beginning with a depth of 6 feet, it would increase to ten feet by the time it reached J Street. Since no more is said, one must presume the effort was successful.

Already but Not Yet

The first five years of Mercy in Sacramento were crisis times. Damp overcrowded housing, the state's seizure of their land, and massive flooding were marquee issues for the sisters during their initial years, but after 1863, the community entered into what might be called "ordinary times." The sisters became part of the fabric of the city—quiet but ever present. They were women of two worlds—that of San Francisco where the majority of the community lived, and that of Sacramento, which had become their home. During this early period, sisters coming to Sacramento never knew how long they would stay. It might be a few months or their stay could expand to many years. All was dependent upon the needs of the whole.

Researching these years is a little like walking in fog. Records have been lost or, if remaining, are skimpy in nature. Sometimes news reports in the papers of the times are misleading or inaccurate. In scanning reports of the day, you find them locating Sisters of Mercy in Italy, France, even persecuted in China. Since Mercy Sisters were never in those countries, it seems like every woman religious was called a "Sister of Mercy." There are internal reasons as well. The community in Sacramento was a branch house, not an independent entity. From its beginning in 1857 until 1886, its future, decisions, and life were shaped by community leadership in San Francisco. The records of those decisions are very brief and lack local color. It is a shadowy past waiting to be explored and brought into the light.

So where do we begin? Well, many families have a family member or friend hooked on tracing family genealogy. They work diligently at piecing together the story of family roots sometimes for years. They seek to know the who, what, when, and where of their family story. So it is with this search, but it is not confined to just one family. Instead, it is about a circle of women, the Sisters of Mercy who left a legacy of courage, compassion, and hope. Who were these women that shaped the Mercy story during the initial years in Sacramento?

The first surprise was the discovery that there were over twenty Mercy Sisters who ministered in Sacramento between 1857 and 1886. Although they were the founding sisters, their names are barely known today. They were a young lot, sometimes newly professed, sometimes even novices.

The first sisters to serve in Sacramento were Sisters Mary Gabriel Brown, Mary Paul Beechinor, Mary Agnes Stokes, Sister Martha McCarthy, and Sister Madeline Murray. Most of the Sacramento sources name only these five sisters but there was a sixth. The *San Francisco Annals* of the community tell us that the day after the sisters came to Sacramento, Sister Mary Francis Benson and a novice arrived.[1] They go on to tell us that the novice returned to San Francisco with Mother Russell who had accompanied the sisters to Sacramento and helped settle them into their new home. Mary Francis Benson, it seems, stayed on to be part of the new foundation. It is significant that Mother Mary Baptist gave Sacramento four of the seven surviving California pioneers. They were already experienced in the ways of the country and had learned how to maneuver the rapids of disease, prejudice, and scarcity.

It must have been difficult for Mary Baptist to part with these pioneer companions but a distant branch house needed all the support it could get. Recognizing that someone there would need to have the authority to make needed decisions, she sent Mother Mary Gabriel Brown to be the superior. Mother Mary Gabriel, professed barely a year before, had just been elected to be mother assistant. A woman sisters esteemed and trusted, she held a leadership role in the community for the next twenty-five years. Mary Gabriel was reflective, introverted, and drawn to the hidden life. You might call her a natural listener who lived the admonition of Catherine McAuley to speak the gentle word, give the tender compassionate look, and patiently listen to another's sorrow.

Mary Gabriel shared one unfortunate characteristic with her sisters. They were all adversely impacted by Sacramento's climate and the unhealthy living conditions of their convent home. The *San Francisco Annals* tell us that twice during the first year of the foundation, Mary Gabriel had to be brought back to San Francisco because of illness. She was consumptive and, for her, Sacramento's dampness and heavy fogs were debilitating. In spite of the hardship and risk, we find that after her recuperation time in San Francisco, Mother Mary Gabriel would return to her Sacramento home. In fact, she spent fifteen years in the Sacramento mission. Sister Mary Francis Benson and Mary Paul Beechnor did not endure so long.

Since the primary purpose of the foundation was focused on education, Mother Mary Baptist had sent two of her best teachers to Sacramento. They were very different personalities. Sister Mary Francis Benson was extroverted, impetuous, and determined.

> Education was the sphere where Sister Mary Francis excelled. Her gifts of imagination and openness led her to develop ways of reaching the many immigrant women who needed education and friendship. It was through her efforts that the St. Mary's Society was formed. This society provided a combination of learning, prayer, and community action. It had its own officers, funds, and policies.[2]

The establishment of sodalities such as the St. Mary's Society was a key element in fostering the spiritual life of Catholic women and it would thrive in Sacramento.

Sister Mary Francis was a woman who spoke her mind. She was an eager correspondent and filled her letters with graphic descriptions of life in California. She must have been very graphic in her letter to Mother Mary Francis Bridgeman about the state of the Sacramento House. The *Annals* quote Mother Bridgeman as writing: "As to dear Sr. M. Francis' exclamation that I would bring you all home if I went out, it is too late for that now."[3] Mother Bridgeman then went on to recommend that Mother Mary Baptist remind the archbishop of the "conditions on which you left your home & were entrusted to him."[4]

Sometimes, Sister Mary Francis's zeal ran ahead of what was expected or permitted. She was more of an "act first" sort of person, but it was that very zeal and passion that made her missteps so forgivable. Whatever was asked of her, she did wholeheartedly but what she could not do was withstand Sacramento's summer. Her time in the city was short, returning to San Francisco in the summer of '58 due to Sacramento's "debilitating heat." She must have returned to St. Joseph's when it was cooler. In March of the following year, the *Annals* once more say that Mary Baptist went to Sacramento to bring Sister Mary Francis back to San Francisco because she was so ill. It was feared she would not recover, but recover she did. This time she remained in San Francisco.

At the time of her death in February 1895, Archbishop Riordan said of her:

> She was not an ordinary woman but a woman of high culture, great refinement, splendid education and yet all those qualities were

spiritualized and sanctified, because they were used in the great service to which Almighty God called her ... So Almighty God led her from one heroism to another, from one year of preparation to another, until at last, after over three quarters of a century passed in His service, she quietly and gently passed away as a child goes to sleep in the arms of his mother.[5]

Sister Mary Paul Beechinor was more like Mary Gabriel in nature. Like her, she was a novice when she came to California, only nineteen years old. She was professed during the time of vigilantes in San Francisco. Sister Mary Paul was quiet, thoughtful, and very calm with a real gift for teaching. Her deeply prayerful spirit caused her to be appointed mistress of novices in June 1861 so she had to leave Sacramento. By the late fall, she began to experience hemorrhaging of the lungs. Since she was always somewhat frail, there was no general alarm about the event. Even with increasing frailty, Mary Paul went about her duties and the formation of her novices. In the August of the following year, she went to Grass Valley with Mother Russell who hoped the foothill air would help her. Whether the air helped her or not is questionable, but the stagecoach ride with its bruising bumps and jumps could not have been all that helpful.

Mary Paul's death came as a surprise to everyone but herself. During December 1862, she began giving small hints that she felt her death was near. When asked what new hymn she wished to teach the novices for Christmas, she said: "You may learn what you please, I will sing my *Adeste* in Heaven."[6] In just two days, she was gone. For the community, it was the loss of a joyful, gentle presence.

Mary Agnes Stokes, another of Sacramento's original group, came to the city as a novice. She is, like so many of the sisters who ministered in Sacramento, a story unknown. We know that she was born in Drogheda, Ireland. She was just eighteen when she entered the Sisters of Mercy in 1856. Received the following March, she took up her duties in Sacramento six months later. We do not know how long she stayed here or what she was like. In that regard, she is joined by others who have untold Sacramento stories: Sisters Mary Polycarp Casey, Mary Aquin Martin, Mary Cecilia Downing, Mary Helena O'Brian, Mary Paul Looby, Mary Assissium Blakeston, Mary Claire Lunney, later a superior of the Sacramento community, and Mary Catherine Fogarty, the only San Francisco sister to die in Sacramento. Perhaps, some who gave Sacramento their love and service will never be known to us.

There are small hints and glimmers of other Mercy women. Nora Bouse entered the community in Sacramento and was received in January 1858, taking the name Sister Mary deSales. Writing in *the Freeman's Journal*,

Dr. Phelan wrote: "This being the first public reception in Sacramento, the church was densely crowded with a very respectable and attentive audience."[7] Mary deSales Bouse went on to teach in Sacramento and later was elected mother assistant of the San Francisco community. We know that Sisters Veronica McQuaid and Madeleine Murray were the first two sisters professed in Sacramento. Their profession, which according to Mercy tradition would have been open to guests, furnished Sacramentans another window into the inner life of the community. Both Sisters Veronica and Madeleine were lay sisters. In some ways, their lives were even more hidden than their sisters who taught, nursed, or held leadership positions.

The Sacramento community had multiple lay sisters during these years; in fact, Mother Baptist once remarked: "We have opened a Branch in Sacramento, a city about one hundred miles from this, but there is daily communication by Steamer. Our community consists of thirty-four, pretty nearly one half of whom are Lay Sisters."[8] The Lay Sisters were abundant because American families rarely had sufficient monies for dowries. Their dowry was their physical labor. They took responsibility for the domestic duties of the community like laundry, cooking, cleaning and the daily care of orphans, elderly, and infirm.

A comprehensive education was normally beyond their reach as well. Due to their lack of education, they did not teach, pray the daily office in Latin, or share in leadership responsibilities. They even ate separately and recreated separately. They were not allowed to have Mary in their name. While we might grieve all the restrictions they experienced, one thing gives comfort. The lay sisters were loved and valued by all their sisters. They were the ones that kept things going behind the scenes. Among these unsung heroines who served in Sacramento were Sisters Rose Smith, Zita Nash, Josephine Denis, Madeline Murray, and Bridget Maher. The latter was a young woman during Sacramento's giant floods of 1861–62. She was so impressed with the witness of the sisters that she joined them as soon as the waters began to recede.

From today's perspective, one can see the courage and contributions of the lay sisters. It is clear from community records that they were loved but they still were denied equal status. Religious communities of the 1800s, like society in general, hung on to class distinctions that emerged in medieval times. Many American bishops found class distinctions abhorrent and considered the practice a waste of talent. Though urging its elimination, they did not forbid the practice. Some made matters worse by refusing religious superiors the permission to waive monetary requirements for prospective candidates. The custom of bringing a dowry to the community endured all the way up to the 1920s because religious orders were dependent upon the dowries brought to the community by new members. Sisters received no salaries at the time, were rarely recipient of church support, and had to support their ministries on their own.

A few lay sisters broke the mold, though. Sister Martha McCarthy was one of those sisters. She was the fourth of the early pioneers assigned to Sacramento. In her case talent trumped custom. A remembrance written of her says:

> Mother Baptist had noticed Sister Martha's quick intelligence and wonderful rapport with little boys and took the risk of putting her in charge of a class of small boys ... As it turned out, she was a natural with a unique gift for dealing with small boys. She was strict with them, but they adored her. She won a reputation throughout the parish as a remarkable teacher of religion and the other basic R's.[9]

The sisters coming to Sacramento must have been surprised by their welcome. Unlike San Francisco papers, Sacramento newspapers printed stories of welcome and support, not censure and attack. In fact, a review of the various news articles of those years consistently shows appreciation and support for the sisters. What is remarkable, though, is that rarely is an individual sister named. The silence around individual sisters even led to the *Daily Union* commenting:

> The regular annual commencement exercises of St. Joseph's Academy, under the conduct of the Sisters of Mercy, whose modest reticence induces them to refuse the names of those who fill the chairs of the faculty, were held at the Convent of the Sisterhood yesterday, beginning at 1 p.m. and occupying the entire afternoon.[10]

This reticence to speak of a specific sister extends to community documents as well. Some clues are only found in the obituaries and surviving recollections of others.

A great example of this dynamic is the picture given to us of Sister Genevieve McCue, another of Sacramento's lay sisters. She was remembered not just for her holiness but for her sense of humor. Her internal community obituary relates:

> This dear Sister devoted herself for many years to whatever domestic employment was assigned to her. For twenty-three years, she was in charge of the kitchen at Sacramento. Some amusing incidents are recorded of her many pranks. On one occasion, she had set before the Superior a delicious-looking pie, which, on being cut, was found to consist of a dish of empty spools covered by a nice crust. At another

time, she sent in a savory dish, saying that it had been donated by a neighboring French Restaurant. After the Sisters had partaken liberally and enthused sufficiently, to Sister Genevieve's amusement, she confessed that the dish was composed of the remains of a previous meal disguised by her own ingenious method ... This good Religious was characterized as "whole-souled" and, no doubt, she received a bountiful reward for her holy, laborious life when her Divine Spouse called her on Jan. 20, 1915.[11]

Sister Genevieve's twenty-three years in Sacramento must have been challenging. She served as cook through flood, summer heat, and sometimes scarcity. Sister Genevieve's final gift to Sacramento was volunteering to stay with the community as it moved to independence in 1886.

Four other sisters contributed to the story of Mercy in Sacramento: Mary Teresa King, Mary Joseph O'Rourke, Mary Ligouri Madden, and Mary Vincent Phelan. All were superiors at St. Joseph's Academy. The exploits of Mother Mary Ligouri and Mother Mary Vincent will be saved until later in the story for these two women were entrusted with the leadership and care of the community after it became independent in 1886. The stories of Mary Teresa and Mary Joseph are interlaced with the story of another Mercy foundation made in 1863—the Convent of the Sacred Heart, in Grass Valley.

The Grass Valley foundation differed in three ways from that in Sacramento. First, it was meant to be an affiliate house, not a branch house. That meant it would be a self-sufficient, self-governing community as soon as it had seven professed members. The second variance flowed from Grass Valley's location. It is nestled in the foothills, above the fog and swampy conditions of nineteenth-century Sacramento. This change in climate, plus a sturdy house, meant fewer health challenges for the small group. The third aspect, however, was a troubling challenge. Eugene O'Connell, the first and founding bishop of the Grass Valley diocese, was not an easy person with whom to work. He could be demanding, authoritarian, and prone to think that the sisters must follow his wishes even when they were in conflict with their own religious rule.

The people of Grass Valley, like those in Sacramento, were eager to have the sisters. Father Thomas Dalton, the pastor, already had a school with 120 pupils, but there was great need for an orphanage. It certainly seemed promising. What almost derailed the foundation was a clash between Bishop O'Connell and the foundation's first superior, Mary Teresa King, over what works could and could not be done. The situation was made even more difficult due to the emotional frailty of Mary Teresa. The *Annals* tell us she was a nervous, timid person quite unsuited to deal with an overbearing bishop.

The catalyst for the conflict was the bishop's demand that the sisters open an orphanage for boys. This was beyond the imagining of Mary Teresa who was a strict interpreter of the Mercy Rule. For her, it was about girls. Since the rule did not name teaching boys as part of the work of the congregation, in her mind, it was forbidden. The bishop was irate, writing to Father Dalton:

> A positive refusal to receive the boys or have anything to do with them I look upon as disobedience to the Bishop of the Vicariate. If the Sisters persist in their refusal to take charge of the boys I will either transfer them or discharge them. Either alternative may be rather unpleasant so I request of you in my name to tell the good Sisters that I recognize no Sisterhood that won't obey me ... My ultimatum is then: Let the holy Sisters in Grass Valley either agree to take charge of little boys or repair without delay to Yreka where they shall have charge of little girls. May God direct them to the best.[12]

Needless to say, this whole situation was a difficult one for Mary Baptist Russell and called for all her diplomatic skills. As was her custom, she consulted widely not only with other sisters but with Mother Bridgeman in Kinsale and with Archbishop Alemany.

A review of the situation surfaced several contributing factors: Mary Teresa did not possess the temperament to handle the demands of her role as she was too nervous, too cautious, and lacked physical stamina; neither Mary Teresa nor Mary Joseph O'Rourke believed in the viability of the Grass Valley foundation as the lack of funds, demands of the bishop, and the pressures of providing formation for new members was beyond what they thought they could do; and there was no prohibition on teaching younger boys, only custom and social propriety—could these be set aside in the face of need?

Mother Mary Baptist had a hard task on her hands. Not only did she need to resolve the dilemma in Grass Valley, but she needed to convey to Bishop O'Connell that he did not have the authority to transfer her sisters or to interpret the Mercy Rule. When Catherine McAuley founded the community, she sought and received papal approval of the Rule. Such approval, received in 1841, meant that only the Pope through his representatives or the sisters themselves, with the approval of papal authorities, could change their Rule. It was left to the community to interpret it. No individual bishop had that power, even if some bishops sometimes thought they did.

All things considered, Mary Russell did what she felt she had to do. She recalled both Mary Teresa and Mary Joseph and sent new, more flexible sisters to the foundation. It was a disappointing failure for Mary Joseph and Mary Teresa, both of whom later served as superiors in Sacramento without tension or incident. Mother Mary Baptist tried to console them:

> Now don't spend time pondering over the past or imagining what may be here after but meekly acquiesce in what has been arranged and keep your mind quiet, attend also to your health. You must pray fervently that God may now in mercy direct all to His own honor and glory.[13]

Sister Mary Baptista Synon, the next superior, did not fare much better. This time, the bishop's complaint was that she was too understanding and had too much "forbearance" with the sisters. Mother Mary Gabriel Brown, just elected to succeed Mother Baptist Russell as superior, comments: "Again we have to speak of the cross in Grass Valley. It will be evident to everyone that the extreme of caution is required to manage well with his Lordship."[14] Once more, another "Head" would have to be found. Mary Gabriel found the ideal "Head" in Mary Baptist Mogan, whom she selected as the next superior for Grass Valley. She was well-suited for the task and well able to deal with the bishop. The foundation thrived under her guidance.

Meanwhile, the Sacramento foundation was quietly growing. The city's newspapers faithfully recorded the successes of St. Joseph's and gave glowing reports. Commenting on the graduation exercises in 1865, *The Sacramento Bee* says:

> All present seemed to enjoy themselves very much, and to feel highly pleased with the progress and proficiency of the pupils. St. Joseph's School is a great benefit to Sacramento and should be assisted by every lover of watchful training and virtuous education of young girls. The Sisters of Mercy could accomplish more if they were free from the pecuniary embarrassment that oppresses their institution. Notwithstanding the past generosity of the people, I am informed that the debt is four thousand five hundred dollars which, until paid, will prevent them from carrying out plans for the convenience and for the benefit of the people.[15]

Throughout the 1860s, Sacramentans were urged by both the *Sacramento Daily Union* and *The Sacramento Bee* to come to the aid of the sisters, primarily to support their ministry to orphans and half orphans.

The full extent of the "pecuniary embarrassment" was outlined in an appeal for support made to the state. In asking for a grant of $5,000 to support the orphans sheltered by St. Joseph's, Sister Mary Teresa King, then its superior, describes the situation:

The block between F, G, Eighth and Ninth Streets now occupied by the Asylum was purchased in 1859 at a cost of $12,000. In 1863 a commodious dwelling was built, which with the school rooms and other improvements, required an expenditure of $10,000, making a total outlay of $22,000. $19,000 of this amount have been paid; of which sum $2,160 was received from the State and the balance from various charitable sources. There is, therefore, $3000 of debt remaining. The Managers have maintained a yearly average of twenty orphans including children deserted by their parents and have provided permanently for ten children. Have twenty-five orphans in charge at present, including children deserted by their parents, and twenty half orphans each of the latter paying $7.00 per month. The necessary expenses of the institution are over $500 per month. It is under the charge of the Sisters of Mercy, and the special object is to maintain and educate orphan girls of all denominations, and as far as possible provide for their future welfare in society. Ask for $5000 appropriation[16]

Sacramentans were generous in giving the sisters their financial support. A review of articles in the 1860s shows such things as "a cow and calf" raffle, a benefit ball held in the state assembly chamber, the Emmets Guard benefit for St. Patrick's Day, May Festivals, and, of course, musical performances and benefit fairs, often hosted at the Agricultural Hall. It would not be an exaggeration to say that the work of the sisters was supported by the whole of Sacramento. *The Sacramento Bee* comments on that reality:

That the school referred to has done much good is acknowledged by all classes of our citizens who have any information on the subject. The festival to be given this evening will, no doubt be largely attended by Protestants as well as Roman Catholics. We know, in fact, that many prominent ladies of Sacramento, who are Protestant, have taken a deep interest in the success of the fair and festival. They have exerted themselves with an eye to the benefit of the orphan irrespective of sect, and with the view to the encouragement of those noble, self-sacrificing women, the Sisters of Mercy.[17]

Philanthropy was key to the sisters' sustainability, but always the fundraising was for the ministry, rarely for the needs of the sisters themselves.

With the school thriving and the community planted firmly in Sacramento, Mother Baptist Russell decided it was time for the community at St. Joseph Convent to become independent. To do that would require the permission of Archbishop Alemany, who was not of a like mind.

Writing to Mother Gabriel in January 1867, she shared that "You will see by this that our good Abp. does not approve of making St. Joseph's 'Stand alone' yet awhile, so of course that point is settled."[18]

We can only speculate on the archbishop's reasons for not granting Sacramento independence. The necessary mediations Mother Russell had to bring to the Grass Valley situation; an episcopal desire for a more centralized authority to guide smaller communities; or, perhaps, the financial struggles of Sacramento itself all might have played a part but, as Mother Baptist shared, "the point is settled," and settled it was, at least for the next twenty years.

What was not settled, however, was the elimination of unhealthy living conditions at St. Joseph's. The growth of the orphanage and school had resulted in overcrowded quarters. Even though the sisters had built a spacious building for both school and orphanage in 1863, it was not large enough to meet the growing need. The chapel was too small to accommodate sisters and residents. Having survived the floods in 1862, the sisters found themselves with other watery problems caused by unhealthy drainage from Sutter slough. The house was left damaged by the great flood and had not been adequately repaired. There were health risks for both sisters and students.[19]

By the winter of 1868, conditions reached an unacceptable level. In March, both the mother assistant and bursar were sent up to Sacramento to check out the situation. Not only did they find crowding, but also a leaky and unsuitable house. The people were more than willing to assist the sisters in building a new home and orphanage, but Archbishop Alemany would not allow such a project to be undertaken until the debt on St. Rose Church was paid. Evidently, he feared that fundraising for the convent would delay paying down the church debt.

The large debt on St Rose's Church was caused by an extensive renovation. Adding cornices and other aesthetic improvements had been expensive and the parish was struggling to erase the debt. The sisters would have to wait, even though it was a danger to their health. The wait was costly. Both Sisters Mary Joseph O'Rourke and Sister Zita Nash, who spent ten years at St. Joseph's, fell victim to malaria while at St. Joseph's. Other sisters became consumptive.

Life for the sisters continued in spite of the difficulties. To their school duties, the sisters added not only visitation of the sick in their homes but also visitation of prisoners. Throughout these years, numerous articles were published on the ministry of the sisters to prisoners at the jail who were awaiting execution. Often the same articles would comment on the solace or change of spirit brought about through those visits to men like Louis Kahl, W. Williams, Col. Frank Hudson, and Au Luck.[20]

Nursing skills were sometimes supplied in emergencies. One such occasion was the explosion of the steamer *Washoe*. The Sisters of Mercy went to the hospital to assist with care of the victims. The small facility, Vernon House Hospital, sheltered the burned and dying. Among the seventeen who died was Father Callen.[21] Unfortunately, such steamboat explosions were not rare. In the October of the following year, the explosion of the *Chrysopolis* claimed their compassion. There were many victims, and government offices were transformed into a temporary hospital. *The Sacramento Bee* commented: "The patients are receiving every attention at the hands of humane men and women. The Sisters of Mercy, as usual, on such occasions, are doing all in their power to alleviate the pains and agonies of the sufferers."[22]

Like the persistent widow of the Gospels, the sisters did not give up their request for a new convent and orphanage. They were back at it in 1871. Once more, the archbishop denied their request, again noting the large debt of the church and insisting that its elimination took precedence. At this point, a group of Sacramento gentlemen decided to act on the need by sponsoring what they called a "Grand Gift Concert" to raise funds for the sisters. Knowing the bishop's position, the sisters had declined their offer but news of the event got into the papers anyway. Planning was already underway and the event publicized. The archbishop was adamant that no fundraising event for the sisters be held. He wrote a disclaimer for the papers:

> It having come to my notice, that a certain project entitled a "Gift Concert" to take place in Sacramento on Thanksgiving Day, is advertised as 'having for its object the building of a free school & Orphanage on the grounds of the Sisters of Mercy in Sacramento" and as it might appear from the advertisement that said project had my sanction, I take this opportunity of informing the public that I disclaim all connection with it, and that I do not wish my name or that of any Religious Body under my charge, to appear as countenancing or encouraging enterprises of this nature.[23]

The question of the new building did not end there. The gift concert was held and the sisters did receive monies from the benefit, but just for the support of the orphans, not a new building. In April of the following year, Archbishop Alemany writes to the Mother Baptist Russell admonishing the sisters to be patient, to not cause "anything that could place us in a bad light or hinder the work of paying the debt," and strongly suggesting that the sisters sell St. Joseph's and relocate to a more central part of the city.[24] He suggests that she go and see for herself, sharing that he has only hinted the proposal to the sisters.

Perhaps the archbishop thought that the sisters would meekly acquiesce to his wishes, but that was not the way things went. The sisters were as determined to retain St. Joseph's as the archbishop was to have them relocate. They loved the grounds, the gardens with fruit trees and flowers, and the spaciousness of the campus. Most of all, the sisters felt a second school was needed for the growing city, not a relocated one. The *Annals* tell us that they prayed, planted four statues of St. Joseph, one on each corner of the property, and declined the proposal. In this position, they were encouraged by men of the city that they trusted. We do not know who these advisors were or what expertise they brought to the sisters, but looking back, it was not a good decision. The archbishop was correct in thinking that the location was removed from the path of city growth and was prone to flooding during wet winters. For the sisters, however, it was their home, a space they had created and shaped. For the future, the die was cast. St. Joseph's would stay where it was.

After all this, it is surprising to read that less than five months later, new buildings were being constructed. Once the sisters refused to relocate, the archbishop must have relented. There are no letters or comments in the *Annals* about what changed the archbishop's mind, but they tell us that on September 8, a groundbreaking for new buildings took place, and on March 19, 1873, the sisters took possession of their new buildings. Without the worries of inadequate housing and poor conditions, the sisters could give themselves completely to educational excellence and care of the sick poor in their homes.

For the next twelve years, education took center stage. Programs expanded, and new courses were added to meet the demands of the day. In 1875, St. Joseph's was incorporated by the state and authorized to confer diplomas of high school graduation. This was a major step in making what was now called St. Joseph Academy, a premier institution for women's education. That became even more significant when, in 1878, a "normal school" was added to the academy.[25] The normal school was dedicated to training teachers and provided Sacramento public schools with women fully trained to provide excellence in education. One graduate of St. Joseph's, Minnie Rooney became superintendent of schools in Sacramento County. She had the distinction of being elected to the post before women even had the vote.

The close ties of St. Joseph's and public education leaders are seen in the attendance lists published at the time of commencement exercises. For the graduation exercises of 1879–80, *The Sacramento Bee* tells us: "The attendance of visitors was large, among them being several members of the Board of Education of this city and a number of leading citizens, all of whom were highly entertained by the interesting programme."[26] Minnie

Rooney was part of that graduating class as was Lizzy King, the first young woman to enter Mercy after its separation from San Francisco in 1886.

Another change visited the St. Joseph's community in 1878, this time unexpected. The state legislature, which provided support for orphans and half orphans, decided to streamline the funding process by supporting only two Catholic orphanages in the North State, St. Vincent's in the bay area, and the orphanage staffed by the Sisters of Mercy in Grass Valley. Unable to sustain the care of dependent children without state funding, the sisters entrusted their charges to the care of their sisters in Grass Valley. St. Joseph's, adapting to the times, added a boarding option for young women whose families lived in rural area. Times were changing but there more changes on the way.

On Their Own

During the years 1865–1885, the Sacramento's citizens witnessed waves of change happening around them. These years saw the advent of the transcontinental railroad, the miracle of electricity, and the invention of the telephone, all making huge changes in society. They witnessed the transformation of Sacramento from a gateway to the mines to an urban center for commerce. The sisters lived through civil war times, the economic depression of 1873, and the raising of downtown Sacramento to prevent flooding. Through all these transitions and more, they had adapted to the signs of the times. Reading the "signs of the time" was not easy. It meant anticipating the next urgent need, projecting what educational focus would be most needed in the future, and what adaptations would be necessary to meet the next societal change. On the horizon was one such change, one that would substantially alter their future. It had to do with changes in church organization.

Significant growth occurred in the Catholic community in Northern California during the second half of the 1800s. In 1860, the vicariate of Marysville was established under the leadership of Bishop Eugene O'Connell. His vicariate stretched to the Oregon border, included parts of Nevada, and stopped north of Sacramento. Pious, zealous, and erudite, O'Connell was not an ideal leader. Bishop Thaddeus Amat of Los Angeles summed it up well: "He has no talent for governing."[1] Bishop O'Connell demanded a great deal of his priests and was not always respectful of the boundaries of authority with women religious. The early years of the Mercy Foundation in Grass Valley attested to that reality. Mother Russell had to use all her finesse to keep Bishop O'Connell satisfied while protecting the autonomy of the young community.

Bishop O'Connell's relationship with his priests might be characterized as arbitrary. He demanded obedience and perfection, overlooking limitations of body and spirit. Father Steven Avella, an authority on the history of the Sacramento Diocese, puts it this way:

> By 1880 Bishop O'Connell's unpopularity with his clergy had reached a nadir and even Roman authorities agreed he needed to be eased out. Two men turned down offers to be Bishop O'Connell's coadjutor. Finally, local priests and even Bishop O'Connell himself (although he later withdrew his support) pressured Father Manogue to accept episcopal ordination.[2]

The soon-to-be bishop would not agree without conditions. Far-sighted in his understanding of dynamics within Northern California, Manogue believed that the center of the diocese should be in Sacramento. The mining towns, once so dominant, were quickly losing their influence. Father Manogue, a former miner himself, would only accept the call to be coadjutor if the center of the diocese moved to Sacramento, a city emerging as a center of commerce and state government. For the sisters, this was a fateful decision.

From its foundation in 1857 until the late 1880s, the Sacramento Mercy Community was under the supervision of the Mercy motherhouse in San Francisco. The Sacramento sisters did not choose who would come to minister at St. Joseph's or how long they would stay. They could not initiate needed ministries without the blessing of their leaders in San Francisco, and they had no voice in selecting who would be their local superior. All of that was determined by the leaders in San Francisco. Mother Mary Baptist herself would come to Sacramento periodically to encourage and support the sisters as well as check on their ministry and well-being. Although she had suggested very early on that they become separate and independent, that had not been approved by Archbishop Alemany. By Mercy custom, however, houses of the congregation that were established in a different diocese became independent. Bishop Patrick Manogue's demand that Sacramento become the center of the new diocese would necessitate the redrawing of diocesan lines, separating Sacramento from the San Francisco diocese. That meant separating the St. Joseph's community from their sisters in San Francisco.

How soon the sisters were made aware of the impending transition is unknown. It took Manogue five years to negotiate the final agreement with Archbishop Riordan, then San Francisco's archbishop, so it is probable that the final decision was not a total surprise. Little is known about how the sisters felt about this development. There would no longer be the flow of members between the convents. No community gatherings or retreats would bring the sisters to San Francisco where they could reconnect with friends. On the other hand, they could put down deep roots in the city knowing that their primary focus would now be Sacramento.

There are no records of the conversations that took place in the community or any hint of what it meant to either the Sacramento or San Francisco sisters. We do know that the sisters living at St. Joseph's were given a choice to be part of the new Sacramento community or to return to San Francisco. The *San Francisco Annals* tell us:

> Early this year the Arch-diocese was re-divided. Sacramento being made the episcopal city for the upper diocese under the jurisdiction of Bishop Manogue. The Sisters were given their choice to remain permanently or for a time on the new foundation or to return to their Mother-house, St. Mary's San Francisco. Sister M. Vincent Phelan, who had nearly the whole of her religious life labored in Sacramento, preferred to remain permanently, though she did not resign her rights to this community also Sister M. Ligouri Madden who had given up all claim on this Community in 1881. Sisters M. Aquin Martin, Cecilia Downing, Helena O'Brian, Genevieve McCue and Rose Smith, volunteered for few years, that is, until the new recruits for that house were professed.[3]

Bishop Manogue, having finished his negotiations concerning the boundaries of the diocese, got his wish. Sacramento became the center of the new diocese in May, 1886 and its episcopal see. One year later, on May 26, 1887, Mother Mary Vincent Phelan was appointed superior of the Sacramento Mercy community and a new chapter in the life of Sacramento's sisters began. Within the first months, fourteen women entered the community. Mother Mary Vincent and Mary Ligouri Madden were assisted by five San Francisco sister volunteers. Forming the new members in the spirit of the institute must have been challenging but the combined wisdom of the senior members guaranteed it a solid foundation.

By August, Bishop Manogue completed his move to Sacramento and the sisters hosted a grand reception in his honor at St. Joseph's. The *Annals* of Sacramento give a sense of what that welcome was like. The entrance to the convent was decorated with evergreens and mottoes, as was the chapel. A large scarlet hanging on which the word "Welcome" was inscribed in gold hung from the stage entrance into the hall. Between the two main pillars of the room, which were wreathed in ivy, was a scroll of purple cloth upon which the words: "Long Live Our Prelate" were printed in gold. The Children of Mary had a three-part program prepared that included an address on the "singular auspicious day," typical of the times.[4] It was effusive in praise of the newly arrived bishop but also expressive of what his arrival in the city meant to the Catholic community. Julia Wiseman, speaking for the Children of Mary, put it this way:

> With reason then may we rejoice today regarding as we do, your Lordship's advent among us as the harbinger of many and great advantages to Sacramento, of untold blessings, both spiritual and temporal, to ourselves.[5]

Bishop Manogue brought energy and focus to the growth of the church in Sacramento. Pastorally, he demonstrated concern about the life and work of the sisters. Not only did the bishop attend the academy commencements and preside at receptions and professions of new members, he also attended planning meetings about the future of the academy. The size of the academy as well as the increasing size of the community itself demanded expansion. Bishop Manogue had just completed building Sacramento's new cathedral. Now he was looking toward the next project. As discussions on the need of the academy continued, the question of relocating the Academy to another site surfaced. Although the bishop was in favor of this option, the "idea of removal was abandoned, and a wing was added facing on 9th Street, containing primary school rooms, recreation halls and dormitories for boarders and music rooms."[6]

Constructing the needed buildings was a leap of faith. The monetary situation for the sisters was highly precarious. We get a sense of the situation from two articles appearing in *The Sacramento Bee*. The first, in November, 1889 relates:

> A festival and fair will be held in Sacramento during the week preceeding [*sic.*] Christmas, for the benefit of the Sisters of Mercy of this city, who are sadly in need of aid. A change in the division of the Order throughout the State has left the Convent here almost entirely dependent upon its own exertions.[7]

While fairs, benefits and entertainments put on for their welfare helped the community, it was not enough. By fall of 1891, the situation had escalated:

> For many months the Sisters of Mercy of this city have been confronted with a condition of affairs at the Convent that has already left that institution in sore financial straits. The school has been in existence many years and was recognized a leading educational Institution, and up to a few years ago enjoyed a liberal patronage ... But of late the sanitation of the place has been so imperfect that the school lost favor with many,

who seemed to think that the health of their children would be impaired if compelled to remain longer in the building.[8]

The coverage in the *Sacramento Daily Union* was even more pointed:

> These good sisters who have done so much for others ... have recently fallen into sore straits. The prevalence of sickness in the vicinity of their convent, caused by the bad sewerage and the accumulating of water on low lots, had done much to keep pupils away, and to lose to them some of their best scholars. The result was that the convent had been gradually but surely falling off in scholarship, and that the various expenses of the institution have had to be met by the contributions of those who knew the wants of the Sisters and appreciated them for the good deeds they had done.[9]

The papers continued at length to make the case that the friends of the sisters and, in fact, the Sacramento community must come to the aid of the sisters. They described all the improvements needed, everything from a new sewage system to an ornamental fence, from new classrooms to improved street frontage. *The Sacramento Bee* notes: "To do this will require an outlay of many thousands of dollars, but the gentlemen who have interested themselves in the good cause anticipate no trouble in securing the amount necessary."[10] Essentially, the *Bee* issued a call to action and made an emotional appeal to the city for a response of gratitude:

> The Sisters' work in this city has been a labor of love. The city has been made better for their presence, and without show or ostentation of any kind they have gone along these many years relieving the distressed, bringing comfort to the sick and dying. It is seldom that the public has been asked for assistance in their behalf, and there should be no delay in accomplishing the good work inaugurated last night.[11]

Looking back from the perspective of time, the whole situation must have been a profound embarrassment to the sisters. They had only been an independent community for five years and their future did not seem promising. To be in debt was a social taboo. They had nothing to sell to raise money. Only the infusion of philanthropy could avert disaster.

The Sacramento Bee continued its call for assistance throughout the coming weeks until it could announce on November 27 that $16,118.50 of the needed monies had been donated. With even more donations anticipated, the work on St. Joseph's could go forward. Eventually, the monies would increase to $25,000. The campaign had another goal as well, "to place the Sisters entirely out of debt and turn over to them an institution which will be self-supporting."[12] In less than two months, the people of Sacramento had contributed today's equivalent of $450,000 in support of the sisters. In April 1892, the final major donation would arrive just in time to pay for the completed work. It was a $5,000 donation from Leland Stanford, one of the four railroad barons of the time and a dedicated philanthropist.[13]

The past months had not been easy for the little community. Its rapid growth meant working in tight quarters. Boarders from the outlying farms had increased as well as day students. While the sisters were now about twenty-eight in number, there was still much to do. In the middle of their busyness, plans of expanding St. Joseph's, and welcoming more members into the community, death visited. Just before the beginning of the campaign to renovate the convent and school, Sister Mary Dolores Liston died.

Sister Mary Dolores was one of the first ten sisters to join the new foundation. She now was the first of the Sacramento community to die. Weakened by a frail constitution, shocked by her father's death just six months after she entered the community, and living in the less than healthy condition of the convent, she died of apnosa at the age of twenty-four.[14] A window into the spirit of this young missionary is given in the description of her found in her published obituary:

> She was truly an "angel of peace and mercy" in their midst, and during her lingering illness was the edification and comfort of her religious sisters by her cheerful endurance and her humility, and the gratitude with which she received their loving ministrations.[15]

A change in leadership came for the sisters in 1893. Mother Mary Vincent Phelan had been the local superior in Sacramento long before the new community was established. Her term of office expired in '93, and the sisters selected Sister Mary Ligouri Madden as their new superior. Sister Mary Ligouri served as principal of St. Joseph's for a number of years but also had extensive nursing experience. This dual interest readied her to take on a major expansion of the Mercy mission in Sacramento.

For many years, Sacramento's medical community saw the need for a public hospital to serve the needs of the civic community. There was a county hospital for the indigent and a hospital dedicated to Southern Pacific patients, but none for the general public. As a result, ordinary folks had to go to San Francisco to seek adequate medical care for illnesses needing hospitalization or serious surgery. Among those physicians seeking to remedy this deficiency was Dr. G. L. Simmons.

Dr. Simmons was the owner of a small private hospital (sanitarium really) called Ridge Home located on Poverty Ridge. It could accommodate a maximum of fifteen patients, but was not equipped to do surgeries or anything major. His hope was that the medical profession in Sacramento would come together in support of a private hospital and he was most willing to turn over the property to such an association without any monetary consideration.[16] That did not happen. Ridge Home would continue to serve the sick, administered by a Mrs. L. Kane, but it was not what Sacramentans needed.

Things would have continued that way except for the intervention of Dr. Thomas W. Huntington, then the chief surgeon of the Southern Pacific Railroad Company, who thought about the possibility of asking the Sisters of Mercy to take on the task. He was both persistent and persevering in his appeals to Mother Ligouri. What Sacramento needed was a sisters' hospital comparable to St. Mary's in San Francisco.

Though the sisters continued to visit the sick in their homes, they were hesitant to take on the responsibility of a hospital. While they had been part of the San Francisco community, there never was a large pool of sisters available for Sacramento. Lack of personnel and monies always stood in the way of moving beyond their work at St. Joseph's. While they could visit the jail, care for the sick in their homes and teach extra religion classes on Sundays, they could not stretch themselves to take on another institution. Now with Sacramento as their center, St. Joseph's renovated, and increased numbers of sisters available, the situation had changed but still there were challenges. Taking on Ridge Home would mean taking on the financial and administrative responsibility for the undertaking as well as providing for the day to day running of a hospital. Having just paid out $20,000 for the renovation of St. Joseph's, the sisters had little to no financial resources to spare. Yet, in the face of scarcity, Mother Mary Ligouri said "Yes." Need triumphed over lack of resources.

The first step was acquiring property. Dr. Simmons was most willing to sell Ridge Home and its adjoining property to the sisters. Never one to think of his own financial advantage, he was reluctant to ask full price for his property. He asked for an appraisal, but the evaluation was so low that Mother M. Ligouri did not want to accept the $12,000 appraisal. She made several attempts to have a just cost determined, but Dr. Simmons would have none of it. He would accept only the appraised amount. Mother Ligouri gave only her personal note as guarantee that the monies would be paid. Grateful for the work the sisters were doing, Dr. Simmons not only settled for $12,000, but returned to the sisters the full amount of their last payment. It took almost eight years for the debt to be paid in full.

The sisters took possession of the hospital on August 1, 1895. Mother M. Ligouri, herself, took charge of the new endeavor with Sisters Mary Agnes Leahy, Mary Columba Somers, Mary Teresa O'Connor, and Baptist Smith as her companions. Aiding the cause was Dr. Stephen Cleary, resident physician and two practical nurses; Dollie Hadlock; and Nettie Barrymore. William Cummings became the first orderly. When they started, there were only two patients at Ridge Home, one with typhoid, the other suffering from septicemia, probably caused by an abdominal problem.[17] During the next week, the volume doubled to four patients. Growth was so rapid that the *Daily Union* commented on the fact:

> There is no physician in the city but is grateful for the favor, and great credit is due to the sisters that such progress has been made within the limited time they have owned the property. When, fifteen months ago, it came to them, two solitary patients were enrolled, while at the present time numbers were being turned away because there is not room for their reception.[18]

There is a saying, "If you build it, they will come." That is exactly what happened. Before the year was over, it became evident that a larger facility was needed, one that would be designed as a hospital commensurate with the medical advances of the day. By October of the following year, the sisters were back in a "building cycle." Since the Ridge Home site was large enough to accommodate a new building, the sisters chose that as the location for a new hospital.

Bishop Manogue did not get to see this new expansion of church ministry. He died in February 1895, just a few months before the sisters took possession of Ridge Home. His successor, long time rector of the cathedral, Bishop Thomas Grace, did the honors at the laying of the cornerstone of the new Mater Misericordiae Hospital on Thanksgiving Day, 1896. The Latin name, *Mater Misericordiae*, means "Mother of Mercy". Most Sacramentans had a hard time saying it so the hospital was frequently called, "The Sisters' Hospital."

Things moved quickly in those days. The new four-story hospital was built by April and ready for use by May 10. The descriptions of the hospital carried in both *The Sacramento Bee* and *Sacramento Daily Union* reflect the sense of pride taken in the new institution. The writer claimed that the hospital will "besides embodying all the improvements of the leading hospitals on the coast, contain many new features which will make this the most modern hospital in California."[19] Of particular note were the "balconies surrounding the building, patient solariums at each end of the building, gas and electric lighting throughout, hot water heaters and electric bells and a "large hose, wound upon rolls and attached to the [water] mains."[20] This latter detail was really important since the whole structure was wooden and at risk for fire.

The sisters were able to attract five nurses, trained at St. Mary's Hospital, San Francisco, to come to help them at the hospital. Mother Mary Ligouri realized that this was not a long-term solution and determined that she would open a training school for nurses at the new Mater Misericordiae Hospital. She already had invited some of her former students to come and help out with nursing, and several had said "yes". With the full cooperation of many eminent doctors in Sacramento, her experiment was successful.

As soon as the new hospital opened, she followed through on her plan and the school of nursing welcomed its first students on August 4, 1897. The first four students were Adele Miller, Frances Kiernan, Ada Kober, and Mary Baxter.[21] Less than two weeks later, Mother Ligouri selected Louise Igo, a recent graduate nurse of the California Women's and Children's Hospital of San Francisco, to be superintendent of nurses. Miss Igo, in collaboration with her executive board, set up the classes, taught daily and partnered with physicians who presented lectures and weekly demonstrations to the students. After two years of instruction and successful completion of a final examination, the students received their degrees.

The beginnings of Mater Misericordiae Hospital came at a critical juncture in healthcare. The field was experiencing a national transition from hospitals that provided comfort and care for patients to ones driven by new scientific discoveries in the field of medicine. At the nursing school graduation in May 1900, both Dr. F. B. Sutliff and Dr. H. L. Nichols spoke about the differences between "old time nurses" and the trained nurses now graduating.[22] Developing technology called for a new type of training and a movement to a higher standard of professionalism. While never using that language, the actions of the sisters during this time indicate a high acceptance of that movement. Sending their resident physician on a month-long study tour of the most noted hospitals in the country, demanding a high level of competency in the nursing school and acquiring the latest in medical technology all witnessed to their commitment to providing the best care of the time.

While Bishop Grace was a great friend to the hospital, he did a lot more than lay its cornerstone. During his long tenure as bishop of Sacramento, he expanded the services the church offered to the poor and needy. To the sisters, he was a friend, having ministered with them at the cathedral. They taught in his religious education classes on Sundays, invited him to all their religious ceremonies and programs and in turn, he did everything he could to support them both in life and ministry. Evidence of the bond of friendship can still be seen today in the articles Bishop Grace donated to what was called "The Natural History Museum" of St. Joseph's. Among the treasures are two of John Sutter's compasses and John Marshall's coffee cup. His support did not stop there. He also was a generous donor to the sisters' ministries, especially the hospital. In 1900, he funded the building of a new surgical suite that was named after him. That same year, he would turn to the sisters to pick up one more ministry—a new orphanage.

An unexpected benefice came to Bishop Grace in April 1900. Mrs. Jennie Lathrope-Stanford, widow of Leland Stanford, returned to Sacramento to make a final disposition of Stanford mansion, which she dearly loved. She had spent many happy days there before the tragic death of her son. She did not want the mansion used for what she considered "profane use." Known for her generosity and concern for orphans, it was her decision to turn it over to the Catholic Diocese as a home for small orphaned children along with a $75,000 endowment. It was to be known as the Lathrop-Stanford Children's Home.

The sisters graciously accepted the call to tend the children left homeless through death and disease, or who were given up by parents too poor to care for them. Within two weeks, the house was ready to receive the first eight children. The children served were from five to sixteen years of age. The home was more than just an orphanage though; it was also a school. The school, open to residents and children in the area, attracted 100 students from the surrounding neighborhood.

Such an undertaking required having another convent established at Stanford Home. The first sisters in residence were Mother Mary Vincent Phelan, Mother Mary Ligouri Madden, Mary Francis Sheridan, Mary Berchmans Kennelly, and Brendan Quirk. Having three convents, Stanford Home, the original St. Joseph's and the residence at Mater Misericordiae brought new questions: "Who was in charge of daily decisions?" "Who was responsible for the spiritual exercises of the community or for calling attention to practices that were not consistent with the rule?" Mother Baptist Russell had tried to figure that out when she first established the Sacramento foundation. Her answer was to place her mother assistant in charge. This time, the community met together in chapter to determine how to deal with this issue.[23] They decided:

> With the approval of the Bishop, whatever Sister may be appointed by the Mother Superior, with the advice of her Council, to preside, in any of our branch houses shall, while she presides, hold in that house the same rank, be invested with the same authority, and discharge the same

functions as the Mother Assistant in the Motherhouse in the absence of the Mother Superior.[24]

For a religious community, this decision carried great significance. It meant that there existed a great amount of trust in each other. No one woman was considered to have all the responsibility. The decision also freed the superior from the pull of having to deal with all the day to day problems that could crop up in a convent community. Without such a chosen practice, Mother Mary Ligouri or any of her successors would not have had sufficient time to deal with pressing ministry issues. One of those issues was staffing all the various ministries.

Prior to the opening of Mater Misericordiae, Mother Mary Vincent Phelan was approached by the Franciscan Friars seeking the sisters for their school at the newly established St. Francis Parish. At the time, Mother Vincent felt the sisters were already pressed in adequately supplying all the sisters needed for their current works. St. Joseph's was just renovated and the new facility was attracting more boarders and day students. Ridge Home was on the brink of opening. To complicate matters, the nation had fallen into a serious depression in 1893, making money short and needs long. The sisters had even opened an employment service for young girls seeking jobs and offered limited boarding to those who most needed it. Notices were placed in the papers indicating that they would help anyone of good reputation and unemployed.[25] They knew how hard it was to get jobs so they had added a commercial program to the curriculum at St. Joseph's. Training persons for self-sufficiency was integral to Mercy education.

Unable to give an unqualified commitment to accept the responsibility for St. Francis School, Mother M. Phelan offered another possibility. The sisters would teach in the school until such time as the pastor found another order to serve in the school. That search went on for six years. Finally, the Franciscan Sisters of Penance and Christian Charity accepted the call to Sacramento and the Mercy Sisters withdrew from the parish school.

Looking back for a moment, it is amazing that within fifteen years of being an independent community, the sisters had expanded their ministry to include three elementary schools, a hospital, orphanage, and had converted the old Ridge Home building into a home for the aged. Few groups of women had such opportunity to make such a difference in a city. Their graduates were formed for leadership and excellence and to bring to their endeavors a social conscience. Well known Sacramentans like Louise Coolot and Ella Kelly, who was now Mrs. C. K. McClatchy, would be examples of such graduates. Most likely one of the reasons C. K.

McClatchy, publisher of *The Sacramento Bee*, was such a strong advocate for the sisters was the influence of Ella.

Reading the stories of these times might lead one to think that the only difficulties faced by the sisters were lack of resources and climatic difficulties like flooding and summer heat. That is not really the case. There were times when the convent was targeted for crime, like the attack on Patrick Riley, their gardener. Riley lived in a detached building on the convent grounds. During the night, two ruffians attacked Riley, beating him and then proceeded to destroy some of the sisters' supplies.[26] No cause was ever determined but, for the sisters, it proved they could not presume safety.

At times, women disguised themselves as sisters to ask for funds, and several times, the sisters had to place public notices in the papers to assure citizens that such solicitations were not legitimate.[27] Of course, there was the ever-present worry about fire breaking out. While all these things fell into the category of daily challenges, there was one situation that caused alarm both in the sisters and in the greater Sacramento community. The catalyst for the alarm occurred in October 1894.

Although the Sacramento sisters were removed from most controversy, that did not mean everyone liked them. Inclusivity was the hallmark of their works. Girls from every religious and ethnic background attended their schools. The advertisements for the hospital were explicit in welcoming persons from all denominations, and the same was true for the orphanage. It was shocking for everyone, therefore, when on the morning of October 2, 1894, the sisters woke to find "A.P.A." painted in large letters 3 feet high on their fence. The letters were spaced in intervals for a distance of 30–60 feet, the paint indelible.

The initials painted on the fence stood for the American Protective Association, a society that was avidly anti-Catholic and anti-immigrant in nature. It was founded in 1887 and in the 1890s grew to almost 2,000,000 members. Considered the successor to the Know-Nothing movement, the A.P.A. attack must have reminded the sisters of the difficult days in San Francisco at the beginning of their California ministry. *The Sacramento Bee* remarked: "The Sisters of Mercy desired that no publicity should be given to the outrage, they evidently being quite willing to let the act of the miscreants go unpunished and unnoticed."[28]

The act was noticed, however, and public outrage followed. It was not just about the vandalism, the defacing of both fence and front door of the convent. It was about attacking women who were seen as women for everyone. The *Bee* proclaimed:

The fact that the Sisters of Mercy, in their thirty-five years and more of residence in this community, have won the hearts of all, and have encountered only praise for their acts of kindness and charity from people of all creeds and of no creed, renders the present incident one well meriting the indignant detestation it has received on the streets today.[29]

This particular action did not find support, even within the A.P.A. Captain W. H. Bradley, a prominent member of the group, told the *Bee*: "The man who did that thing should be tied naked to the tail of a ___ and cowhided through the streets, and I would take great pleasure in wielding the lash."[30] Fortunately, that did not happen. The vandal was never caught.

A more intimate sorrow was the death of cherished members of the community. Sister Mary Dolores had been the first but others would follow. Two losses came in 1897 just as the community was opening Mater Misericordiae Hospital. Sister Mary Stanislaus Keane, an invalid due to tuberculosis, died after a five-year struggle. The second loss was unique for it was Nora O'Donnell, the community portress.

Nora was not a sister, but she was an integral part of the community. For thirty-three years, she opened the doors of the convent, guarded the privacy of the sisters, and was "a good old soul, and was beloved by the Sisters of Mercy and all the pupils of the Academy."[31] The role of the portress was important in these times for the portress literally controlled who was admitted to the property and who was not. Prior to her death, "Faithful Nora" lived in what was called the "Lodge" on the convent grounds, but in her last years, she was moved to the hospital where the sisters could care for her. She is buried with the sisters at St. Joseph's Cemetery.

Two more deaths came in 1902. First, Sister Mary Antonia Irwin, another victim of tuberculosis, returned to God in March. Known for her spiritual wisdom, she was made mistress of novices in 1893 and at the time of her death, she was in charge of Stanford Home. This was felt keenly since her sister, Sister Mary Michael Irwin, was also a member of the small community.

The final death was, perhaps, the most difficult. It was the death of Mother Mary Vincent Phelan on April 29, 1902. Her death was not just a loss to the sisters; it was felt throughout the Sacramento community. For Sacramentans, Mother Mary Vincent embodied everything they valued about the Sisters of Mercy. C. K. McClatchy wrote a heartfelt tribute to her carried in *The Sacramento Bee*:

If ever the Almighty placed an angel in Sacramento to do His will, to love and cherish His creatures, to comfort the widow and help the orphan, to smooth the pillow of pain and dry the eyes of grief, to be in all and through all a ministering spirit of gentle kindness, and love, and all-pervading charity—that angel was Mother Mary Vincent.

Her forty-three years of life in this community have been years of thought, and care, and doing for others. One of the noblest of her sex, and one of the grandest of her Order, she has grown into the affections of all the people of Sacramento, irrespective of creed, and now her memory will be enshrined in their hearts almost as at an altar.

There is no man in Sacramento today—no matter at what alter he kneel—no matter if he kneel at none—who will not doff his hat at mention of the name of Mother Mary Vincent. There is no woman who knew her who will not hold her in her inmost heart of hearts as a type of all that is best, and noblest, and most lovable in womankind.[32]

The contributions of Mother Vincent were multiple. Trained in classical music, she was the moving spirit behind St. Joseph Academy's reputation for musical excellence. A fine educator, she saw the importance of good literature and established a subscription library of 2,000 works to which the public had access. She spent much of her life in governance and shaped the way in which the community engaged in a mode of inclusive ministry. In his sermon at her funeral, Bishop Thomas Grace said: "She led the hidden life of a saint, spending hours daily in the presence of her sacramental God from whom she received a plentitude of blessings, as bees draw honey from the fragrant flowers."[33] Hundreds attended her funeral and lingered throughout the day.

Mother Vincent had seen forty-three of Mercy's fifty years in the city and died just five years before Sacramentans would celebrate the golden jubilee of the community's presence among them. In a sense, her death was an end to an era. She was the only remaining Sacramento pioneer. The San Francisco sisters who stayed to nurture the new community had returned to their motherhouse in 1890, and Mother Mary Ligouri had only come to Sacramento in the early '80s. The community was on the cusp of a new beginning but first, Sacramento wanted to celebrate.

Plans for the fiftieth celebration began in May with the organizing of a St. Joseph's Academy Alumnae Association for its seventy graduates. Providing Sacramento this many fully educated women, many of whom had assumed professions in education, nursing, and business was a significant contribution to furthering the role of women. One of the first goals of the Alumnae Association was to celebrate the anniversary.

By August, plans began to be formalized. The mayor, R. R. Beard, presided at the first planning meeting. It was to be a floral fete with entertainment held in the gardens of the academy. In promoting the event, *The Sacramento Bee* reported: "To a very large extent the history of charity, the history of humanity, the history of beneficence, in this community is the history of the Sisters of Mercy."[34] To be sure, this description is a bit of an exaggeration, rooted in the florid writing style of the day, but it illustrates the place of the sisters within the community.

The actual event must have overwhelmed the sisters in its scope. Pope Pius X sent his special blessings and members of the Jesuits, Franciscans, and Dominicans joined diocesan priests from all over Northern California at the Pontifical Mass presided over by Bishop Grace. The *Bee* estimated that 4,000 people attended the reception with at least 3,000 of them staying to greet the sisters.

At St. Joseph's, the garden was strung with sparkling electrical lights and filled with floral pieces while the newly elected superior, Mother Mary Gertrude King, greeted the guests and the State Fair Chorus provided musical accompaniment. The event was truly an extravaganza of gratitude. The sisters were particularly thankful for the $6,000 donation raised by the event that allowed them to have heat and light in the convent for the first time in fifty years.

The anniversary was also a transition point. Society was standing on the brink of crisis. The memory of this day was food for encouragement in the dark times to come.

Light and Darkness Mingled

At the dawning of their fifty-first year in Sacramento, the sisters found themselves responsible for three major Mercy institutions: St. Joseph's Academy, Mater Misericordiae Hospital, and Stanford Lathrop Home. In addition to these major works, the sisters taught religious education classes at Immaculate Conception parish, conducted a nursing school, and continued to visit the homes of poor and sick Sacramentans. Since the sisters received no pay for their services, they coped with trying to do it all with the limited resources they could raise from music lessons and through philanthropy. At the time, there were only about thirty professed sisters. It was daunting but they were undeterred. In the middle of these commitments, the sisters, along with all Sacramentans, were plunged into "hard times" during the 1918 flu epidemic, World War I, and the depression that followed.

At the beginning of 1908, all that was far away. What was not far away was the need to enlarge and upgrade the physical facilities that housed the sisters' ministries. Expanding needs as well as advancements in both education and healthcare demanded that the sisters constantly adapt to the changing circumstances. Excellence was always the hallmark of the sisters' ministries, whether in education or in healthcare. It was what prompted them to work diligently to see that St. Joseph's Academy acquired certification from University of California and what caused their music program to gain widespread acclaim. What had been done for education was now needed for health care.

When the sisters accepted responsibility for Ridge Home in 1895, it could only accommodate fifteen patients. Mater Misericordiae Hospital was initially built for thirty patients, but that was now insufficient. It could not accommodate the number of sick seeking help. Plans were made to double that capacity with a new wing added in 1908. At the same time, an upgraded surgery and an X-ray department were put in place. Soon even that capacity proved too small, and in 1914, a men's wing was opened increasing the hospital's capacity to seventy-seven beds. In the next year, another twelve beds were added.[1]

For anyone familiar with modern healthcare, the constant expansion, renovation, and upgrading of facilities are commonplace. New discoveries in medical technologies, demographic changes, and diagnostic advances create an unceasing demand to adapt facilities and acquire the equipment needed. In 1908, that dynamic was just beginning. One small example illustrates this dynamic. The medical application of the X-ray only began in 1895 when William Röntgen took an X-ray of his wife's hand. The full significance of this discovery caused its rapid distribution throughout the hospitals of the period. Within five years, X-rays were considered essential for clinical care.[2] Before 1910, an X-ray was used primarily to diagnose persons with fractures. These images were only read by physicians. That would change over time as its usage became more widespread.

Dr. Roy Jones tells us in his history of medicine in Sacramento that Mater Misericordiae's first X-ray department was organized by Dr. F. E. Shaw in 1908. To make sure that the hospital was fully equipped with the more up-to-date facilities and medical practices, Drs. F. E. Shaw, J. H. Harris, and Charles McKee spent a month touring the hospitals of the east, including the principal Catholic hospitals in Chicago, Illinois, and Rochester, Minnesota. Upon their return, Dr. Shaw noted that the doctors had discovered little in their visit that was not already known and practice here.[3]

In what we might consider a visionary stance, the Mercy community began to train the sisters for medical leadership. The first were Sisters Mary Angela Desmond and Mary Berchmans Kennelly, both earning graduate degrees from the California College of Pharmacy in San Francisco. The regents of the University of California conferred the degrees. The accomplishment was celebrated at a private celebration with Very Reverend Thomas H. Horgan presenting the degrees to the sisters. Other sisters went through the Mater Misericordiae nursing program and obtained the status of graduate nurses. Sr. Mary Lourdes Cook was trained to be Mater Misericordiae's first X-ray technician, and she took charge of the department in 1918, joining with other sisters trained to provide the hospital with professional staff.[4] All of this was consistent with the high value the sisters placed on excellence of care.

The results were acknowledged by the public. The *Sacramento Union* extolled the level of scientific surgery and advanced hospital equipment in the vanguard of modern progress.[5] The article goes on to speak of Mater Misericordiae specifically:

> It has grown and developed with the municipality, adding improvements and extensions as they became necessary to keep step with the rapid progress of modern medicine and surgery, until it now stands as one of the best equipped in all the empire of Northern California.[6]

Having a hospital that was among the best in California was a good thing for Sacramento, a city prone to health issues arising from its location between two rivers. Deep fog, sometimes called tule fog, rolled over the city in the winter, while in the summer, the city baked. While Dr. Shaw and his medical friends examined the state of medicine in the east, Sacramento leaders worried about how to prevent an outbreak of bubonic plague resulting from a rat infestation. The possibility was serious enough for the mayor to visit every school and distribute flyers on how to prevent the infestation.[7] Even today, it is not uncommon for Sacramentans to look out a window and see river rats scurrying across the telephone wires in their back yards. Disconcerting to say the least, but at the turn of the twentieth century, it must have stirred fear in the hearts of citizens.

Two years later, in 1910, St. Joseph's Academy had to close for several days when three students came down with smallpox, causing a city-wide alert.[8] These unusual occurrences were added to the hospital's usual combination of tuberculosis, cancer, and other serious diseases afflicting Sacramentans. If that were not enough, the hospital frequently had to treat patients with terrible injuries from explosions, accidents, and the occasional gunshot wound.

As the sisters dealt with the expansion of the hospital, the nation began its journey to full involvement in World War I. President Woodrow Wilson had been reluctant to enter into the war, but once he made the decision to take up arms, he was all in. John Barry, author of *The Great Influenza*, sums up Wilson's mindset this way:

> To Wilson this war was a crusade, and he intended to wage total war. Perhaps knowing himself even more than the country, he predicted, "Once lead this people into war, and they'll forget there ever was such a thing as tolerance. To fight you must be brutal and ruthless, and the spirit of ruthless brutality will enter into the very fibre of our national life, infecting Congress, the courts, the policeman on the beat, the man on the street."[9]

Such a spirit touched every aspect of American life. Barry suggests that any kind of dissent was seen as treachery. Everyone was expected to engage fully in the war effort, expected to prove their patriotism. Congress, urged on by the Wilson administration, passed a new Sedition Act that made the publishing or proclamation of anything considered "disloyal, profane or scurrilous" a crime punishable by twenty years in prison.[10] Patriotism was the god of the day. A special Flag Dag service at the Cathedral of the Blessed Sacramento illustrates that reality. The benediction service that even the papers called "intense," resounded with the strains of "Over There," the national anthem, and the solemn presentation of the flag for blessing.[11]

· Father Humilis Weise, OSF, pastor of St. Francis Church, spoke to the people on patriotism and loyalty of Catholics to the American cause:

> We are here to give an open expression to the sentiments of our souls in the determination to co-operate with our Government to the fullest extent of our power. We must show the true spirit by putting our shoulder to the wheel ad move the machinery of war ... Religion cannot be placed above patriotism.[12]

A century later, it is really hard to understand how a church leader could have encouraged people to put patriotism above faith, but Catholics of the time were intent on proving that they could be loyal citizens. German and Irish citizens were under special scrutiny.

Germans in the United States were looked upon with suspicion because they might still be loyal to the motherland. The Irish were suspect because they were at the height of the struggle for Irish independence and at enmity with our British allies. Added to those factors was a suspicion that American Catholics took their direction from the Pope not the president. Could you be a loyal Catholic and loyal citizen at the same time? The hierarchy wanted to make sure that everyone knew the answer to that question was a resounding "Yes."

Church leaders did everything they could to encourage full participation in the war effort and the sisters, through their ministries, joined in that cause. The nursing school sent fourteen graduate nurses to the war in Europe, while the sisters contributed to the home front. It is hard to know exactly how the sisters dealt with day-to-day life during the war itself. The only hint comes from a memoir written by Sister Mary Gabriel Spadier who tells us: "We were rationed but somehow didn't think about it."[13] We do know that they had to deal with shortages of staff since both doctors and nurses had been called for active service. The emphasis of the Wilson administration was making the folks at home see their every choice as a contribution to the war effort.

For the public of World War I days, there were limited channels of information. In an effort to build support for the war, Wilson created the Committee on Public Information and appointed George Creel as its head. Creel flooded the country with patriotic posters and press releases. Barry asserts that Creel demanded "100% Americanism." Every word was planned for maximum impact.[14] Fear of public disapproval or even jail was to be fostered. It is no wonder that a review of the entertainments given by the St. Joseph Academy students reflect an abundance of patriotic songs, speeches, and readings. Two are particularly noteworthy.

For the commencement exercises of 1918, the girls performed an original dramatic reading of a work called "President Wilson's Vision." The storyline was simple. Wilson, wearied by the stresses of war, is revived by the vision of the goddess of liberty ruling the world. The dramatic presentation was vigorously applauded, and the sisters sent a copy of the production to the President himself. His response, communicated by Secretary Tumulty, was one of appreciation and thanks.[15] C. K. McClatchy quickly published the response and left us a record of this small window into the stance of the sisters.

A second indicator of the sisters' full engagement in the war effort surfaced after the armistice was signed. It is a lengthy poem written most likely by Sister Mary Aloysius Nolan. Following the customs of the time, *The Sacramento Bee* says only that the poem is written by a Sister of Mercy at St. Joseph's Academy. It was called "Lafayette, We Are Here!"

> *Pershing, our General, with wreath in hand*
> *Stood by the tomb of a hero grand*
> *Who had answered Colombia's call of woe,*
> *And helped her to Freedom, long ago*
> *And looking a-down the ranks he led,*
> *With the Stars and Striped high overhead.*
> *He placed the wreath on the tomb, and said:*
> *"Lafayette, we are here."*[16]

The poem continues for several stanzas but ends with the words: "They will utter these words from a nation-wide—Fair France, our debt is paid."

For many Americans, that debt was costly. Not only were the wounds of war devastating, but the drive to get new recruits trained and to the battlefields created incubators for the flu of 1918. Every area of American life would be touched by this pandemic. Sacramento was not exempt. Even though the flu had visited the country yearly since 1892, nothing like this influenza had been experienced. Sister Mary Berchmans Kennelly wrote in the *Annals* of the community:

It spared no one, even the healthiest and most robust men and women. The fathers were taken today; the mothers, tomorrow; and the sons and daughters soon followed and numerous children were left helpless orphans.[17]

The havoc caused by the flu was the result of many factors. First, the cause of the disease was not understood although medical scientists worked round the clock to identify it. There was no vaccine or even a tried-and-true treatment for the ailment. Secondly, it was rapidly spread in places that were crowded, lacking in fresh air and sanitation and into which came anyone infected with the virus. Public health officials rushed to contain the disease. Their efforts were impeded by the rush to get as many soldiers, doctors, and nurses as possible to the war front. In spite of warnings, recruits were transferred from one base with contagion to other bases that were not yet infected, thereby spreading the disease.

Signs of influenza first surfaced in 1917 when soldiers being transferred from Camp Funston, Kansas, to Hot Springs, Arkansas, brought the disease with them. Cities soon began to run articles on protecting yourself against the flu. *The Sacramento Bee* ran a series by H. Addington Bruce, which warned folks to refrain from sneezing and coughing "recklessly in crowded street cars, churches, theaters, and other public places."[18] Other articles in his series warned about such things as poisoned air, germs clinging to clothes, and rushing convalescence. Health departments tried to track the disease by requiring doctors to report new cases but since many of the poor died without medical care, it was hard to gather accurate statistics.

While eastern cities like Philadelphia languished under the epidemic, Sacramento remained disease free until mid-October 1918. On October 5, the *Sacramento Union* suggested that the influenza might not get a grip on Sacramento. By the middle of the month, however, cases in Sacramento began to increase. As late as October 17, Dr. G. C. Simmons, commissioner of public health, declared "So far Sacramento is entirely free from 'Spanish' influenza."[19] Dr. Simmons was wrong. The "Spanish" flu had arrived.

Officials moved to close stage performances, movie theaters, dance halls, and churches until the danger was past. Churches like St. Francis and Immaculate Conception held outdoor masses, while other faith communities met in parks, church grounds, or on the sidewalk in front of the church.[20] By the last week of October, Sacramento was in crisis mode. Sacramento had already sent forty-five nurses to the war front and was now hurting for nurses at home. Mary Ribzinski, a graduate of Mater Misericordiae Nursing School and supervisor at the hospital, was in charge of the committee entrusted with rounding up nurses. While her efforts in June proved successful, there was renewed urgency in the fall.

By the end of October, *The Sacramento Bee* published a call for nurses. They reported a dire need for women volunteers to nurse influenza sufferers in Sacramento. Hospitals were full and families were prostrate with the virulent disease.[21] The response of the sisters to these needs was the same as at other times of major health crises. They volunteered their services to the city. Sister Mary Berchmans tells us:

> Our schools were closed for several weeks in October and November and this gave our sisters an opportunity of devoting their time and energies to the poor sick and afflicted in their homes and in the County Hospital. With the permission of Bishop Grace, six sisters volunteered to serve at the County Hospital.[22]

The sister volunteers included Sisters Mary Gertrude King, Mary Francis Sheridan, Mary Berchmans Kennelly, Mary Dolores Soto, and Mary Regina Higgins.[23] The sixth volunteer, Sister Mary Gabriel Spadier, having contracted a bad cold, was sent back to the convent.

The work must have been exhausting. We can get an idea of the situation from a description of the County Hospital reported by *The Sacramento Bee*:

> In one ward a Sister of Mercy, with one assistant, is caring for forty patients. In another ward an entirely inexperienced volunteer with an orderly have charge of twenty-seven patients. So overworked are the regular County Hospital nurses, that one nurse fainted from sheer exhaustion.[24]

Since there were no sleeping accommodations at the hospital, the sisters commuted daily between the convent and the hospital. They continued this work until the flu ended in late November.

Meanwhile, the sisters at St. Joseph's and Stanford Home were busy caring for the sick as well. Many of the boarders at the Academy were stricken with the disease, one so ill that she died within a week. The sisters at Stanford Home took on a special work, caring for as many stricken babies as they could accommodate. "These babies had occupied a room at the County Hospital which was needed for adults. These hopeless little cases were kept at the Home during the epidemic and one sister devoted her entire time to them. Only one little tot died."[25]

The work of the sisters and other valiant volunteers did not go unnoticed. *The Sacramento Bee* drew attention to the service of the sisters:

Working heart and hand with the Red Cross women volunteers and the few trained nurses left at the Sacramento County Hospital, five sisters of Mercy, who voluntarily went to the institution to give their service in nursing and caring for the Spanish influenza patients, are doing a great good for humanity.[26]

The article goes on to speak of the dangers of exposure to the disease voluntarily embraced. Mary Berchmans tells us that daily twelve to fourteen persons died at the hospital.

The illness did not pass by the sisters. The *Annals* tell us that many became seriously ill, although none died. But the sisters were not alone in their outreach. Others joined them: the Christian Brothers, Franciscan Sisters, Red Cross Volunteers, and Protestant ministers like Rev. Mr. Harvey Miller were all part of the effort. With only five nurses from the County Hospital staff still well enough to remain on the job, all were needed. Before 1918 ended, there were 3, 262 confirmed cases of influenza, and 243 deaths ascribed to the disease.[27] The cost of the winter epidemics was not only in human lives. It would cost the city $8,227.09 and Sacramento County, $16,454.19.[28]

Writing about the pandemic of 1918 in the middle of the pandemic of 2020 gives one the feeling of *déjà vu*. Masks were required and, not wearing one, would result in fines or jail. Sister Mary Gabriel Spadier notes in her memoir that the sisters even wore them in the chapel. That would have been quite a challenge given the religious habit of the times, which encircled the face with tight, white linen. Public gatherings were prohibited whether religious or cultural.

The flu moved fast, sometimes because its symptoms were misleading. It was both difficult to diagnose and difficult to treat. The virus spread rapidly with as little as two day's incubation. Not only did the disease often progress to pneumonia, but people sometimes lost their senses of taste and smell.[29] Just like today, the disease spared no one but unlike today's frontline healthcare workers, the medical folks of 1918 had little personal protection and few of the respiratory aids. Recognizing how challenging it is for us to deal with COVID-19, the enormity of the efforts to save lives under those conditions in 1918 is almost beyond comprehension.

Toward the beginning of December, it looked like the worst was over, but a second wave came in February and the last wave in April. Only then was life able to return to normal, but what was normal? For the sisters, it meant reopening school, tending the orphans at Stanford Home, now expanded by children orphaned by the flu, and deciding how to meet the demand for even more hospital beds. It also meant embracing the rhythm of death and new life.

The first urgency was replacing Mater Misericordiae Hospital. Plans to build were actually started in 1914 since the current building, being made of wood, was considered a fire trap. A campaign manager, Bert Wells, was engaged to start a drive to raise funds. When all was in readiness, committee member Alden Anderson, a prominent Sacramento banker, strongly proposed that the campaign be delayed until after harvest time when money would be more available. For the sisters, this delay was very costly for before harvest arrived, World War I began and prices soared. No campaign could be held. The war and the flu epidemic consumed available resources. They would have to make do.[30]

After the war, with prices high and resources low, the sisters again started plans to move. Unfortunately, there was no monies available since the campaign never happened. Bishop John Keane, the new Sacramento bishop, encouraged them to act. Mother Mary Michael Irwin, superior at the time, went "site shopping" with the sisters. After visiting several locations, they selected a seven-acre site in East Sacramento. The land was owned by the Inderkum family and, in some ways, seemed like an unlikely place for the new facility. Originally used as dairy land, it was a bit swampy but that was not an insurmountable problem. They purchased the site for $18,837. Now they only needed another $500,000 to build.

There was a restlessness in the medical community at the time. Doctors desired state of the art equipment and facilities and hoped that the sisters would be able to supply that need. From their perspective, the existing Mater Misericordia Hospital was no longer feasible. An article in the *Sacramento Union* of November 28, 1919, was headlined: "Say Hospital Must Be Built." It noted that there were some differences between the manner in which the doctors wanted the hospital to be conducted and the vision of the sisters.

The Sacramento Bee mentions the differences of opinion in an article on May 21, 1921. It seems to indicate that initially the plan was to combine with the doctors who had ideas about hospital facilities they wanted to see carried out. That vision did not seem to match the vision of the sisters or, perhaps, the Sisters at that point lacked the funds to build.[31] The difference of opinion might also have been tied to another medical conflict experienced across the nation. Doctors were divided about having hospitals be staffed by a selective group of physicians or be open to all practicing physicians. Added to that conflict was a struggle for control of how things would be done. Sisters, viewing hospitals as a mission, ardently preserved their autonomy to make choices that they believed were in the best interest of all.[32] Whatever the differences, it seems they were not resolved, and the group of physicians went on to build a new hospital,

Sutter General Hospital, near St. Francis Church. Meanwhile, the sisters continued with their plans.

Because need was critical, time was of the essence in replacing the old hospital. Bishop Keane arranged for a $400,000 loan from the Bank of Italy, now the Bank of America. Plans had to be scaled back from a seven-story building to a four story one. In an effort to raise the needed monies, Sister Mary Aloysius Nolan, then the superior of the community, sent out "The Dollar Letter," both a poem and an appeal to all the friends of the sisters. Sent a few months after breaking ground for the new hospital took place, it read:

Dear Friend:
Here's a dollar, yes, a dollar: crisp and clean and bright and new.
You may keep it if you want to, when you've read this letter through.
"Tis a bid for an investment, based on our urgent need,
For with loyal friends to help us, we'll be sure we shall succeed.
There is much of human kindness in this great old world of ours;
Oft it turns the hard to easy, with its wondrous, magic powers.
It has been our past experience in this Eden of the West
That when wants are clearly stated, friends rise up and do their best
We are putting up a building our on Fortieth and "J"
That will beautify our city, growing fairer day by day;
Up-to-date in every detail, well-equipped in modern style,
We'll invite you to inspect it; 'twill be more than worth your while.
'Neath its roof the sick and suffering will have tender, watchful care,
While the very best of MD's will perform their labors there.
There the lonely, poor, and needy ever shall a welcome find
For the very name of "Mercy" bids us to the poor be kind.
But we must have many dollars to complete this work so great,
So we mail our paper dollar, hoping for a happy fate.
Someone gave a thousand dollars in a humble, quiet way
Which we've changed to current paper to gain interest on the way.
You who give will be remembered in our fervent daily prayer
And in every work of mercy, you will have a generous share.
Every name will be recorded, be the offering great or small;
And God's blessing for your bounty will descend upon you all.
Your humble friends, The Sisters of Mercy.[33]

By Thanksgiving of that year, the cornerstone for the new hospital was laid. Bishop Keane called it the beginning of a new era in the work of the sisters. It was an accomplishment that took many hands. The sisters visited the site frequently keeping up with progress. Mr. Rudolph Herold, the architect, always had time to explain the plan, listen to suggestions, and asked the opinion of the sisters even on small things like color schemes. The sisters sought advice from others as well. Once, they asked Bishop Keane about what color he thought the new hospital should be. Pretending discouragement at the rising indebtedness, he said: "Paint it black!"[34] In that, the sisters did not acquiesce.

The design for the new hospital was quite striking especially for the time period. It was designed in the form of an "X," a design that allowed an abundance of fresh air and sunlight for every room. All the various medical departments had the most up-to-date equipment, and the sisters made sure solariums were included in the building for the enjoyment and comfort of the patients. The new hospital would allow the sisters to continue their tradition of excellence in care long into the future.

It would be easy to overlook all the background pieces that went into moving from the old Mater Misericordiae campus to the new site on 40th and J Street where it remains today. It took massive planning, and that work fell upon the shoulders of Sr. Mary Carmel McNaughton, who was hospital superintendent at the time. A born organizer, Sister Mary Carmel enlisted the help of Brother Lewis, then director of Christian Brothers' School on 21st and Y Streets. Brother Lewis sent several of his strongest boys with a large truck to assist with the move. For days, the boys loaded up truck load after truck load of furniture, supplies, and other items and hauled them to the new hospital. This was no easy task since there was no elevator in the hospital convent and the boys had to carry everything up and down three flights of stairs.[35]

Even St. Joseph's was pressed into service and became a storage site for chapel furnishings too large for the temporary chapel at the hospital. Lack of funds had meant eliminating the original chapel design that was included in the plan. As the sisters sought another way of providing a chapel, they landed on the proposed roof top garden as an alternative site. Mr. Herold, learning of the dilemma, offered to transform the garden into a chapel, making all the needed alterations as his personal donation to the sisters.

One last arrangement had to be made before closing the chapter on the first Mater Misericordiae Hospital. When the hospital was first built, the sisters had converted Ridge Home into a home for the aged. At the time of the move, four elders were still living there. Not wanting to leave them behind, the sisters fixed up apartments for them in the old Inderkum home where they peacefully ended their days[36]

Finally, after ten years of planning, the hospital was ready, opening its doors on February 11, 1925, the feast of Our Lady of Lourdes. It was such a big event that the February 7 *Sacramento Bee* devoted its entire issue to the upcoming opening. Sister Mary Aloysius Nolan tells us it was "a splendid account of the new hospital, giving names of all the Sacramento firms connected with its erection and equipment, as the sisters had arranged with the architect and contractor—Mr. Herold and Mr. Keating—that our Sacramento firms were to be patronized as far as possible."[37] The memory of that day was cherished by the sisters long after its closure.

Having paid almost $1,000,000 for land, buildings and equipment, it was truly a leap of faith.[38] Bishop Keane spoke to that truth: "The Sisters of Mercy go into this magnificent building today under the shadow of a huge debt, but they do not fear, for they have faith."[39] He pointed to another truth as well. Only with the support of the civic community was such an accomplishment possible. Bishop Keane put it this way:

> Unfortunately the insistent demands of the people for greater comforts, and of the doctors for the very best and most modern equipment to make their work more efficient, the multiplicity of state laws with regard to health—all more or less praiseworthy—make the cost of building and operation so great that it is no longer possible to carry on the work of caring for the sick in modern hospitals without the willing and generous co-operation of the public, for whose benefit they have been erected.[40]

The new facility was more than a hospital. It was also a home for the sisters and the new site of Mater Misericordiae Nursing School. It allowed more space for the burgeoning numbers of student nurses seeking admission. At its opening, Dr. James W. O'Brian, house physician for the old Mater Misericordiae Hospital, called the new nurses' home "a model of its kind."[41] The building was three stories high and contained lecture halls, a recreation room, a parlor, and a library. Each bedroom on the second floor had a basin with hot and cold running water—an improvement over the old home. There was also a kitchenette and snack room. The *Annals* tell us the, "home was designed with a view of giving them (the students) a real home."[42] It also had such things as a piano, a screen for movies, a garden, and a radio.

No matter how much we delight in new beginnings, there is also a stirring of past remembrances that claim attention. When reminiscing about her student nursing days, Alice Doyle Brunner once shared that being a nurse in the early 1920s was like learning to be a good mother. You learned how to make patients comfortable, prepare wholesome food, and tend to their needs. She added rather quickly, "Nothing like today." Nursing school alumnae fondly gathered remembrances of their experience for the golden anniversary of the nursing school. In addition to their memories of various sisters, religious experiences and studies were memories of things like forbidden tamale parties in the dorms, the one hour of recreation allowed nightly, lost toast found under beds, and taking Jimmy the skeleton across town to the new hospital.

There was a strict discipline that came as much from the doctors as the sisters. In the beginning, ten physicians taught all the classes. One of the memories passed down was of Dr. Parkinson and Sister Margaret Kennelly. Dr. James H. Parkinson was quite strict. Sister Mary Gabriel referred to him as "a master of novices if ever there was one. He had been a doctor on a British warship and never got over it."[43] As a teacher, he was determined to demonstrate bone structure to his students.

Dr. Parkinson made an early morning (4.30 a.m.) trip to the slaughter houses in Broderick across the Sacramento River, bringing back lots of bones wrapped in newspaper. Leaving them on the porch, he went inside. Meanwhile, Sister Margaret had ordered soup bones from the local butcher and went out to claim her bones. Seeing the pile of bones wrapped in newsprint, she was quite put out that they were not properly wrapped but, since they were needed for lunch, she took the bones inside and started to brew her soup stock. The story goes that the air around Dr. Parkinson was "quite blue" when he discovered he had lost his "exhibits."[44]

There were memories of the hardships of the old hospital as well—no running water in patient rooms, the rigor of nursing typhoid patients in the summer and trying to disinfect everything before it went to the laundry. Pneumonia had to be treated without the help of sulfa drugs or penicillin. Since the building was not fireproof, each floor had three buckets of water stored in case of fire.[45] Creativity sometimes compensated for the absence of modern technology. Sister Mary Gabriel tells of how a friend of the sisters helped supply them with the first and only incubator in town. He fixed up an old gas chicken incubator. Someone, usually herself, sat by it all night to make sure no accident happened.[46]

While one can look at building a new Mater Misericordiae as a natural progression of growth based on need, it is important to understand that it also was part of a natural movement. In 1915, the seeds for a network of Catholic hospitals was planted with the birth of the Catholic Health Association. It started small but grew to enfold hospitals across the United States. One of the goals of the movement was to establish criteria for excellence of care that fit both the demands of medical excellence and the mission of healing. This is what Mater Misericordiae expressed in concrete, brick, and mortar. It combined the elements of new technology while providing for patients a spiritual environment of care and compassion.

The opening of the new hospital was both an opening and a closure. It was a new beginning for Mercy healthcare in the city and the culmination of a vision that started years before. There was only one great sadness. Among all the guests, dignitaries and sisters gathered for the dedication of what would later be called Mercy Hospital, two significant people were missing, Mother Mary Ligouri Madden and Bishop Thomas Grace. Neither lived to see their vision fulfilled.

Keeping It All Together

If you were searching for an apt metaphor to describe the life of the Sisters of Mercy during the early years of the twentieth century, you might choose "A Juggling Act." Multiple threads were woven into their lives within the community and in their ministries. Not only was the hospital project constantly calling for attention, resources, and effort, but so were St. Joseph's Academy and Stanford Home. St Joseph's needed to keep up with evolving certification needs of academic institutions as well as an aging building. Stanford Home needed funds to support the orphans. In spite of all these worries and concerns, the internal life of the community did not come to a stop.

There were still deaths to grieve and new members to integrate. Add to this mix another question emerging at the same time: Was it the right time to join with other Mercy communities and create a larger group, or should the Sacramento Mercies remain separate and independent? No matter how important that decision might be, they still had to embrace the daily challenges of life and loss.

Just as plans for the new hospital were underway, the community experienced two significant loses in the deaths of Bishop Thomas Grace and Mother Mary Ligouri. In life, the two leaders were close collaborators and friends. They shared a "like heartedness." They died barely within six months of each other—Bishop Grace on December 27, 1921, Mother Mary Ligouri on June 22, 1922. Their deaths were amplified by the deaths of Sister Joseph McEnerney and Sister Alphonsus Browne.

Bishop Grace was the first to die. From 1908 on, he was physically frail, yet not eager to have the assistance of an auxiliary bishop. The bishop was an interesting blend of qualities. At the time of his death, *The Sacramento*

Bee called him, "A beloved man, a prelate who endeared himself to people of all denominations."[1] That would have been a valuable quality for any church leader in Sacramento, a religiously diverse community. That sense of inclusivity was matched by the inclusive nature of the Sisters of Mercy's ministries. The advertisements for Mater Misericordiae Hospital were explicit in noting that it welcomed persons of all religious faiths. In fact, an article in the *San Francisco Call Bulletin* of November 28, 1897, noted:

> A Sister of Mercy will meet you at the door and extend a welcome that is given everyone who enters. There are no class distinctions here, no sectarian restrictions, no questions of belief to answer, no pledges to make, no hinderances of creed; the saint and the sinner, the pure and the defiled, the godly and ungodly pass side by side through the open door of the Sisters' Hospital.

This same quality was found in Bishop Grace. An editorial by C. K. McClatchy said: "Catholic, Jew, Protestant, agnostic and atheist mourn today the passing of a true Christian, of whom unfortunately there are few."[2] Bishop Patrick Keane said of his predecessor: "He never failed to support every cause that made for the moral and social betterment of his city and State."[3] While Bishop Grace was known for his gentle spirit, acceptance of persons as they were, and forgiving nature, he also was most frugal. According to the diocesan historian Steven M. Avella, "he exercised almost penurious caution when it came to money and building projects."[4] This caution might explain his reluctance to renovate or replace the aging St. Joseph's Academy.

In spite of his fear of spending too much money, Bishop Grace was a strong support to the sisters. He gave of his own monies to build the surgery at Mater Misericordiae, attended the commencement exercises at St. Joseph's, and gave his full support to Stanford Home. According to community legend, concern for the health of the sisters prompted the bishop to direct them to purchase a home by the ocean where community members could recover from the heat of Sacramento summers. Given that the sisters wore heavy woolen serge habits in a time before air conditioning, some respite was greatly needed. One example of the extreme heat occurred on July 17, 1925, when Sacramento's temperature soared to 114 degrees. The sisters embraced the suggestion and just before Christmas in 1918, purchased a cottage in Moss Beach, CA. The price was a $10 gold coin.[5]

Just after Bishop Grace's funeral, the community experienced the first of three deaths. All were long-time members of the small community; indeed, two were among the first members of the newly independent foundation.

On January 2, 1922, Sister Mary Alphonsus Brown died. Hers was a sudden, unexpected death, taking her within twelve hours after falling ill. She was a member of the community for thirty-three years serving at both St. Joseph's and Stanford Home. The second death was that of Sister Joseph McEnerney, who was one of the first four young women to join the Sacramento community. She had served at both St. Joseph's and Mater Misericordiae since 1890. The papers of the day tell us that over forty Sisters of Mercy were present for her funeral. Sister Joseph was seventy-two years old when she died. We know little about the lives of these two women of mercy except that both were seen as faithful women, beloved by both their sisters and the wider community.

The third death was that of Mother Mary Liguori Madden. Mother Liguori enjoyed a long and fruitful life as a Sister of Mercy. She entered the community in 1867, just ten years after the founding of the Sacramento house. In the minds of Sacramentans, the lives of Bishop Grace and Mother Ligouri were braided together. *The Sacramento Bee* attested to this understanding in Mother Liguori's obituary:

> And it is no exaggeration to say that few of any faith in this vicinity have been so universally respected and loved as Bishop Thomas Grace and Mother Mary Ligouri. Their ages were about the same. Each bore the Cross of Christ in religious life for over half a century. Each held in the highest respect the good work of the other ... Their careers in religion ran along somewhat parallel lines for many, many years, each doing faithfully all those things which religion and dearest hopes pointed out as their work decreed by the Master. And Death separated them but little in that call to the Everlasting which both grew to welcome.[6]

Mother Ligouri must have possessed a burning desire to be of service to those who had no one to help them. Community tradition tells us that in the early 1880s, she embarked on missions to establish convents of Mercy in Arizona and in Butte, Montana. Her generosity went against the custom of the time. Sisters did not normally move back and forth between foundations that were not sponsored by the community of which they were members. So great was Mary Liguori's zeal, however, that she was willing to give up her membership in the Mercy community in San Francisco to respond to need. Neither of the attempts to root Mercy in Arizona or Montana succeeded, and she returned to California in 1885 to begin her long ministry in Sacramento.

At the time of the separation from San Francisco, Mother Mary Liguori was principal of St. Joseph's Academy. Two years later, in 1889, she took on the added responsibility of mistress of novices, meaning she was helping new members absorb the meaning and practice of their religious commitment. She was asked to serve in the leadership of the community either as superior or assistant superior for twelve years. It was during these years that she planted the seeds of Mercy Healthcare in the city.

To say that Mother Mary Liguori was exceptional would be an understatement. She had a particular talent for training women for leadership. Not only did she form women for leadership and self-sufficiency through the academy, but she also sought to train them for leadership in the medical community through the nursing school. The *Catholic Herald* wrote of her:

> She gave freely of her exceptional talents to the training of youth, and thousands of women scattered throughout the Coast gladly acknowledge their debt of gratitude to this very able and zealous educator for the loving and effective efforts which she bestowed upon all who were entrusted to her guidance in the formative period of their lives. She possessed a remarkable faculty for imparting to those who came under her care a reflection of her own strong character and rare mentality. She was a woman of brilliant mind and all-embracing humanity, wonderfully kind and considerate of all who needed sympathy and help in the manifold trials and difficulties of life ... here was no more reverenced or influential figure in the quasi-public life of Sacramento of other days than Mother Liguori in the heyday of her service and activity. She was honored and respected by all sorts and conditions of people in California for the unusual qualifications of intellect and character which she brought to the execution of her chosen life-work; and the delightful personality which captivated all who came in contact with her, no matter how casually.[7,8]

The legacy of Mother Mary Liguori was preserved in the cornerstone of the new Mater Misericordiae. Along with a picture of Catherine McAuley, foundress of the order, was a picture of Mother Liguori, a golden jubilee poem in her honor, and two other pieces, "A Tribute from the Sisters" and "In Memoriam." Her absence from the realization of a vision long sought must have been keenly felt by all the sisters. Sister Mary Aloysius Nolan, always ready with a poem for special occasions, summed it up this way:

> *She needs no monument of stone*
> *No lettered shaft of costly worth:*
> *The Hospital she toiled to build,*
> *Will keep her name revered on earth;*
> *Will teach as it has ever taught,*

How much a generous heart can do,
Which bravely welcomes trials grave
That work like this be carried through[9]

The poem's final stanza is full of emotion and gratitude:

Her work is done, and now she lives
In realm of bliss where God abides;
Untroubled by the cares of time,
Regardless of life's changing tides.
Yet still her work goes calmly on
In 'Mater Misericordiae' blest,
Round which her name through the years
Will like a Benediction rest.[10]

Records indicate that between 1915 and 1920, no new members joined the community. Perhaps in this period, things were just in too much of an uproar due to the twin crises of war and epidemic. As things began to normalize, five young women sought entry into the convent—Catherine Connelly, Mary Kate O'Donnell, Mary Helen Readman, Ellen Connolly, and Mary O'Brian.

The joy of new life quickly turned to sadness as death took both Mary Kate O'Donnell and Mary Helen Readman. Mary Helen, called Sister Mary Immaculate, died just a month after her first profession. Mary Kate, called Sister Mary Mercy, died after three years, having been weakened by the flu. Mary O'Brian and Catherine Connelly left the community, realizing they were not called to religious life. Only Ellen Connolly, now Sister Mary Ignatius, endured.[11] Cumulative loses must have been disheartening for the small community, seeing not just the deaths of long-time members like Mother Liguori and Mary Alphonsus, but also the deaths of sisters who had entered more recently.

In the middle of sadness, life continued. Just as society was changing quickly, so were things changing in the church. Church leaders desired more clarity and unification of church rules, and in 1917, the church had promulgated what was called the Code of Canon Law. What this meant was that all the diverse rules, regulations, and norms guiding church life were gathered together in one place and published as a guide for all church members. Embedded in the law were norms governing the manner in which women religious were to live the vowed life. Since it was church law, it was expected that all women religious would follow that guidance. While such a development does not seem to be so significant, it really was. The new code meant that sisters would need to revise their Original Rule to match the requirements of the revised canons. How would this be done? How would all the various Mercy communities across the world remain one in spirit without the same rule for all?

To understand the context of the dilemma, we have to go back to the beginnings of the congregation. When Catherine McAuley founded the Sisters of Mercy, she was doing something new. She did not originally plan on starting a new religious order within the Catholic church. It simply happened due to circumstances of the time. Having started her work, there arose a need to provide for its continuation. Relying on the inspiration of the Holy Spirit, Catherine set out to provide a shelter for young women needing protection from exploitation. Along with that desire, she saw education as a pathway out of poverty and committed herself to do what she could to provide such education for those who were poor. Finally, she was keenly aware of the need to comfort the sick poor in their homes. Those desires shaped her way of life and ministry.

Catherine, having received a large inheritance, built a large sheltering home on Baggot Street, Dublin. Other women like Mary Frances Warde and Mary Clare Moore joined her in the work and came to live with her. They did not make vows, nor were they recognized as religious. They prayed and worshipped together, lived and worked together, and shared everything in common. In other words, while not members of a religious community, they looked and acted like other communities of women religious with the exception that they were out amid the people. It was that aspect that later won for them the title, "the walking nuns."

In a way, Catherine's first companions shared much in common with the Beguines of the thirteenth century. The Beguines were also not women religious, but they did share life in common and engaged in service of the poor. As lay women, they reached out to meet the evolving needs of their towns or communities and were outside church regulation. Whether Catherine knew anything about this movement within the church is unknown, but there were some common threads. Catherine started a lay community. She supported herself and welcomed others to share life with her. She helped them deepen their love of God and God's people. Just by doing this, opposition emerged for Catherine just as it had for Beguines centuries before. The criticism focused on their way of life—looking like a religious community but holding themselves outside church regulation. The criticism hurt, and clerical opposition to the circle of women made their lives more difficult.

When Bishop Murray, the bishop of Dublin, shared this concern with Catherine, she realized that for her work to continue and her community to endure, she would need to formalize their lives as a group of vowed women religious. She willingly entered the Presentation Sisters with two others and was formed in the way of religious life. After the required time of training, she and her companions made their vows as the first Sisters of Mercy. That was in 1831.

The next hurdle was to receive approval for their rule from Rome. A rule is the document that defines a religious order, its way of being, and its vision. In founding the Sisters of Mercy, and writing her rule, there was one thing Catherine was unwilling to do. She could not accept the rule of cloister, which kept women religious confined within their convent walls. Catherine and her sisters would be out in the midst of the people. She was successful in her wish. When the rule for the Order of the Sisters of Mercy was approved by the church in 1841, it did not require that the members be cloistered. The change was significant, providing the flexibility and freedom to serve the poor no matter where they were.

Things in the Catholic Church usually move slowly, and that is reflected in the manner in which the 1917 Code of Canon Law addressed religious life almost sixty years after the Order of Mercy started. Catherine McAuley had founded what is now called an apostolic religious community, one which organized its life of community and prayer around their lives of service. This departed from the pattern of life consistent with monasteries. The monastic pattern centered life around the hours of prayer core to their life.

When the 1917 Code of Canon Law took effect, this distinction was not yet clear. In other words, some of the rules did not fit the reality of the new form of religious community. For instance, Canon 604 stated that for all congregations of women, no matter whether they were diocesan orders or one of papal approval, "the law of enclosure shall be observed so that only who by law have a right to enter, as specified in Canon 600, shall be admitted."[12] The code went on to say that bishops had the obligation to see that enclosure was observed. The code also indicated that sisters were forbidden to leave their house unless accompanied by a companion.[13] These provisions simply did not fit Mercy life.

It was not so much what the canons imposed upon the sisters but more how it was interpreted that impacted the lives of the sisters. While apostolic religious life was now a reality, the rules regulating such a life had not caught up. A monastic pattern was imposed upon apostolic religious by interpreters of the law. Even though not an enclosed community by rule, the sisters were enclosed by contemporary customs. Jean Leahy, a long-time friend of the sisters, remembers it this way:

> The Sisters did not really interact with parish families. They didn't visit our homes, parishioners were (to my knowledge) never invited to the convent. Few nuns would attend the school events. A nun could not go

"out" alone, two nuns had to go together. Also, I don't remember the
nuns eating in public. In describing the nuns, you would probably say
they were cloistered—somewhat shut off from the world, protected,
secluded, etc.[14]

In spite of the restrictions, the sisters continued to meet the needs around
them. In ending her reflection, Jean Lahey notes that even with the
difficulties they experienced, the sisters "remained pleasant and friendly.
Their ministries were their priorities and main concern."[15]

There were other movements within the various Mercy communities
that called for the sisters' attention. When Catherine McAuley established
her first convent outside of Dublin, she had it become independent from
the "motherhouse" as soon as possible. That was the custom in mercy,
separate houses but one common rule. Each house became independent
as soon as feasible. In California, that practice continued. Mother Baptist
Russell's request that the Sacramento foundation become independent in
1868 was rejected by Archbishop Alemany, delaying that independence
by almost twenty years. The Mercy community in Grass Valley became
independent as soon as it had sufficient sisters because it was established
in a different diocese under a different bishop. As time went by, some of
the small houses that dotted the west languished because they could not
attract newer members.

Bishops worried about how such small communities could properly
form new members should they have them. Bishop Manogue shared such
concerns prompted by the situations of two of the smaller communities of
Mercy Sisters in Yreka and Eureka. These foundations were besieged by
internal conflicts and, in Manogue's opinion, were giving scandal. It led
Manogue, familiar with the challenges experienced by the sisters in Grass
Valley, to believe that bringing the communities together under a single
leadership was important. Writing in 1881 to Cardinal Simeoni, prefect of
the Sacred Congregation for the Propagation of the Faith, Manogue said:

> One may ask why such dissentions do not exist in the Archdiocese where
> there are three Mercy communities as well. The answer is that they are
> under the same house and are ruled by the authority of the Motherhouse,
> and if our communities were ruled in the same way, dissentions and
> difficulties would, by the same token, be removed.[16]

The bishop went on to ask the cardinal to bring the groups together under
one rule and one central authority.

He was not successful, but Manogue was not alone in his sense that
centralization would lead to stronger, holier communities. A year later,

Archbishop Alemany expressed the same idea. Writing to all the Mercy communities in California in the name of the Provincial Council of bishops, he noted that many convents were able to have only a few sisters to meet the many pastoral needs of the diocese. He realized the limits under which they worked:

> We are always desirous of establishing a house wherever it can be supported, but since, as we have seen, if often happens that in such places only a few Sisters can be maintained, we consider it undesirable to have a novitiate in every small convent and believe it highly useful to the welfare of each to be aided by others[17]

The bishop went on to name other benefits, such as caring for incapacitated sisters or extending mutual support. He then went on to state that such benefits could be attained by having one superior for all Mercy convents or, at least, one superior within each diocese if that was what the sisters wanted. The plan was to be put to a vote within three weeks of receiving his letter. Each sister was asked to freely express her view, sign the vote and seal it. The sisters did as they were asked but their answer was "No."[18] The matter was dropped for the present.

It was not just the bishops who thought unification would be a good idea. As early as 1851, Mother Mary Agatha O'Brien of Chicago suggested the possibility of creating one motherhouse for all the U.S. Mercy communities. In a letter to Sister Elizabeth Strange, she writes:

> It seems to me that the Order of Mercy is destined to do immense good in the United States, but I think there is one thing that is a great drawback to it and that is our not having a Mother House such as Emmittsburg is to the Sisters of Charity, where the young might be trained for the different missions and brought up according to the Spirit of our holy Institute.[19]

Mother Mary Magdalene de Pazzi of St Louis took the unification of all Mercy communities on as her personal project, contacting the Congregation for the Propagation of the Faith with a petition for general governance in the United States in 1875.[20] In this case, she did it on her own, not as a representative of a group of Mercy superiors. Bypassing a process of collaboration and consultation did not win a lot of support.

The concerns raised by Archbishop Alemany were very real. A number of Mercy convents throughout the west were forced to close due to lack of members or resources. Debt stalked some groups as the small cities in which they ministered faded away. One example is the Mercy Convent in Yreka, CA, established in 1871. It struggled from the beginning. The sisters, seven in number, arrived shortly before the town itself was devastated by a fire on July 4, 1871. The advent of the railroad undercut the town's commercial importance, mining was waning and, finally, the Modoc Indians, seeking a just treaty, were in open conflict with settlers and the government.[21] By 1876, the decreased population of the town, concerns for safety and their own poverty made some sisters welcome an invitation from Archbishop Alemany to establish a foundation at Rio Vista, CA. Four sisters, including the original foundress, Mother Mary Camillus McGarr, accepted the invitation.

By 1881, the sisters who remained in Yreka found that they could no longer continue. Although the work of the sisters thrived after the Indian war was over and stability returned, they still had to deal with massive debt and a lack of new members. The new coadjutor bishop of the vicariate of Grass Valley, Patrick Manogue helped relocate them to Red Bluff, where they started over again. He arranged for creditors to take the Yreka property in partial payment for the debt.

From the time of their arrival in Red Bluff until 1906, six women entered the community, but only two stayed. Sister Kay O'Brian tells us that "the community was in deep trouble, if not actually dying."[22] The intertwining of various Mercy stories emerges at this point. The Red Bluff sisters were to elect new leadership, Sister Mary Helena Dickson, having served her maximum time as superior. They could not agree on who should succeed her. After three ballots, the Mercy Rule authorized the bishop's delegate to appoint a superior. He appointed Sister Mary Joseph Boyland.

Oral tradition tells us that Sister Mary Joseph, trained by the sisters at St. Joseph's Academy in Sacramento, initially sought to enter the Sacramento community. Father Thomas Grace, then pastor at St. Rose Church, was aware of the great need in Red Bluff, and convinced her to enter there.[23] It was a graced appointment as Sister Mary Joseph brought new life and energy to the foundation. Her drive for excellence and keen perception of what was needed for the community's future set the community on a firm foundation.

Like Mary Liguori Madden, she opened a hospital, St. Elizabeth's; saw to the continued upgrading of the school's curriculum; and addressed the need for new members. Sister Mary Agatha Marie O'Connor, a member of the community at the time, asserts that "if Mother Joseph had been around when the sisters were in Yreka, they might never have had to leave."[24]

Mother Mary Liguori would have understood these experiences since she had been part of at least two failed missions. She was not alone in the experience. In fact, the bishop asked the Sacramento community to accept two sisters whose small foundations had failed. Again, Sister Mary Gabriel tells the story:

[Sister Mary Stanislaus Lydon] was a dear soul from a community which had to be disbanded. As we got older we learned about these small communities in the State which had been working for years—but could not get subjects [a name used for new members], so the Bishop closed them and asked larger Communities to take the Sisters in."[25]

Another religious, Sister Mary Aloysius Banks came from Ferndale, CA, where the same thing had happened. According to Sister Mary Gabriel, she was "tops in lots of things." She did the bookkeeping at Stanford Home, coached foreign born priests with their English, taught French, mended clothing, and read stories to the children and to the sisters. She was, in the opinion of Mary Gabriel, "a pet."[26]

We do not know what the sisters in Sacramento felt about all the various closures and turmoil since there is no mention of it in extant community records, but one can see from Mary Gabriel's memoir that the sisters were most conscious of the reality. Right at the beginning of the century, James Cardinal Gibbons of Baltimore had written to every Mercy community, surveying their wishes around unifying. He was not successful either.[27] As the closures continued, the bishops returned to their desire for unification. With each convent closure, bishops found themselves having to deal with the financial consequences as well as helping to find welcoming communities for sisters like Mary Aloysius and Mary Stanislaus.

Another chapter in the story about Mercy fortunes in California in the early twentieth century revolves around Mother Mary Josephine Cummings. A native New Yorker, Mary Josephine was sent to Eureka, CA, as superior of a small group of sisters. The young community struggled and that struggle was heightened by being surrounding by a hostile environment. Sister Mary Athanasius Sheridan tells us:

The A.P.A. movement was rampant in the area and persistently hampered their efforts. Under the guise of patriotism, this group carried out an intensive campaign of bigotry similar in expression to that fomented by the Know-Nothings in the 1850's.[28,29]

After two terms as superior, Mother Mary Josephine asked to return to New York. Bishop Manogue prevailed upon her to open a new foundation in Ukiah, California, instead. Here she and three companions did much good for a few years, but like many other small communities, they discovered they could not continue.

Bishop Patrick Riordan, then archbishop of San Francisco, arranged for the group to amalgamate with the Rio Vista community which was within his diocese.[30] Having achieved success with this union, Bishop

Riordan desired to join all the Mercy communities in his diocese together. Riordon looked to the San Francisco Mercies as the pillar upon which he would shape this union. Mother Mary Camillus McGarr was a frequent visitor at St. Mary's, Rincon Hill, and was a friend of Mother Mary Baptist Russell. He began to work for the union as early as 1894 but did not live to see it realized in May 1917.[31]

There was continued movement. In 1918, the Mercy communities of San Diego and Los Angeles came together with the Mercy community in Phoenix joining them in 1921. Finally, in 1922, the vision of Archbishops Alemany and Riordan became concrete with the formation of the Sisters of Mercy of California and Arizona, encompassing the former communities of San Francisco, Rio Vista, Los Angeles, San Diego, and Phoenix. The official name of the newly amalgamated community was "The Sisters of Mercy of California and Arizona." Later, they were less formally referred to as "the Burlingame Sisters of Mercy."

Sacramento's sisters were not involved in the mergers of these years except as spectators. They had other concerns that demanded their time and focus. That changed in the later 1920s when another attempt at forming all the Mercy units into one group emerged. There were a mixture of Mercy leaders and U.S. bishops behind the initiative. Given the times, little face-to-face contact, and all the dynamics arising from history, location, and heritage, it was a formidable ideal.

Reading through correspondence between American bishops and Rome's delegate to the United States during this period reveals a shared fear held by some bishops. These bishops feared that some autonomous Mercy communities were too small to properly provide training for new members, manage financial debt, and provide alternatives for members who needed a new living situation for emotional and spiritual well-being. Some communities, they felt, failed to follow the mandates of the church law. All this played a part in the push to unification.[32]

The changes in the Code of Canon Law brought another set of concerns. The original Mercy Rule would have to be updated, revised and aligned with the new code. Adjustments and revisions would need to be made, but would every house be different? There was only one Mercy Rule approved by Rome. Would all these small groups now have to have their rules approved? The problem was only resolved in 1926 when arrangements were made with the original community at Baggot Street to submit to Rome their revised rule and then have all other revisions made by the various communities patterned on that rule.[33]

While the Mercy community in Sacramento enjoyed stability and a vigorous mercy life, that was not true everywhere. Encouraged by local bishops, mergers began to happen throughout the country. Little is said of these amalgamation efforts in the Sacramento records of the mid-1920s. In late 1923, a meeting of twenty-four Mercy groups decided to once more survey the forty-five Mercy foundations across the U.S. By the next year, the results were in: "Opposed to the movement nineteen; in favor of general government in the broad sense fourteen; in favor of provincial government three; undecided nine."[34] Still, behind the scenes, strong women like Mother Mary Carmelita Hartman of Baltimore and Mother Mary Bernadine Clancy of Chicago worked to bring one union into being. By 1929, their efforts once more brought the questions before all Mercy communities.

It is here that the Sacramento records provide insight into the mind of the community. Pietro Fumasoni-Biondi, apostolic delegate to the U.S., wrote to the bishops asking them to facilitate the vote by communities who had not yet decided whether or not to become part of the union. In the letter, Bishop Fumasoni-Biondi emphasized two things: the wish of the Holy See that all Mercy communities in the U.S. join as one and the freedom of conscience for them to say "No."[35] The Sacramento sisters met to discuss and vote on the proposal on June 21, 1929. The vote was thirty-four against, three in favor of amalgamation. The annalist states that the primary reason was that, using the numbers listed in the Catholic Directory, the community calculated only 1,200 sisters out of 6,000 were in favor. They needed greater support to say "Yes."[36]

As usual, there probably was a story behind the story. In a letter from Sister Mary Aloysius Nolan to Mother Mary Carmelita Hartman, Mary Aloysius shared that the sisters were strongly opposed to the idea of union. Reasons were not given, but it is reasonable to surmise that, after becoming an independent house, the sisters found greater freedom to expand ministries, embrace new needs, and retain Sacramento women who were entering the community. It is possible that the challenges encountered in the Burlingame amalgamation also might have added to their hesitancy.

The question did not end there. Bishop Armstrong, Sacramento's Roman Catholic bishop, evidently greatly favored the union and hoped that the three Mercy communities in the Sacramento diocese, Grass Valley, Red Bluff, and Sacramento would all become part of it. None of the three said yes at the time of the first vote. When Bishop Armstrong again tried to make his case for union, the sisters in both Grass Valley and Red Bluff voted to join. It did not happen that way in Sacramento. The bishop called the sisters together on October 13, 1929, and once more explained the purpose of amalgamation. The letter from the apostolic delegate outlining the hopes of Rome was once more read. The sisters delayed the vote until they had time to talk among themselves. The next meeting was convened on October 15. When the vote was taken, it was twenty-six against amalgamation, sixteen in favor.[37] For the Sisters, the discussion was closed.

Expanding with the City

Although healthcare consumed much of the sisters' energies at the beginning of the twentieth century, education remained a passionate focus. Between 1857 and 1894, they had only one school, St. Joseph's Academy. That changed in 1895 when, in the absence of other religious communities, the sisters started a school at St. Francis parish with the understanding that the pastor would continue to look for another community to serve there permanently. They relinquished that responsibility when they took on the Stanford Home ministry in 1901. That too had a school for a brief period of time, but the sisters soon found that it was more workable to walk the children across town to classes at St. Joseph's. The walk, a little over a mile long, must have been challenging during the winter rains and late summer heat. In spite of such hardship, that practice continued until 1936 when the home was turned over to the Sisters of Social Service.

Looking at the struggles of these years, the lack of monies, the challenges with deteriorating buildings, and the task of providing training for new sister teachers, one has to ask: Why? Why were the sisters so willing to sacrifice so much to educate children of every economic class in society? The answer lies in the commitment to education articulated in the rule of the order.

Catherine McAuley believed that education was the most effective tool to eliminate poverty and despair. In her rule, she wrote:

> The Sisters shall feel convinced that no work of charity can be more productive of good to society, or more conducive to the happiness of the poor than the careful instruction of women, since whatever be the station they are destined to fill, their example and advice will always

possess influence, and where ever a religious woman presides, peace and good order are generally to be found. (Chapter 2, Article 5)[1]

From its beginning at the House of Mercy on Baggot Street, the sisters had incorporated the work of education into every setting. Sometimes, it followed the pattern of Stanford Home where care of orphans was twinned with a school. At times, it was going out after a day's work at the hospital or at a school to teach religious education classes to children at local parishes. At other times, it was providing adult education opportunities to help new immigrants or adults lacking education break the cycle of poverty. Education for the sisters was not just about the mind. It was about the whole of life. It also was a challenge to the society of the period. By providing education for girls of every social class, rich or poor, regardless of ethnicity or religion, Catherine challenged the injustices of her time.

In her own life, Catherine left a model of educational excellence for her sisters to emulate. Conscious of her own shortcomings in religious knowledge, she sought out the best teachers she could find to help her become better equipped to respond to the challenges to faith she encountered.[2] Prior to opening the school at Baggot Street, she travelled to France to learn the most up-to-date teaching strategies for class instruction.[3] In the early years of the community here in the United States, much time was given to transcribing books for the sisters to use both for personal growth and for teaching.

The sisters in Sacramento followed in that tradition. The subscription library started by Mother Vincent Phelan, was part of that effort. The *Annals* note: "This antedated the establishment of the City Free Library. St. Joseph's supplied hundreds of professional and business men with the best English literature, and incidentally made many friends for the Sisters."[4] Among those who made great use of the library was *Sacramento Bee* publisher C. K. McClatchy, whose paper often carried stories of the sisters. The library, housed in what was called "the Lodge," was not only a way of providing adult education but, as a subscription library also provided the sisters with monies to support the academy. Today, some copies of original library books can be found in the holdings of the sisters in the Auburn heritage collection at the Convent of Our Lady of Mercy, Auburn, California.

Mother Russell took special interest in the accomplishments of the students at St. Josephs and in the early years of the foundation often came to Sacramento for commencement events. She had a special gift for utilizing whatever resources became available to provide educational opportunities. The establishment of a natural history museum at St.

Joseph's Academy illustrates this educational strategy. In September 1985, Mother Russell sent to Sister Mary Aloysius Nolan what she called a "box of sundries" for the museum. It contained such things as corals, a pair of walrus' teeth, a plate of whale bone, and bark from a pear tree planted at the San Raphael mission. Ever the teacher, she then went on to break down the items according to species, genus, order, and class.[5]

The yearly programs hosted by St. Joseph's both for commencements and special occasions during the year reflected a combination of academic proficiency, elocution, and musical abilities. The quality of the presentation prompted people to pay to attend, and *The Sacramento Bee* often noted that the crowds overflowed to the balconies.[6] All levels, primary through secondary, contributed to these events, showcasing the level of education provided by the academy.

Perhaps no aspect of the curriculum at St. Joseph's was more reflective of excellence than its music program. At the commencement ceremonies in 1912, this excellence was seen in the selections chosen: 'Humoresque' by Dvorak, 'Mazurka' by Chopin, and a solo from Tannhauser were just a few of the pieces shared.[7] A later report on a St. Joseph's commencement program notes that six pianos were used by twelve to eighteen performers. The musical part of the event was always blended with an extended dramatic presentation.[8]

It was not enough for the sisters to provide their students with quality education and Christian formation; they also wanted to make sure that their students could pursue higher education. This was evident in the efforts to achieve accreditation from the University of California. Accreditation was essential for the girls and for the school itself. The one thing standing in the way of achieving such accreditation was the absence of science labs. Once again, monies were short and so, in the fall of 1915, the alumnae undertook the task of raising sufficient funds for new laboratories. Two years later, they were still at it. *The Sacramento Bee* tells us:

> The graduates of St. Joseph's Academy have held their own with credit in normal school and university. Now that it is announced that the crowded condition of the normal will preclude their accepting any pupils, except such as come from schools accredited to the University of California, it becomes necessary that the laboratories of the academy be brought up to the required standard in the matter of apparatus.[9]

By December 1917, enough money was raised to complete the laboratories. Accreditation from the University of California followed in July. St. Joseph's Academy was also a "normal" school, a term that might seem strange or unfamiliar. In the early twentieth century, it was the term used to refer to training schools for teachers. St. Joseph's was like a nursery for emerging teachers, and many of its graduates entered the sphere of public education.

One of the most remarkable aspects of Mercy education was the empowerment of women. Beginning in primary school, young girls were challenged to show confidence and competence, whether that was in the oral recitations of school programs, the musical performances, or the recitation of original writings. An example of this dynamic is found in a series of articles published in the *Sacramento Union* in 1922. The articles, all written by St. Joseph's students, dealt with literary topics. Rosemary McEnerney contributed a book review on "The Dragon's Teeth" from *A Wonder Book*. She was only a freshman. Carola Diepenbrock, a junior, showed her literary prowess through sharing the life and accomplishments of Longfellow while Lillian Donahue shared her love of Shakespeare's *The Merchant of Venice*. Carola Diepenbrock continued her contributions with a piece on George Eliot. She took great care in telling the story of this woman author whose real name was Mary Ann Evans.[10]

From their beginnings in Dublin, the Sisters of Mercy were concerned about the empowerment of women. This concern prompted them to provide two forms of educational experiences aimed at fostering women's self-sufficiency and dignity. In addition to providing young women with quality education, the sisters also provided job training. This was true at St. Joseph's where a commercial department was an integral part of the school. In his study of the Catholic Church in Sacramento, Father Steven Avella notes:

> While the academy provided a number of teachers for Sacramento's growing elementary-age population, St. Joseph's also offered course work to students entering the ranks of clerical workers in city businesses. In 1893 a commercial course was introduced, promising that "young ladies will receive a thorough business training."[11]

The sisters delighted in the accomplishments of Minnie Rooney O'Neill, Sacramento County's superintendent of schools; Emma Van Hatten, a member of the examining board for education; principals like Nettie Hopley and Lizzie Griffen; Rose Sheehan, who after obtaining a law degree, became the assistant deputy district attorney; and high school teachers, such as Margaret Morgan and Rose Mary McEnerney.[12] Sister Mary Berchmans Kennelly spoke enthusiastically about the role of St. Joseph's graduates in the *Sacramento Annals*:

> Not a single branch of the Business world but can be found a graduate of St. Joseph's Commercial Class holding positions in Banks, Legal

and Merchant firms, Motor Vehicles, Electrical, Traffic Companies, railroads, Social Service and Welfare work and last but not least, in the all-important profession of Nursing the Sick in Private and County Hospitals.[13]

Religious communities also benefitted from the work of St. Joseph's. By 1957, the school had thirty-nine of its graduates enter religious communities.

Students were encouraged to exercise creativity and gain organizational skills through sponsoring public fundraisers and benefits. All the planning was done by students. Students enrolled in the commercial courses took responsibility for the myriad details of bookkeeping and monies. For young women, it was an impressive enterprise. *The Sacramento Bee* took notice of these efforts, reporting in March 1914 that the girls had raised $1,000 for the benefit of the sisters—a formidable sum for the time. Such activities not only provided students with a sense of confidence and success, but also developed in them a sense of philanthropy.[14]

The same focus on excellence that was placed on student formation at St Joseph's was evident in the internal formation of young sisters. At the beginning of the twentieth century, it was not common for young women to earn college degrees. Even a high school diploma was a major achievement. For the sisters, such education became imperative. While St. Joseph's was working on accreditation from the University of California, the community began sending teaching sisters like Mary Gabriel Spadier and Bernard Artz on for college degrees. It began a long period of sisters attending universities after school, over summers and weekends until degrees were earned. Some sisters like Mary Evangelist Morgan and Mary Cecilia Nealis were sent to complete Masters programs, but they were exceptions to the norm.[15]

This same dynamic was seen in relationship to the nursing school. In the beginning years, not all prospective nurses had completed elementary school. For such students, the sisters taught both basic education and the best of medical training. At the hospital, there was spirit of professionalism and study. Doctors sought out best practices from other medical institutions and brought them back to Mater Misericordiae.

Sometimes, unexpected barriers emerged, which inhibited the freedom of sisters to acquire professional degrees. One such barrier was a church policy that prohibited sisters from being present at child birth. That automatically excluded them from a nursing degree. Mary Gabriel shares that the Irish Medical Missionaries of Mary petitioned Rome for a revision of this policy. When it was granted, there was great rejoicing as that opened the way for nursing sisters to obtain their licenses and degrees.[16]

For women, the closing years of the nineteenth century and the beginning years of the twentieth century were years of struggle. Women's place within society was at stake and the campaign for women's suffrage was in full swing. The sisters saw women as influencers both within the home and in society. While the sisters were not directly involved in the campaign for women's suffrage, their efforts provided their students with foundational tools for leadership. Providing high school degrees in 1875 and developing a "normal school" for future teachers three years later was part of that work.

The sisters were not simply passive participants in the civic and political spheres. They understood the need to be actively engaged in advocacy for the needs of those served. From the early days of the community, the sisters consistently petitioned the state assembly for public funding for their orphans and for exploited women. The legislative records of the state show the extent to which these appeals were successful.[17] They saw to it that their students understood governmental action as well. Visits to the state assembly were among the learning experiences provided to the girls, especially after California awarded the vote to women.[18]

Indirectly, the sisters had another impact on the empowerment of women. That was by way of witness. The ministry of the sisters showed the capacity of women for leadership and displayed the business acumen needed for those works to be successful. In speaking of the autonomy of women, Father Avella reflects:

> Religious sisters tended to their own business affairs, managed increasingly complex personnel issues and technological advancements for their health-care centers, and maintained control over their living space—all within the context of a church structure totally dominated by men.[19]

In some ways, the sisters jealously guarded their autonomy. This took various forms, including their refusal to move from the St. Joseph's property. They safeguarded their freedom to determine how they would be governed. An interesting anecdote from the *Annals* tells us that in 1893, Bishop Manogue had appointed a sister to succeed Mary Michael Irwin as mistress of novices. The community did not take this intrusion lightly. The *Annals* tell us that the sisters, wanting to assert their privilege of electing a sister to this post, decided to have an election even though the bishop had appointed Sister Mary Antonia Kellaghan to the job. This they did the next day, "casting their votes to the satisfaction of all."[20]

This same determination to plot their own course is seen at the time of the 1929 amalgamation. Even though it was clear that Bishop Armstrong desired them to join with other Mercy communities, the sisters followed their own counsel. Having built strong relationships with those in ecclesial authority helped to safeguard that stance. Differences did not dissolve into conflict, but were talked through, compromises were crafted and life went on.

One of the challenging aspects of providing excellence in education was space. If St. Joseph's was to maintain its high standards, it had to have improved classrooms. The old buildings were not only inadequate, they were dangerous. Plans to replace the old buildings created a new reality for the sisters. Up until that point, they were the owners of both property and buildings. In other words, the schools literally belonged to them. That would not be true for the new buildings erected in 1926.

Plans for the new buildings were announced in 1924. The idea was to provide a new cathedral parish school for the elementary classes and use the existing buildings for the academy. Monsignor Thomas Horgan, rector of the cathedral, attributed the need to congestion. There were simply too many students.[21] It took eighteen months to complete the project, dedicated right before the start of school in September 1926. The cost of adding some sixteen large classrooms plus administrative offices was somewhere between $65,000–75,000 to complete.[22]

The sisters found themselves in a new relationship with the parish. Prior to this time, everything was part of the academy. Now, the sisters would have administrative responsibility for the elementary school, but not bear the full fiscal burden. It was a model that would be replicated as the sisters expanded their educational ministries beyond St. Joseph's. Still, the academy or secondary department was the full responsibility of the sisters. Some remodeling of the old structure was necessary to make the building suited to the needs of an exclusively secondary school.

The original plan for the new buildings included an auditorium. This did not materialize in 1926. No reasons are given for the delay in spite of an auditorium being publicized as part of the plans in the articles of the day. While it was planned to have such a facility provided, it was five years later when it moved from "hoped for" to "realized." A possible clue for the delay is found in the minutes of the chapter book, which recorded the decisions of the sisters. It indicates that the Cathedral parish lacked the property to build the new auditorium until they negotiated with the sisters for more land:

In January 1931, the community decided to sell the quarter block 8th and F Streets to the Cathedral Parish for $12,000 as Monsignor Horgan wanted it for a site for the school auditorium. The lot takes in "The

Lodge" but Monsignor did not want to buy this so he agreed to lease it back to the Sisters for $1.00 a year for fifty years. The $12,000 was credited to the account owed by the Sisters' Hospital to the Cathedral Parish.[23]

This arrangement was a win-win for Monsignor Horgan. Not only did he get his land for the auditorium, but he did not have to pay hard cash for it, only deduct the cost from the debt owed. While the sisters relinquished part of their coveted garden space, they gained a new and much-needed indoor gathering space for performances and other social events. In addition, it was a relief for them to erase part of their debt, especially with the country deep in the depression.

There was another motive behind Monsignor Horgan's desire to build in 1931. It was part of the church's efforts to help the unemployed and down trodden. The depression of the 1930s had completely overwhelmed the churches. Income dropped as members lost jobs and could barely feed their families. The church found itself unable to follow its usual way of providing help. What Monsignor Horgan could create was jobs. In order to provide hope and employment, he went forward with plans to build the new auditorium for St. Joseph's. People understood what he was doing.

Construction has been undertaken at this time in adherence to the appeals of the social leaders for contracting all necessary work in the current depression as an aid towards industrial rehabilitation.[24]

Since these were depression days, such considerations loomed large.

The 1930s were not easy for anyone. Desperate families migrated out of dust bowl areas seeking work. Some came to Sacramento and settled in "Hoovervilles" on the outskirts of the city.[25] Avella tells us that the huge increase in transient persons coming into the city overwhelmed Sacramento's social services. "Homeless men created at least five sprawling shanty villages on the banks of the Sacramento River."[26]

Even with such economic hardships, the depression years were a time of expansion for the church. Bishop Robert J. Armstrong succeeded Bishop Keane in 1928, just before the stock market crash of the following year. He was an avid advocate for parish schools, and this passion expanded the educational ministry of the sisters.

During his 28 years as bishop of Sacramento, Bishop Armstrong built more churches, schools and religious facilities than had been built in the entire previous history of the Sacramento Diocese. In addition to opening 21 chapels and 31 mission churches, he increased the number of parishes from 52 to 79. During his administration, 21 schools were built and Catholic school enrollment increased from 3,000 to 11,500.[27]

One of the first of those schools was Sacred Heart School, Sacramento. East Sacramento was a fast-growing part of the city during the early 1920s. Bishop Keane recognized the need to establish a parish to serve the needs of the Catholics who had moved to that area and purchased land for the new parish. When the sisters selected that area of the city for their new hospital, it was only a short distance away from the site purchased by Bishop Keane for the new church. On January 1, 1926, the parish was established, beginning with a temporary building. That temporary building would eventually become the school. The *Sacred Heart Community Annals* preserve the story:

> August 27, 1934. On this morning the school in Sacred Heart Parish, opened its doors in St. Stephen's Hall, which had been fitted up for the purpose with an attendance of fifty-nine students. Only the first four grades can be accommodated at present, and these will be taught by two sisters from St. Joseph's Academy—Sisters M. Mercy [Longwich] and Mary Vincent [Kirby].[28]

This pattern of "make-do" was repeated as new parish schools were staffed by the sisters. Rarely was everything in place. In the case of Sacred Heart, Sisters Mary Mercy and Mary Vincent had to commute from St. Joseph's Academy by street car every day. They started out at 8 a.m. and returned home around 4.30 p.m. Weather was not a consideration that was factored in. Once they got to school, Sr. Mary Vincent taught a combined first and second grade while Mary Mercy took the third and fourth grades. Part of their task was to make the parish hall suited for classroom use. Each year, more grades were added but the costs of building the church and the impact of the depression delayed the parish's ability to build a proper school. That did not happen until 1939. A convent for the sisters would wait until 1941 when Monsignor Michael Lyons purchased a private home and converted it into a convent.

Another major change came for the sisters in the mid-1930s, their withdrawal from Stanford Home. Many divergent threads came together to require that change, one not sought by the sisters themselves. During the Great Depression, the Catholic diocese struggled to provide for the needs of the most vulnerable. This struggle provided the needed incentive to upgrade and expand Catholic social services.[29] A Catholic Social Welfare Bureau was formed to oversee the diocesan agencies including both Stanford Home and the Grass Valley orphanages. Mary Francis Grogan was hired to head the new office.

To grasp the whole story, one must understand what was happening in Grass Valley. At the beginning of the 1930s, social service outreach was becoming professionalized, especially those services that offered care to vulnerable children. Licensing and inspections were now the norm. Avella tells us that "Grogan visited the decrepit Catholic orphanage buildings in Grass Valley and was shocked by what she found."[30] The nineteenth-century-era buildings housed two separate institutions, one for girls and one for boys. Avella continues sharing the vivid description of Bradley Riter, a correspondent for *The Sacramento Bee* that listed such things as jerry-rigged fire escapes, a study hall used as dormitories, and unacceptable heating, ventilation, and plumbing.[31]

The description is pretty dismal but not as alarming as the series of articles appearing in *The Sacramento Bee* throughout the early months of 1931. For months, *The Sacramento Bee* appealed to Sacramentans to support a drive to build a new orphanage to replace the dilapidated orphanage buildings. In March 1931, Riter asserts:

> It was heart rending enough to view the ancient and tottering St. Patrick's Orphanage for boys and St. Vincent's Orphanage for girls in Grass Valley, but it was terrifying to see the outside stairs called "fire escapes," and then to vision how almost hopelessly they might be used if a fire should break out.[32]

In an aside comment, Riter notes that while the Sisters of Mercy in Grass Valley were aware of the danger, they were absolutely unable to do anything about it.

Riter's comment about the sisters was partially true and partially inaccurate. True, the sisters had no resources to rebuild the orphanages; indeed, they struggled to keep all their charges fed and sheltered. He missed the mark in thinking they had no way to change things. As early as the mid-1920s, the sisters looked for ways of improving the situation, even considering a farm that the boys could run to provide extra food. A committee was formed to explore options. Now, with the buildings condemned and declared uninhabitable, there was dire urgency. With Bishop Armstrong in charge, things moved quickly. A new solution was formulated. The orphanage would be moved to Sacramento, where it would have greater financial support and fireproof buildings that could accommodate up to 100 children.

As the depression deepened, the idea of raising the $250,000 needed was daunting. Bishop Armstrong appealed to all the parishes of the diocese to support the effort. The papers of April 1931 extolled the project as not only providing safe haven for the children but as one which "will be of immense benefit to the local building trades."[33] It was thought that the project would be one of the largest undertaken in that year. Both the new auditorium at St. Joseph's and the new St. Patrick Orphanage slated for construction were part of the church's efforts to provide employment.

Although the transfer of the orphans from Grass Valley to Sacramento might initially seem to have little to do with the Mercy Sisters in Sacramento, it brought a major change in their ministry. From 1900 until 1936, the Sacramento Sisters of Mercy had cared for orphaned girls at Stanford Home. While they did receive some state subsidies and funds from the community chest, it was not enough to cover costs. The gap was filled by the sisters and sometimes they struggled financially. Sacramentans were usually generous in their support, but in hard times, philanthropy was limited.

How much of his plan Bishop Armstrong shared with the sisters is not noted in any of the community records. There was no mention of an intent to move the orphans from Stanford Home to St. Patrick's in various stories carried by the newspapers, but that is exactly what happened. The purpose of Stanford Home had been to care for girls between the ages of five and sixteen. It was focused on young girls who needed care and training for self-sufficiency because their parental or family conditions could not provide such care. While the sisters administered the home, they did not sponsor it. The diocese did that and when St. Patrick's opened in 1932, the bishop decided to transfer all the younger girls to St. Patrick's, leaving the sisters at Stanford Home with only a few teens under their care. Even that was not to last for long.

Monsignor Thomas Markham took the helm of Catholic Social Welfare Bureau in the mid-1930s. A trained social worker himself, he saw a different future for Stanford Home and prevailed upon Bishop Armstrong to replace the Sisters of Mercy at the home with the Sisters of Social Service, a newly founded religious community specialized in settlement house work.[34] Since the Chapter Book is silent on the matter, it must be presumed that there was no consultation with the sisters on the transfer.

For the sisters, this was different from their other dealings with diocesan leaders. Sister Mary Gabriel Spadier gives us the only indication of how the decision was received, saying "Monsignor Markham made things unhappy for a time but..."[35] No more was said. Sister Mary Gabriel does add one last insight into the experience writing: "Sisters of Social Service took over Stanford (for which the sisters were grateful as it was a drag on us—as it is still of S.S. Srs)."[36]

For the Mercy sisters, it was a bittersweet decision. Working with orphans was a long-treasured part of their charism, and they had done so whenever need arose. However, another abiding value brought them comfort. It is a core part of their charism to hand over their ministries to others who can carry on that ministry into the future. For the sisters, letting go is part of responding to the next urgent call.

Widening the Circle

The sisters had little time to grieve the loss of their ministry to orphans. In the middle of expanding their school ministry to Sacred Heart Parish, responding to challenges arising from medical advances, and saying goodbye to Stanford Home, the sisters had a population explosion. Applicants to the community increased, causing great crowding at St. Joseph's Academy. Even though there were new classrooms, there were no new bedrooms. In hopes of easing the crowding, the sisters closed the boarding department in 1935 to make room for new members seeking to join the community. It was just in time, too, for the community welcomed twelve new members in the fall of 1936. They were bursting at the seams.

Realizing that the possibility of expansion at the St. Joseph's property was not feasible, plans were initiated to relocate the novitiate and motherhouse of the community to a new site. The selection of a new location was guided by the needs of young women entering the community as well as the needs of the elder members of the community. An editorial in the *Superior California Register* summed up the situation:

> To continue St. Joseph's as headquarters for the novitiate means imperiling the health of the Sisters who are to come. Novices, and indeed all the Sisters, lead a hard and exacting life. A certain modicum of fresh air, outdoor exercise, and sunshine is a necessity if they are to do their work and avoid contracting the diseases which follow the lack of these blessings. But exercise, fresh air, and sunshine are almost out of the question for the community at St. Joseph's.[1]

Time and circumstances had not been kind to the original St. Joseph's site. The main house was built in 1861 and expanded thirty years later. Like many other older structures in the city, the house was built of wood and began to deteriorate over time. What was once a location filled with trees and garden was now filled with the buildings needed for both the grammar school and academy. Little open green space remained. The house itself had only acquired a heating system in 1907.

Cooling the convent in Sacramento's summer months was another thing entirely. On hot nights, the sisters would drag mattresses out to the third-floor balconies seeking a cool breeze. Surrounded with the additional buildings provided for the school made the practice a less than satisfactory solution. Sister Mary Evangelist Morgan, writing in 1937, put it this way:

> Seventy-six years of service has left the building far from comfortable, very far from modern. Too, the city has grown so much in the past few years that the Sisters have been surrounded until now they are in crowded quarters with the railroad almost next door.[2]

Monsignor Thomas Horgan, according to *The Sacramento Bee*, estimated that the project would cost approximately $150,000 to complete.[3] To make it a reality, the sisters would need support and financial assistance. Only once in eighty years had the sisters asked for help for themselves. That request, thanks to the efforts of C. K. McClatchy, had raised sufficient monies to add a wing to St. Joseph's convent. A similar undertaking would be needed now.

A fundraising drive was designed both for the Sacramento area and for outlying communities like Roseville and Auburn itself. Mr. Dom Civitello took the lead on the campaign in Sacramento while Mr. Robert E. Shields chaired the Auburn drive. Other long-time friends of the community gave freely of their time and talent to meet the $26,000 goal. Among them were Bishop Robert Armstrong and the rector of the cathedral, Rev. Thomas Horgan; Mrs. M. J. Desmond; Mrs. Andrew Lagomarsino; and Mrs. Thomas Patterson. Mrs. C. J. Nealis and Mr. Frank Fay rounded out the executive committee[4]

Mother Mary Antonia Kellaghan and her advisors started the hunt to find a location that would meet their needs. Their search brought them to the Auburn foothills, a location above Sacramento's fog, still possessing a rural character and providing quiet and solitude to support the formation of new members. With this in mind, the sisters purchased the Teagarden Ranch, a 35-acre tract with vineyards, orchards, and lots of space to walk. Getting accustomed to rural space would prove to have its own challenges.

It took almost two years to raise sufficient monies to complete the project. Finally, in the fall of 1939, construction began. Yet there was more to be done. To relocate a novitiate or motherhouse, there must be approval from the church authorities in Rome. That permission arrived on April 8, 1940, just before the completion of the new building.[5] The next step was a legal one. Since the main administrative center of the sisters would now be in Auburn, Placer Co., the legal title of the community had to reflect that reality. Although the majority of the community lived in Sacramento, the sisters would now be known as the Sisters of Mercy of Auburn, California.

The Convent *Annals* tell us that the first sisters to live in Auburn included five novices, two postulants, the community leadership, and eight professed sisters—seventeen sisters in total. The space issue at St. Joseph's must have been greatly relieved. In reviewing the names of the first residents, it is easy to see that the sisters had been true to the vision of providing for both new members and elders in community. Among the eight professed sisters were six who were advanced in age, most born in the 1860s: Sisters Baptist Smyth, Rose Cagney, Bridget Brennan, Margaret Kennelly, Brendan Quirk, and Imelda Brennan.[6] These women had carried the burden of demanding domestic work for decades and could do so no longer. Their new home allowed them peace and solitude in their later years.

There were challenges to rural living, though. One of the most vexing was water. To supply water for the convent, a well was dug by Mr. Frank Stormfedder. The well, begun in July, was finished in November and began to supply water to the house but, unfortunately, the *Annals* tell us that there was only enough water for two days.[7] It was early summer the following year before sufficient water for the house was provided by the well.

Shortly after the move to Auburn, World War II broke out and the sisters joined with other Americans in facing rationing and war time conditions. The sisters noted the rationing of butter, gas and other items simply by saying: "rationing, rationing, rationing!" Sister Mary Laurence McCabe had the daunting task of feeding the community, now over twenty in number, while working around the various food scarcities. Other things were also rationed. Of particular note was the absence of a Christmas tree due to the war.[8] The sisters also had to say goodbye to their groundskeeper, Peter Duffy, as well as to their first chaplain, Father Thomas Bracken, as the two left to join the armed services.

Farm life had its share of challenges, too. The *Annals* are dotted with comments about the number of turkey eggs collected, the first newborn lamb, and the various guard dogs that were charged with warding off any attacks on the chickens. Evidently in the solitude of the foothills, there was not a lot to write about. One anecdote recorded focused on sixty or more turkeys perched in the trees, refusing to come down and be quiet so all could sleep.[9] They also spoke often of the beauty of spring blossoms, bee hives, and harvests. Being in harmony with the earth and rhythm of the seasons was an integral part of the sisters' experience. It fed the contemplative part of their lives.

By the summer of 1941, the convent was a gathering place for the sisters. Throughout the *Annals* of the convent, mention is made of sisters coming for a rest, for convalescence, or for community gatherings. The new convent provided a place of retreat for sisters preparing to make their final vows. Among the young sisters retreating in Auburn were the group of sisters that arrived from Ireland in 1936. Eight of them—Sisters Mary Oliver Farrell, Laurence McCabe, Attracta Mahony, Concepta Lynch, Ita Cunningham, Patricia Nolan, Dympna Beglin, and Teresita Durkin— were the first to make their final profession at the new motherhouse on September 8, 1941.[10]

The move to establish a novitiate in Auburn was the first venture the sisters had made beyond the city limits of Sacramento. From the time of their independence in 1887, all their energies and activities had served the needs of the city. Fundraisers for the new novitiate had to do more than gather the necessary monies. They also had to assure donors that such a move would not diminish the ability of the sisters to continue responding to the urgent needs of the city. Solicitations for funds all stressed that the new house would be devoted to training sisters and providing for the care of elder sisters who were not longer able to continue in ministry. Today, Our Lady of Mercy Convent in Auburn is no longer a center for training new members but retains its original purpose of providing a home for the infirm and aged sisters of the community. In addition, the sisters provide a sacred space for those seeking a place of solitude and prayer at Mercy Center, a retreat center sponsored by the sisters.

The life of the sisters in Auburn was not all about prayer and study, however. Immediately after settling into their new home, sisters, including novices, were assigned to teach summer school at neighboring parishes while Sisters Mary Evangelist Morgan and Mary Kevin Redmond traveled out to Folsom for the same religious education work.[11] Some requests to assume new ministries had to be declined, however. Just two months after arriving in Auburn, the sisters were asked to accept responsibility for Highland Hospital located near them. Given their efforts to join with the Auburn parish in starting St. Joseph's School, organizing music lessons to help support the convent and managing the day to day demands of the "Mercy farm," there simply were not enough personnel or resources to accept the request.[12] In spite of such limitations, the community would soon embark upon a new outreach to the people of Northern California.

When Mother Mary Baptist Russell first visited Sacramento to assess its possibilities as a site for a new foundation in 1857, she made an additional trip to the Shasta area. Finding it quite remote and lacking in the supports needed for a new convent, she had to decline Bishop Alemany's request for her sisters to go there. Now, almost ninety years later, another request came from Redding, located in Shasta County. Redding needed someone to take responsibility for St. Caroline Hospital whose major stock holder was Dr. Ferdinand Stabel. Family connections might have encouraged the outreach since Dr. Stabel's sister was a member of the San Jose Dominicans and his nephew was a Sacramento physician, Dr. Alois Stabel.[13]

Organized under the direction of Dr. Ferdinand Stabel, the forty-five-bed hospital provided care of local citizens until the time of his death in 1943. Monies from the sale of his majority shares in the hospital were needed to support his children, Marianna and Paul, both of whom were still young. Just a few days after his death, the superintendent at St. Caroline Hospital issued an appeal for nurses due to a shortage of graduate nurses. Help was needed if the hospital was to thrive.[14]

In June 1944, Mother Mary Carmel McNaughton, superior of the community, and Sister Mary Benignus Redmond, superintendent of Mercy Hospital, traveled to Redding with eight other sisters to inspect the hospital.[15] The sisters did not take long to make up their minds about the purchase. By mid-July, William Quinlan, chairman of a citizens committee tasked with bringing the sisters to Redding, told the Shasta County board of supervisors that the sisters would come if financial arrangements could be worked out. Bishop Robert Armstrong had already given his approval for the venture.[16] Once more, the sisters accepted the burden of large debt to meet the needs of the sick. Even with the uncertainties of wartime, they committed themselves to providing $35,000 toward the purchase but asked that the remainder of $15,000 be raised by local contributions. By October, *The Sacramento Bee* tells us that $10,000 had been raised.[17] In spite of the shortfall, the sisters assumed responsibility for the hospital on October 12, 1944. Mercy Hospital in Sacramento loaned the new facility $20,000.[18]

The first sisters assigned to the hospital were: Sisters Mary Francis Sheridan, Mary Therese Farrell, Mary Augustine Holzworth, Mary Berchmans Kennelly, and Mary Gerard Schmitt. You might call the first sisters "pilgrims." They moved houses three times within the space of ten years. The first convent was a little home on Court Street formerly owned by Mrs. Anna Bucher. With limited transportation options, its distance from the hospital forced the sisters to look for another option.

Seeking proximity to the hospital, now renamed Mercy Hospital, the sisters converted two hospital rooms into a new home. This arrangement contributed to "community legend" for the space was so limited that sisters on the day shift used the beds at night while night shift sisters used the same beds during the day. Needless to say, this arrangement was not at all satisfactory and soon another convent on Pine Street was rented. This third dwelling was also very small to accommodate the community. Initially, the bathtub had to be used as a bed until another temporary solution was found. Finally, in October, 1947 the sisters moved again, this time to a house on Court Street next to St. Joseph's Church.[19]

The move proved auspicious for the next expansion of Mercy ministry in Redding. The new house provided sufficient space to enlarge the community, this time with sister teachers. The community already had responsibility for four elementary schools—St. Joseph's in Sacramento, St. Joseph's, Auburn, and Sacred Heart in Sacramento. Holy Spirit in Sacramento, while not yet ready for a full school, had initiated kindergarten and first-grade classes in the parish hall in 1945. Now, just a year later, the sisters would replicate in Redding a pattern already experienced at schools like Sacred Heart, Holy Spirit, St. Joseph's in Auburn, and Our Lady of Fatima. In each case, the small beginnings of a school were conducted in the parish hall. In Redding, that task fell to Sisters Patricia Nolan and Mary Eileen Brannigan.[20]

As the need for sisters to staff schools throughout the diocese increased, church leaders looked for new ways to attract vocations to the community. Monsignor Thomas Horgan, then vicar general of the diocese, had an idea. Why not set up a pre-postulancy house in Ireland to attract young women to serve in Sacramento? Over the years, Ireland had provided a steady stream of zealous men and women to serve the needs of the diocese. A house dedicated to the recruitment and preparation of young women would help to ensure that the stream of church workers continued. Monsignor Horgan took his idea to Bishop Armstrong and Monsignor Thomas Kirby.

Monsignor Kirby was given the task of going to Ireland to find such a house. His task was two-fold. He not only needed to find a location, he needed to find an Irish bishop willing to welcome the endeavor. Kirby sought out Father Patrick Kennedy, a retired priest of the Sacramento diocese then living in Ireland. Kennedy took on the task of finding both bishop and house. With the blessing of the bishop of Kerry, Bishop P. O'Brien, Father Kennedy was able to purchase a 6-acre site in the village of Ardfert, Co. Kerry.

In August 1948, with the financial assistance of the diocese of Sacramento, the land, known as Abbeylands, was purchased for £4,000.[21] Due to the cost of the building being higher than expected, Mother Mary Barbara Ley was notified by Monsignor Kirby that the community living there would need to purchase all the house furnishings out of their own monies.[22] The estimated cost of the building was $50,000, which the sisters repaid to the diocese over time. Abbeylands was the Irish home of Sacramento sisters until 1979.

The location of what was to be called Immaculate Heart Convent was ideal for prayer, study, and stepping aside from the usual busyness of everyday living. The first contingent of sisters to staff Abbeylands were Sisters Mary Antonia Kellaghan, Veronica Banks, Emmanuel Farrell, and Agnes O'Halloran. Since the house needed renovation to accommodate its new residents, the four sisters resided with the Sisters of Mercy in Tralee for their first year. By the summer of 1950, they were moved into their new home and welcomed six pre-postulants.

Sister Maureen Costelloe, one of the early pre-postulants in Abbeylands, remembers the beauty of their rural setting. She shares that "looking out the window you could see a field of bright yellow daffodils. The convent cow provided milk for the sisters. What they did not need was sold to neighbors providing needed revenue."[23] Since monies were scarce, the sisters made and sold blackcurrant jam. Sister Hannah Mary O'Donoghue, born and raised in Ardfert, describes the area as one of small farms and rural setting. While the village numbered less than 1,000 people, it had two churches and two schools. There were a number of places nearby that fed the spirit: the ruins of a thirteenth-century Franciscan monastery, St. Brendan's Cathedral, and, just 2 miles away, Banna Strand.[24]

Once the convent opened, the two-fold task of inviting girls to the California mission began. At first, school visits were initiated by Father Kennedy. His school visits always included two sisters to share their own stories. A look at the Auburn register shows that during the 1950s, Abbeylands sent sixty-two women to Sacramento to join the community.[25] As time went by, only the sisters went on their recruiting trips. Sister Maureen remembers that even in the early days, the convent was busy with visitors. At the time Abbeylands opened, 90 percent of the priests in the Sacramento Diocese were from Ireland, and of that number, 45 percent were from Kerry. The linkage between Kerry and Sacramento was strong and the newly established convent was a natural meeting place.[26] Visiting priests from Sacramento home on vacation, families of the sisters, and friends would all drop in as they enjoyed the beauty of the area. In spite of all the hospitality given to visitors, however, strict pre-Vatican rules were in place. Sister Hannah Mary remembers being scolded for talking with her mother at the convent gate.

There was another blessing attached to having a pre-postulancy house in Ireland. For sisters entering the Sacramento community prior to the 1970s, going home was not a possibility. Like the early sisters, saying goodbye frequently meant not seeing your family again. Opening a house in Ardfert meant that at least sisters serving in that mission would be able to reconnect with family. It also provided a welcoming place for sisters who were called home by emergencies or death. When, after Vatican II, the priests of the Sacramento Diocese created a fund to send the sisters to Ireland on regular home visits, Abbeylands provided welcome and hospitality.

The program for prospective members varied across the years. In the beginning Sister Maureen Costelloe tells us that her first class in Abbeylands was Latin. Later, other classes like English literature, United States history, and mathematics were added. In addition, some prospective sisters needed to complete their secondary level studies. Sister Hannah Mary remembers meeting some of the prospective novices on the bus to Tralee where they attended school.[27]

The work of church leaders to procure a pre-postulancy house in Ireland was part of a larger dynamic moving in the church in the United States. Initially, Archbishop John Carroll, the first Catholic bishop of the United States, had a vision of a system of Catholic schools across America. This system would not only help to more deeply root children in the faith and help enculturate generations of immigrants to U.S. culture, but it would also protect young Catholics from tides of anti-Catholicism that emerged at various times and places.[28] This potential hope had to be made concrete. What was needed to make it happen would be many women religious to staff those schools.

In 1884, the Third Plenary Council of Baltimore transformed that vision into church practice. At the council, U.S. bishops adopted a policy that required a parochial or Catholic school to be built within two years after the establishment of a parish. In addition, Catholic parents were directed to send their children to these schools, some of which were free and some of which were tuition based. It was like an all-hands-on-deck moment that called women religious to become a teaching core for the accomplishment of the vision.[29] With schools multiplying, the need for sisters in the classroom was urgent.

Catholic parishes tended to be short on funds and big on needs. Due to their vow of poverty, the burden of sisters working for little pay was not seen as unreasonable by church leaders. The actual picture was rather bleak. While women religious were provided housing in most cases, sometimes transportation, all other expenses—like food, medical care, clothing, education, and basic things like blankets, etc.—were the responsibility of the religious community.

The true picture of the situation was reflected in a study by the National Catholic Education Association. Between 1940 and 1950, sisters had received only a 25 percent increase in stipends, although the cost of living rose 93 percent. "Women religious teaching in parochial schools received an annual salary of $511.25 but living expenses consumed $489.50 of that amount, leaving a paltry $21.75 contribution to the support of their congregations."[30]

The inadequacy of teaching stipends presented a dilemma to religious communities including the Sacramento Mercy Community. There existed an unevenness to sisters' education. While records indicate that efforts were made to send sisters away for their degrees, it was not a short process. Most went to study over summers or weekends. It was a long endeavor, sometimes taking up to ten years. In that process, sisters sometimes faced classes with little preparation. Usually, new teachers were mentored by a more experienced teaching sister. To further complicate matters, women were not allowed to pursue theological degrees through Catholic colleges until 1944, when graduate degrees in philosophy and theology were first offered by St. Mary's Graduate School of Sacred Theology in South Bend, Indiana.[31]

It is difficult to know just what impact the struggle for education had on the sisters during these years. Since many applicants to religious life were fresh out of secondary schools or, in the early years, had not yet finished their high school degrees, religious communities had to provide such opportunities for new members. During the 1940s, sisters with expertise in various subjects were tapped to add teaching the new members to their already heavy teaching duties. For some sister students, it meant weekend trips to Catholic colleges in the bay area to attend college classes. A few sisters attended other Catholic colleges outside the state. Some like Sister Mary Evangelist Morgan were able to complete Masters degrees, but that was not the norm.

While the sisters worked to resolve the challenges of educating new members, life went on. Shortly after moving to Auburn, World War II broke out and the sisters worked to support the war effort both in the schools and hospital. Mercy Nursing School initiated a cadet nurses training program, preparing nurses to serve on the front lines as well as the home front.

At St. Joseph's Academy, student involvement in the war effort is best seen in a review of school's newspaper, *Academy Hi-Lights*. Throughout the war years, the paper carried reports of various activities: a fundraising campaign to purchase three jeeps for the army; establishing a Red Cross knitting center at St. Joseph's; learning the basics of first aid; and purchasing war bonds and war stamps.

It was not only activities that filled the columns; patriotic poetry, columns on women's role in war, and struggles of conscience all peppered the pages.[32] Of particular note was an opinion piece written by Betty DeCuir, class of 1943. In the article, she reflects that every nation has its good and bad points. For Americans, she saw racial hatred as a wound in the country's spirit. She challenges her countrymen for their sense of superiority. DeCuir goes on to reflect on how such dynamics led to the persecution of the Jewish people in Nazi Germany and to ask other questions about what the role of believers should be in such situations.[33]

This and other articles written by students during this period reflect a deep sense of patriotism woven together with a social consciousness. Another powerful example of the level of thought and discussion fostered by the sisters is a long piece written by Barbara McDonald who would later enter the Mercy community. The future Sister Mary Loyola wrote on the "why" of the war:

> We did not want this war. We have openly declared through our leaders that we thought war, with all its hate, bloodshed and death, to be nothing more than a brutal unleashing of savage hounds on the innocent peoples of the world.[34]

She then went on to speak of the horrors that impelled the country to war:

> Having awakened, we look to the countries who have fallen beneath the heel of the fiendish aggressor; we look with opened eyes, and we shudder at the sights we see, at the miseries we contemplate. Listen well, oh, America! Listen to the cries of the starving women and children in famine-stricken lands, shots of the firing squad as innocent hostages are murdered before a martyr-marked wall. Their crime? Loving God and freedom above the state.[35]

In evocative language, McDonald describes sufferings of the world and the cost to our national spirit if we do not respond. She challenges her readers to "strive for the unity that comes with solid strength, fervent faith, and persistent prayer while we wait for the day when we present to the world not only a better life but a common brotherhood."[36]

While the education of young women attending St. Joseph's might have thrived in the early 1940s, the convent did not. A word that summarizes its condition would be "woeful." When funds were raised for the new motherhouse of the sisters in Auburn, Mother Mary Carmel shared with the public that plans were being made to replace the ancient house following the completion of the motherhouse. The wooden building would be replaced with a concrete building.[37]

The urgency of that decision might be linked to an episode recorded in the memoir of Sister Mary Gabriel. Our storyteller describes the scene. The convent's fourth floor was comprised partly of bedrooms, one of which was assigned to Mother Mary Gertrude King. Another part of the floor was used for storage, and the flooring was not great. Mary Gabriel gives a rather vivid picture of what happened:

> One day, M. M. Gertrude, (known by some as the "Big Woman from G. Street" as she was six feet tall and rather heavy set), ventured back into the storage area and must have stepped on a weakened board— for suddenly, her foot appeared, sticking through the ceiling of the third floor Chapel.[38]

The image of a "nunly leg" dangling down into the chapel says everything about the state of the building.

It took almost ten years for the plans to replace the deteriorating convent with a new one to become reality. The condemnation of the place by the Sacramento Fire Department helped bring things to fruition. That act of condemnation was long past due. Community legend has it that the convent withstood condemnation only because the bishop had forbidden the Catholic fire chief to condemn it. Fearing for the sisters' safety, the chief left on vacation, leaving directions for his second in command to condemn St. Joseph's in his absence.

Before its demolition, the sisters held a farewell tea to mark the passing of this Sacramento landmark. Several thousand alumnae, along with their families and friends, attended the event. Photographs of the old building were taken and sold to raise funds for the new building. The new convent was to be large enough to house twenty or more sisters and was a welcome change to those who lived and ministered at St. Joseph's.

Today, the importance of this site to the city of Sacramento is memorialized in the naming of the jury parking lot, its former site, as the St. Joseph's parking lot. With the motherhouse in place, Abbeylands settled, and the war over, the community paused on the brink of another wave of expansion, this time initiated by its healthcare ministry.

Just Before the Earthquake

The 1950s were a *déjà vu* experience for the sisters. Their ministries continued to follow a cycle of build, extend, and build again. This was especially true in healthcare. The early Mater Misericordiae Hospital went through multiple expansions during its twenty-eight-year existence, and the new Mater Misericordiae, now called Mercy Hospital, was replicating that pattern. Within a year of opening the new hospital, P. C. Drescher endowed a fourteen-bed ward for children at the hospital. This endowment made it possible for the sisters to provide free or partial payment services for children in need. To sustain this, the sisters knitted together a collaborative partnership with physicians, civic groups, and individual donors to provide the needed care and underwrite the funding gaps.

By 1931, the Drescher Ward was matched by the establishment of Mercy Clinic, which opened its doors on February 11, the feast of Our Lady of Lourdes. This feast had special significance for the sisters and is associated with healing the sick. Dr. G. N. Drysdale was the first director of the clinic. Its goal was to serve children from infancy to sixteen years of age, providing needed health services for them regardless of their race, creed or inability to pay.[1]

It was not only children that benefitted from new services. On non-clinic days, the space was given over to a cancer clinic. When polio swept the country, patients needing treatment were accommodated. The hospital also offered a unique "fever therapy" department. The efforts of the sisters to keep abreast of medical developments caused *The Sacramento Bee* to name Mercy General as one of the finest hospitals in the west.[2]

The sisters' commitment to excellence was highlighted in a statement issued at the opening of Mercy Hospital in 1925. In the statement the sisters said: "We searched diligently for the best and most modern plans working out details with the greatest consideration, that nothing which could contribute to the better care of our sick and suffering might be omitted"[3] They honored the commitment for the next twenty years, but the population growth of the city after World War II presented new challenges in providing the kind of care they desired.

The main challenge standing in the way of achieving excellence was space. A study presented to the Sacramento Chamber of Commerce in 1949 predicted that Sacramento would need 400 hospital beds within a ten-year period. Facing an estimated $2,500,000 price tag, city leaders debated whether such funding could be raised through private donations or whether a hospital district would need to be established.[4]

Something needed to be done, but while coping with this space problem, the sisters had another pressing urgency. Sacramento was not the only area running out of hospital beds. The recently acquired hospital in Redding was also running out of space. Hints of "tight quarters" are found in the Redding community *Annals* as early as October 1945. The *Annals* record the various rearrangements needed as the hospital updated its equipment and integrated the latest medical technology into the facility. Even when the newly built Shasta Memorial Hospital was completed, patients could not always be accommodated.[5] Bishop Armstrong visited in October and inspected property for a new hospital. It would take another six years before it became a reality. Finally, in May 1947, the first concrete step was taken to build a new Mercy Hospital when a $1,000 deposit was paid on an 11.5-acre parcel of land sitting upon a hill which overlooked the city.[6]

The hospital was not the only place that was full to the brim. There was a steady stream of sisters moving between Sacramento and Redding for visits, time for retreat, and celebrations. The convent was very small so sisters had to fit wherever they could find space. By fall 1946, the hospital sisters were joined by school sisters who were preparing for the opening of St. Joseph School, a new parish elementary school. Sisters Mary Patricia Nolan and Mary Redempta Scannell arrived to prepare for its opening. As usual, the school would not yet have a real school building to call home but instead started out in the basement of the church.

Father A. Gavin purchased a home on Placer Street for a new school and convent. This did not work out since the property was not sufficiently large. Instead, Father Gavin made the home his rectory and turned the rectory over to the sisters for their convent. While the sisters did not have the responsibility for funding the building of a new school, they were busy preparing for its first students. It opened with an enrollment of 130 students and three teaching sisters, Sisters Mary Teresita Durkin, Mary Eileen Brannigan, and Mary Monica Burns.[7] The school opened before the

Above left: Mother Mary Baptist Russell, founder of the Sisters of Mercy in California, brought the sisters to Sacramento on October 2, 1857.

Above right: Mother Mary Gabriel Brown, first superior of the Sacramento community.

The Sacramento Sisters of Mercy, *c.* 1893. Mother Mary Vincent Phelan, center front row, became superior when the sisters in Sacramento became a separate community in 1887.

St. Joseph Academy on 9th and G Streets was the center of the sisters' lives and ministry from 1860 until 1940.

The first graduating class from St. Joseph Academy, Sacramento.

Sister Mary Aloysius Nolan and the nurses of Mater Misericordiae Hospital.

Mater Misericordiae Hospital, built in 1897.

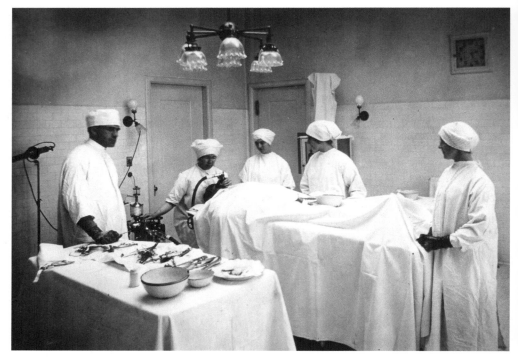

Grace Surgery, named after Bishop Thomas Grace, allowed the medical staff at Mater Misericordiae to provide the finest care of the period.

Dedication of the new Mater Misericordiae Hospital in 1925.

Above: Postulants newly arrived from Ireland are Srs. Ellen Philbin, Mary Michael Murphy, Anne McCrohan, Mary Raphael Doyle, Mary Martin Mulroy, and Mary Celine Heneghan.

Right: Novices harvest fruit in the Auburn orchard.

Convent of Our Lady of Mercy, Auburn, California, in the 1940s.

Immaculate Heart Convent in Abbeylands, County Kerry, Ireland—a welcoming house for young women seeking to join the Sacramento sisters.

Mercy Convent, home for the nursing sisters ministering at Mercy Medical Center, Redding.

A reception ceremony in 1965 at the Cathedral of the Blessed Sacrament, presided over by Bishop Alden Bell.

Left: Sister Elizabeth Marie Farrell chats with Bishop Manogue High School students on the school's front lawn.

Below: Sister Mary Loretta Dowd confers with Sister Mary Peter Carew (Mercy General Hospital's superintendent from 1950–1968).

Right: Sister Mary Peter was passionate about forming a healing culture that put people at the heart of the hospital.

Below left: Sister Mary Virginia O'Sullivan signs a memorial beam, which was incorporated into the structure of Mercy Folsom Hospital.

Below right: Sisters Connie Raymond and Anne Chester prepare lunch for guests at Loaves and Fishes.

Russell Manor, Sacramento—an affordable housing complex for seniors in South Sacramento sponsored by Mercy Housing California.

Mercy San Juan Hospital, Carmichael, which opened in 1967.

Mercy General Hospital was blessed with a circle of Mercy nurses. Front: Sisters Glenda Shaw, Mary St. John Hall, Nora Mary Curtin, and Mary Peter Carew. Back: Sisters Mary Philomene Gogarty, Marilee Howard, Mary Gregory Rogers, and Mary Kevin Redmond.

Sister Sally Dominic Torres places symbolic crosses during an anniversary ritual. Each cross represented one of the regions of the Institute.

Above left: Sister Margaret Mitchell stands with the Cedar Rapids quilt given to the Auburn sisters during the Grand Right and Left.

Above right: Sister Michelle Gorman next to the commemoration of the Sisters of Mercy on Sacramento's Pioneer Wall.

The memorial statute in honor of Mother Mary Baptist and the Sisters of Mercy at the California State Capitol was created by sculptress Ruth Coelho.

Sisters Terese Marie Perry (left) and Maura Power (center) welcome Sister Nadine Foley, OP (right), into CHW. Sister Nadine's community, the Adrian Dominicans, were the first non-Mercy community to join the healthcare system.

Sister Nancy McInerney joins with other Mercy sisters in protesting military aid to El Salvador.

Sister Brenda O'Keeffe examines data collected during a consultation process conducted at a community assembly.

Above left: Sister Sheila Browne (left; community president 1998–2008) joins with Sister Susan McCarthy (right; community president 1990–1998). Both sisters guided the community through years of transition and change.

Above right: Mercy Associates Sue Thompson (left) and Barbara Ghattas (right) plant a memorial tree in Mary Grove.

The "Promises Kept" campaign of 2004 was only one of the major fundraising initiatives led by Mercy Foundation. This campaign was held to help remodel the Auburn campus for the elder sisters.

Sister Anne Sekul responded to a call to iconography as sacred ministry. The icons she has written include one of Catherine McAuley as well as others done for churches and private oratories.

Above: The air ambulance *Sister Patricia* was dedicated to Sister Patricia Mulderrig (left) for her service at Mercy Medical Center, Redding. Joining her at the dedication were Sisters Alice Spohn (center left), Mary Grace O'Flaherty (center right), and Margaret Ann Walsh (right).

Below left: Sister Marilee Howard began her ministry as a lab tech and went on to serve as an ethicist for CHW.

Below right: Sisters Marita Cunningham (left), Mary Raymond Holzworth (center), and Maura Bowie (right) enjoy a community celebration.

sisters could move out of the small Pine Street convent to the larger house on Court Street. This would end the cycle of bed-sharing. Small things were celebrated, especially the purchase of four new beds just before Christmas.

Movement on the new hospital was slow. Since the purchase of the site for the hospital, the sisters had elected a new superior, Mother Mary Barbara Ley. She came up to Redding in December to meet with doctors, Father Gavin and Harry Devine, the architect. It would take until June, 1948 before plans were made for a professional fundraising drive to build the new hospital under the guidance of Mr. G. Everman. The campaign started in August of that year.[8] A full year had passed since the initial purchase of land. When the plan for a new hospital was first proposed, the estimated cost was around $300,000. By the time the campaign started a year later, the cost had ballooned to $1,000,000. The Redding community was asked to contribute half the cost of the building. The sisters would find money for the rest. Charles Dicker took the lead in raising funds.

The longer the campaign went on, the higher the cost. By December, the price tag was $1,267,290. For a while, it looked like it would be an impossible task to find enough funds for the project, but in December 1949, the sisters received word that they would receive a Hills-Burton grant from the federal government covering one-third of the cost. This plus the $250,000 already raised by citizens reignited hope and put the proposed hospital back on track. The only hurdle remaining was raising the last $173,000 of the Redding community's contribution.

Just how difficult this challenge was is only hinted at in the *Redding Annals*. In early January, they tell us of a donation received from Pacific Gas and Electric Company for $20,000, multiple meetings with governmental officials and doctors, and of the "disappointments" that occurred at intervals. Without trust in Divine Providence and in the people of Redding, the project could have been abandoned. In February, the Chamber of Commerce took over the task of fundraising. Patterned on the experience of their sisters in Sacramento, the sisters had formed a partnership with the civic community that was vital. The city council helped by extending water and sewer lines to the site on the hill, and put a booster pump in at the its bottom, sharing the cost of this work with the hospital.

In March, things came to a critical juncture. The board of directors of the Chamber of Commerce held a meeting to determine whether the results of their work were sufficient to continue. The contributions of federal government and the sisters were guaranteed, but could the city meet its goal? On July 12, 1951, ground was broken for the long-awaited hospital. The Central States Construction Company had won the bid at a cost of $1,144,440, but additional costs for items like elevators had to be added into the overall cost. Ultimately, the city was able to donate $365,000 toward the hospital leaving the sisters with an additional debt of $50,000. Even though they recognized the heavy debt they would carry, the sisters went forward with the hospital.

It took until April 1953 to complete the hospital. Construction was delayed due to two strikes, one of carpenters and the other of steelworkers. In spite of the delays, all came to completion and the hospital was dedicated on April 11, 1953. It would become the hospital on the hill, keeping watch over the city. Mr. Dicker had given five years to this cause. The dedication was a huge event for Redding. Bishop Armstrong summed up the feeling: "This is the greatest thing that has happened to Redding since the Shasta Dam."[9]

Twenty-seven sisters attended the dedication, sixteen coming from Sacramento for the great moment. They were joined by five Sacramento doctors and multiple friends who also made the journey to celebrate with the sisters. The dedication was in the morning and open house was held that afternoon. The *Annals* tell us that almost 4,000 people toured the facility. The large turnout reflected the sense of ownership felt by the Redding community. This was a hospital welcoming everyone. It was also the result of partnership and perseverance to say nothing of Divine Providence.

The hardships the sisters endured during these years were matched by a spirit of joy and generosity. The Court Street convent provided more space than the earlier arrangements but by 1952, the community had grown to eleven sisters. Sisters had to use space where they found it or, as the *Annals* indicate "various places."[10] In addition to the regular community, guests were frequent as meetings were held about the hospital plans and Sacramento sisters came to visit. The *Annals* tell us that, to complicate matters, "everything is wearing out at 1733 Court Street, our present convent. Electric switches, blinds, roof, plumbing, etc."[11] A new convent would come none too soon. Packing up the convent was a major project taking many days. Boxes were everywhere, but finally, on March 25, the sisters moved to their new home next to the hospital. For the first time in over a decade, they would have enough space for everyone.

The opening of the hospital in April was quickly followed by the opening of a new Catholic school for Redding, St. Joseph's School, in May. The sisters barely had time to catch their breath. Within a week of the hospital's opening, moving began again as they moved from the makeshift school to the new St. Joseph's. For the first time in ten years, building was at a standstill.

Things were not at a standstill in Sacramento, however. While the community was struggling to build a new hospital in Redding, it was deeply involved in plans for expanding Mercy General, Sacramento. Plans for the expansion of the hospital did not begin with the sisters. Like the first hospital established by the sisters, plans were initiated by city leaders. The original proposal was for a unified public campaign to finance expansion of Sacramento's private hospitals to provide the needed 400 additional beds.[12] Waiting times for admission sometimes stretched to three or four months.

A committee comprised of Beverly Gibson, president of the Sacramento Chamber of Commerce; Rev. T. H. Markham, Mercy Hospital; James T. Harvey, Sacramento–Yolo Federated Trades Council; Stephen Downey, Rotary Club; and James A Callaghan, city school system was appointed to study the matter and recommend a course of action.[13] By November, the committee leaned toward a voluntary drive instead of the creation of a hospital district which would fund the expansion of medical facilities. In January 1949, the formal report and recommendation was made to the Sacramento Chamber of Commerce's board of directors. The emphasis was upon the role that the city's hospitals played in the public interest and included a plan to expand the capacity of Mercy Hospital by 100 beds.

It took two years for the proposed campaign to be launched. In March 1951, a community-wide campaign began. Bishop Robert Armstrong enthusiastically endorsed the plan, guaranteeing the full participation of the diocese in the endeavor. The total cost of Mercy General's expansion would be an estimated $1,500,000. Hopes were that one-third of the cost would be funded through a Hill-Burton grant. The sisters were to contribute $250,000 while the civic community would fund the rest. Considering the difficulty of raising adequate funds in Redding, this was really a leap of faith on the part of the sisters who had absorbed the unsubscribed debt of Mercy Redding.[14]

The Sacramento effort was a very different experience. It was a total community effort. Archie Mull, Jr., was selected as chairman for a newly established Mercy Hospital Expansion Fund Committee. The *Catholic Herald* notes: "Serving with Mull is an interdenominational group, some of whom served on a hospital fact finding committee under the chairmanship of Stephen W. Downey in 1948."[15] In fact, the committee was comprised of major business leaders throughout the city. Among the group were Kenneth Anderson, Orrin Cook, Dalton Feldstein, Thomas Gormley, Dr. Hermann Lorenz, Peter Mitchell, and B. F. Vandenberg to mention a few. When introducing the committee, Mull stated:

During the years following the war the citizens of the Sacramento area have become increasingly aware of the fact that the community's hospital

facilities have not been keeping pace with the needs. Today the situation
is serious.[16]

Throughout the month of May, *The Sacramento Bee* ran almost daily
articles highlighting the need. The kitchen facilities at Mercy were deemed
inadequate and equipment needed upgrading. Lack of space was illustrated
by statistics showing that over a ten-year period, patients ballooned from
5,738 patients to 10,701 patients without any expansion of the facilities.[17]
Laboratory and X-ray departments, pediatric care, and new surgical and
obstetric facilities were all part of the plan.

The importance of this drive and its significance to the city was
highlighted when Governor Earl Warren accepted the honorary
chairmanship of the campaign. The design for the new wing was presented
at a kick-off dinner where members of the committee painted a vivid
picture not only of the need for the project but of the civic obligation
to provide healthcare for the people of Sacramento. Dalton Feinstein
summed up the inclusive nature of the hospital saying: "Disease never asks
the religion of any man, woman or child. And neither, thank God, do the
Sisters of Mercy."[18]

The actual fundraising drive began on May 29 and was planned
to last until late June. The high level of organization, enlistment of key
business leaders of the city, and the full support of the Catholic Diocese
all contributed to the high momentum of the drive. In mid-June, Bishop
Armstrong declared a "Mercy Hospital Pledge Sunday" asking the
Catholics of the city to contribute to the campaign. In his letter to the
people, the bishop said:

> Every Catholic in this area should be moved to give generously to this
> fund drive. In justice, we owe an inestimable debt to the Sisters of Mercy
> who have given of themselves so unselfishly through the years to make
> it possible for them to serve us more completely and more effectively.
> In charity we owe a generous contribution to this institution through
> which the suffering are served with Christian love.[19]

The combined efforts of the city resulted in the "city's most successful
drive."[20] The fundraising campaign exceeded all expectations by raising
$836,672 dollars. The remarkable aspect of the event was that the drive
itself took only six weeks to complete—a stark contrast to the six years
needed for the Redding campaign. At the dinner celebrating the completion
of the drive, Dr. Orrin Cook shared a message of gratitude from the sisters.
After expressing their regret that they could not be with the group, the
letter states:

The most outstanding feature of this campaign is not the money which has been collected—though we all agree that this is of tremendous importance—but the spirit of friendliness, the gracious giving of your time and service, the many contacts made by you who have borne the burden of the drive, the knowledge that Mercy Hospital has so many loyal and devoted friends—these are the things that make our hearts glad and that will live forever in the memory of the Sisters of Mercy of Sacramento.[21]

The east wing expansion of the hospital was not the only construction going on. A parallel project was taking place while construction of the new wing went forward. When the nursing school was closed in 1950, plans went forward to create a special children's hospital. Financed by the sisters, this facility would provide Sacramento with a dedicated hospital designed to meet the special needs of pediatric patients. It could provide for up to forty children, including eight bassinets. A playroom was provided for children who were ambulatory. To support the work of the children's hospital, the Mercy Children's Hospital Guild was organized with Mrs. Hermann Lorenz as its first president. In addition to raising funds to support the hospital, guild members provided non-professional volunteer service by providing company and activities for the children. Their innovative ways of fundraising included a traditional headdress ball, which was a major civic event for over forty years. When children's hospital closed, Mercy Guild members continued to contribute vital volunteer service to the hospitals.

Inside the main hospital, more reorganizing and remodeling was taking place as the whole facility was upgraded to provide the most advanced medical technology possible. Finally, in 1956, all was complete. Almost 100 years after their arrival in Sacramento, the sisters opened the doors to the expanded Mercy hospital and promised to continue their tradition of compassionate care to everyone. Governor Goodwin Knight summed up what the moment meant in his words at the dedication:

It is more, however, than a mere structure of stone and steel. It is representative of man's thoughtfulness for man, of man's desire to provide every improved means of alleviating pain from the wounds and the ills which beset the flesh. It is symbolic of our community progress, of scientific achievements and of a prudent desire to prepare for future community requirement. This magnificent structure is a dedication to Him who knew suffering and through suffering gave us a better world and a better life to follow.[22]

Money was not the only benefit arising from this major drive. As the fundraising group transitioned to a Mercy Hospital expansion committee, it became apparent that for the future of the hospital more was needed. Such a group would both provide for long-range planning on a continuous basis as well as becoming a legal entity capable of accepting and administering future gifts. This was the birth of Mercy Foundation, Sacramento.

Fred Read, assistant general manager of the California Fruit Exchange, accepted the presidency of the foundation. In accepting his responsibility, Read commented on the non-denominational character of its newly elected board, which included persons from diverse faiths and a broad coalition of business and labor leaders—people like Dalton F. Feldstein, Phil R. Hullin, A. I. Diepenbrock, Arthur Luddy, and Dr. John Walsh. He was quick to point out:

> For our public-spirited citizens who desire to contribute to a worthwhile cause no field is more deserving or will better serve the community. We invite participation from everyone, and the Foundation will see that all donations, large or small, will be devoted to the purpose intended by the donor.[23]

In its sixty-five years of existence, Mercy Foundation has raised $147,650,000 in support of the work of the Sisters of Mercy in the Sacramento area. Without it, the mission of the sisters would have been greatly limited.

There were also sad goodbyes during this time. When Mater Misericordiae Hospital was built in 1897, the sisters established a nursing school to provide fully trained nurses for the hospital. It continued to function when the hospital moved to the 40th and J Street campus. Over 500 nurses were trained by the sisters between 1897 and 1947. During World War II, the classes were made up entirely of nurse cadets. Thirty-nine entered the service. When the war ended, those seeking a nursing degree decreased to the point where it was no longer feasible to continue the school. In a poignant letter written to nursing alumnae, Sister Mary Benignus, superintendent of the hospital, wrote:

> It has so happened that I have been with you through the trying years of war, those years when things were difficult everywhere, but particularly so in our hospitals, staffed with less than half the usual number of nurses, and filled with an unusually large number of patients. Much can be said, must be said, for those who answered the call of their country and who enlisted in the Service; but much, too, can be said for those who stayed

at home and worked in the hat of the gray on the home front. Looking back over those years, I recall how often I had to ask "my girls" to do extra duty, to return to the floors and wards after a few hours' rest to do double shifts. I realized then and now that you did it all with a sense of love and loyalty that is not found everywhere. The war is over; the need is not quite so crying; but in my heart I know that if it were, if I needed you again in the same way, I could count on you, everyone to respond.[24]

The bond of relationship was strong, but recognizing that the school was no longer needed, the sisters moved on to the next greatest need.

The amount of time, planning, resources, and faith that went into the expansion of two hospitals at the same time seems quite overwhelming, but those were not the only building projects the sisters had underway. In addition to young women entering the community from Sacramento, the pre-postulancy house in Abbeylands, Ireland, was sending the sisters a steady stream of new members. Between 1949 and 1952, twenty-three women joined the community and were in formation. Once more, beds were in short supply. The sisters needed more room.

Expansion plans began in July 1949 when an initial conversation took place with the architect, Harry Divine. With the scope of the project defined, permission was obtained from Bishop Armstrong in late October. It was decided that the sisters would fund it themselves and then work to pay back the loan. The expansion was no minor undertaking. It added sufficient sleeping accommodations for twenty novitiate sisters, rooms for classes, library, sewing, and conferences as well creating twelve new rooms for professed sisters and a new chapel that could hold 120 people. While the preliminary surveying of the site took place in November, the actual construction did not start until April of the following year.

The *Auburn Annals* tell us that the sisters were surrounded with noise when the construction set in: "Noise and more noise! The breaking of the steps into the novitiate is being done and the noise is almost unbearable."[25] Construction continued with its usual delays, rain, muddy ground, waiting for things to dry out so windows could be sealed, and roofing tiles laid. It took just a little more than a year to complete, and an open house was held for the public on July 8, 1951.

The beauty of the new chapel was the highlight of the expansion. The *Mary Book* of May 1953 described it through the eyes of a young Anne Chester soon to be Sister Anne. Prior to her entrance, she visited the chapel:

We entered the "chapel-in-the-making" finding it unfinished, but near completion as far as structure was concerned. It seemed like a cathedral since its pitched beamed ceiling, which arched thirty feet over us, threw back the echoes which resounded through the emptiness. Despite the skeletal appearance, the gray moss green walls, the oak wainscots, the pink, green, black and white of the marble and terrazzo floor showed promise of future beauty.[26]

When she entered the community four months later, the chapel was complete. In her reflection, she notes that some visitors said the chapel was like a League of Nations since every part of the world contributed to its making. The blond oak pews and church stalls were from Japan; the reredos and canopy hand-crafted by a German woodcarver; the carved crucifix from Italy; the marble steps from Tennessee; and ten glorious stain glass windows hand-made by the artisans at Clarks and Sons studios in Dublin.

Expanding the motherhouse was not the only challenge the sisters faced in the beginning of the 1950s. Increased membership meant an increased need to provide education for the young women who would carry the mission into the future. It had to be an education equal to the task before them. As increasing numbers of new members flowed into the novitiate, a practical and do-able plan for the education of new members emerged. Given the numbers of novices, it seemed feasible to establish a special college for the sisters. An article in the November 20, 1952, *Catholic Herald* notes that there existed a co-operative arrangement with Placer College in Auburn, through which young sisters attended the college as special day students as well as utilizing instructors from its evening college for on-site classes.[27] At this point, the College of Our Lady of Mercy, a three-year college, was established at the motherhouse. This new college, which was just for sisters, was accredited by the Catholic University of America.

A description of the course of studies is found in a little set of books called the *Mary Book*, written by the novices. In it, they outline the typical course of study: philosophy and psychology, apologetics, English and history, public speaking and economics, Latin and choral, chemistry and foods as well as Americanization. Just in case that did not suffice, they also were trained in music, typewriting, sewing, cooking, domestic science, and physical education.[28]

At the end of their novitiate years, new members would have completed at least an associate of arts degree and be ready to complete their baccalaureate degrees and teaching certificates at an outside university. Later, in the 1960s, this affiliation with Catholic University of America was transferred to the University of San Francisco.

The drive for degrees was not without its humor, however. When Sister Elizabeth Marie Farrell attended the University of San Francisco in the mid-1950s, she was the only woman in her classes. The university did not yet admit women students. In sharing her experiences, she reflected that somehow sisters did not count as women. She also noted that her university experience brought her into contact with a wide variety of persons from different backgrounds including her classmate, the great Bill Russell of basketball fame.[29]

The Sacramento sisters were not alone in their push for better educational formation of new members. There was a national movement among sisters of the time called the Sister Formation Conference. In September 1951, Pope Pius XII at the first International Congress of Teaching Sisters had encouraged religious superiors to do everything they could to foster the training of sister teachers. He did not just want adequate training; he called for excellent formation. Mercy leaders like Mother Bernardine Purcell of the Union of the Sisters of Mercy called for such training to expand beyond the professional and provide a thorough grounding and training in religious life.[30] This would not be easy. In past years, the demands of providing sister teachers for Catholic school was achieved by funneling sisters into the field before they received full training. That would have to change.

While not part of the union of the Sisters of Mercy, the leadership of the Auburn community were in communication with changes being made in regard to sister formation. Like other Mercy groups, the sisters extended the time before vows to eight years. A curriculum that stressed theological formation was implemented and instruction became less lecture and more discussion oriented. Training new members in catechetics through the Christian Doctrine Program was also incorporated into the process. None of this happened instantly but was phased in incrementally between 1955 and 1965. Mother Mary Rita Bathurst, elected superior in 1956, was a strong advocate of this new direction.

The education of significant numbers of sisters was not only a logistical challenge, it meant the investment of resources for college tuition. Although Universities like Dominican College, San Raphael and the University of San Francisco were generous in their tuition discounts, it still was not easy to fund the costs. Once more, friends and partners came to the aid of the community. The Mercy Auxiliary was established in 1950 out of concern for funding the education of young sisters. The group was spearheaded by Mrs. James Mulderrig and Mrs. B. Andrew Lagomarsino.

[The group was committed to] pursue such undertakings as will aid in enriching the spiritual life of its members, to make known throughout the Diocese of Sacramento the works and objectives of the Sisters of Mercy, to foster vocations, and assist through membership dues and special fundraising projects, in supporting the Novitiate in Auburn.[31]

The Mercy Auxiliary grew quickly. By 1952, it numbered over 300 members. The membership was a combination of the parents of younger sisters, parents from the various schools taught by the sisters, alumnae of St. Joseph Academy, and partners in ministry. Together, they crafted numerous benefits to raise monies such as an annual Christmas sale, a spring luncheon, retreats for members, card parties, and raffles with profits going directly to the education fund. The Mercy Auxiliary transitioned with changes in the Mercy community. In 1995, they adopted a new purpose. They would now focus on assisting in the care of aged sisters and changed their name to "Friends of the Sisters of Mercy."

From the perspective of time, the adoption of sister formation principles and practices seemed vital to religious life in the twentieth century, but implementation was not without consequences. Retaining young professed long enough for them to complete their college degrees meant fewer sisters available for the expanding Catholic school system. Pastors had to accept the reality that religious communities, including the Auburn sisters, could no longer provide enough sisters for every class. Catholic lay teachers were needed to share the educational ministry. St. Joseph Academy, many years previously, had shown what a gift lay teachers could be to a school. It was now up to the pastors to find monies for lay salaries which could not be as minimal as the stipends provided for women religious.

Catholic education during the 1950s continued to expand. For Mercy, this meant that Our Lady of Fatima School reached its full eight grades while a new school, Holy Cross, West Sacramento was added to the circle of Mercy-administered schools. All these educational centers were parochial schools, meaning they were owned and funded by the parish not the sisters. Only St. Joseph Academy was a community-sponsored school. It had long been the cherished symbol of the sisters' commitment to the education of women and, in particular, those who were poor. The alumnae had a deep bond with the sisters and continued to meet yearly. A change in the diocesan vision of secondary education would irrevocably change that long tradition.

Bishop Armstrong, in the final years of his episcopacy, had a vision of creating a unified educational center for Catholic secondary students. The catalyst for acting on the plan came from the need to relocate Christian Brothers High School from 21st and Broadway to a more adequate site. The buildings housing Christian Brothers College needed upgrading and the site lacked adequate space for burgeoning sports teams. To answer the need, a new school was planned. It was to be Sacramento's first co-institutional high school, meaning that both girls and boys would comprise the student body but not attend classes together. To accomplish this plan, the seniors and juniors from the three city high schools—Christian Brothers, St.

Francis High School, and St. Joseph Academy—were to be transferred to the new site. The plan was not popular.[32] For the sisters, it meant that there would be no more graduates from St. Joseph Academy.

Bishop Armstrong never saw the completion of his vision. He died before the school opened, his funeral cortege passing by the school that would be named after him, Bishop Armstrong High School. The school's success was hindered by a complex of factors. The potential of shared classes was eliminated due to a prohibition in the Christian Brother's Rule of that period which forbade the teaching of girls. Classes could not be shared, so there was no economy of scale when it came to smaller classes like advanced languages or sciences. The students could mix at lunch, for activities and events but instruction was strictly separate.

The experiment lasted only ten years. For young women merged in their junior year with many new peers, there was a sense of lost identity. For the boys, that was not a factor since they stayed together. A track system was in place grouping students according to proficiency. Long-time friends sometimes found themselves sharing neither classes nor lunch periods. Relationships formed early in high school had to be renegotiated, old loyalties set aside. When the co-instructional experiment ended in 1966, female students were transferred to new diocesan high schools. Both the original St. Francis High School and St. Joseph Academy were closed leaving some of Armstrong's women graduates with a felt sense of displacement. Where did they belong? What school held their story? For male students, it was different. Bishop Armstrong changed its name back to Christian Brothers, thus reestablishing a continuity of identity. For St. Joseph graduates, that was not to be.

In 1957, the sisters paused to celebrate not the expansion of hospitals or education, not even their renovated motherhouse. They paused to celebrate 100 years of service in Sacramento. It was a week-long celebration marked by a Pontifical Mass, a senate resolution saluting the services rendered by the sisters, a reception for all the friends of the sisters on the St. Joseph Academy grounds, and a linen party to "restock" the convent linen closet. The centenary was also the occasion for storytelling and the local papers recounted the history of the sisters' works in Sacramento, Redding and Yolo County. As part of preserving the story, Sister Mary Evangelist Morgan wrote *Mercy Generation to Generation,* the only published history of the sisters until the present time.

The centennial celebration was a moment of savoring the beauty and contributions of the past while embracing a future yet to come. It was a recommitment to the legacy of mercy which was the living witness of sisters since 1857. At that moment, all was calm. Little did the sisters anticipate the revolution of spirit that was about to erupt.

Seismic Change: Revisioning of Charism, Life, and Mission

As the curtain went down on the 100th anniversary of the sisters in Sacramento, plans were already underway for new initiatives and ministries. The post-war years brought the emergence of a new spirit in the country, a spirit of adventure and courage. Returning soldiers from World War II used the G.I. Bill of Rights to attend college and achieve economic stability. Entering the middle class, many of these veteran families helped to populate an expanding suburbia, bringing a need to establish more Catholic parishes and schools. The one constant of the period was change.

Sacramento, with Mather and McClellen airbases, the signal depot, and Aerojet, was profoundly influenced by post-war demographics. With a high influx of military families and all that went into supporting the life of the bases, Sacramento County grew from a population of 170,333 to 634,373 within a ten-year period.[1] Church authorities were challenged to meet the spiritual needs of this new reality. Nine new parishes were established in Sacramento's north area, each designed as a total complex of church, school and gathering place.[2] The Sisters of Mercy did not initially move into this suburban context. Instead, their educational presence moved to Holy Cross parish, Bryte in 1957 and only later to St. Rose parish, Roseville, in 1961.

The events of World War II were not all benevolent. The United States had introduced the world to atomic warfare, a warfare that did not discriminate between combatants and civilians. The atomic bomb had quickened the surrender of the Japanese government, but it also introduced the fear of annihilation into the psyches of young Americans. The same wartime technology that led to atomic warfare brought other more benevolent uses of atomic power to provide energy as well as new uses in medicine.

The growing impact of scientific enquiry was highlighted when space exploration became a reality. Russia's ability to launch the first successful rocket to outer space shocked the U.S. and sparked a national quest not to be left behind. The exploration of the space not only brought new understandings of the universe, it caused philosophers and humanists to reflect upon the place of humankind within this cosmic reality. In spite of such heady concerns, however, there were the day-to-day needs of Sacramento citizens calling out for attention. Mother Mary Rita Bathurst, then superior of the congregation, frequently found her mailbox filled with requests for more teaching sisters and for sisters to facilitate religious education programs in outlying parishes. There were always more requests than sisters to fill them.

In 1957, just at the time of the centenary celebration of the sisters' arrival in Sacramento, Pope Pius XII started his eighteenth year as pontiff of the Catholic Church. Having assumed the papacy in 1939, Eugenio Pacelli began a re-visioning of the mission and ministry of the people of God. In a series of papal encyclicals, he called for the increased involvement of Catholic scholars in biblical studies (*Divino Afflante Spiritu,* 1943); the recognition of the role of the laity and the interconnectedness of all believers (*Mystici Corporis,* 1943); and finally, a renewal of liturgical life (*Mediator Dei,* 1947).

These encyclicals gave birth to developments such as dialogue Masses, increased numbers of Catholic scholars devoting themselves to critical biblical scholarship, and, particularly important for young Catholics, dedication to what Pius XII called "Catholic Action." In addition to his encyclicals, Pope Pius issued a call to simplify religious dress. The chapter records of the Auburn community from the 1956 allude to this call, noting that Pope Pius XII asked that religious habits be simplified, efficient, appropriate, responsive to climate, and religiously modest.[3] These threads of thought led the Catholic church to examine its practices and prayer life. At the beginning of the 1960s, both church and society were in the throes of upheaval.

Not every American enjoyed the prosperity of the 1950s. Racial segregation trapped persons of color in situations that deprived them of their human rights. Black soldiers fought and died for freedom and justice. They stood shoulder to shoulder with their comrades as they fought for equality and protection for those marginalized by the Nazi regime. Returning home to the reality of segregation was an unacceptable reality. The post-war years saw the long journey to social equality become a national movement. The struggle for civil rights for all peoples converged with the deepening faith understanding of the Body of Christ and the conviction that all are brothers and sisters in God. Religious leaders, including sisters, were drawn into the movement and, at times, the public demonstrations.

Black civil rights workers were not the only group struggling for equality. Sacramentans had to deal with the truth that they had allowed their Japanese neighbors to be confined to internment camps. While some Sacramentans acted as guardians of their neighbors' properties and goods, others exploited their situation. Too often, Japanese families returned to discover that all was gone. Sacramento's history contained within it seeds of prejudice against the Asian communities, excluding them from public schools in 1863.[4] Sacramento's civic leaders established a separate school for Asian students in 1895 to avoid the need to mix Asian and Caucasian students in the city's schools. Black and Asian communities were not the only victims of discrimination. They were joined by their Mexican brothers and sisters.

For all these groups, the pathway to achieving their rights and dignity led through education. While there is little documentation of the Sisters of Mercy in Sacramento being actively involved in public demonstrations or marches during the civil rights movement of the later 1950s and early '60s, they were actively engaged behind the scenes in working to provide quality education for children from all racial groups and economic circumstances. That was particularly true of children from Mexican families in the neighborhoods surrounding their schools. Sisters, like Sister Mary Patrick Kellaghan who taught at St. Joseph's grammar school, worked to assist Mexican students and their families.[5] In the mid-1920s, the Mercy sisters joined with Father Stephen Keating in providing religious education classes for Mexican children. The six-week sessions were held during the summer at St. Joseph's.[6] By the beginning of the 1930s, attendance grew to 325 children.[7]

In the 1940s, Mexican families began to cluster in what is called Alkali Flats, just north of downtown Sacramento. It was not only a residential area, but also a commercial center for restaurants and business. Part of cathedral parish, many of Alkali Flats' children attended St. Joseph's, which, prior to the building of Our Lady of Guadalupe Church, provided a gathering place for a two-day festival held after summer school was over. Supported by Father Anthony Maio, the festival helped raise monies for a permanent gathering place for the Catholic Mexican community.[8]

It was not only through the use of their property that sisters supported the Mexican families. Part of the outreach of the sisters to the families was a school bus to pick up the children. City bus transportation was most limited and the fares sometimes exceeded what families could pay. Cash-strapped cathedral parish could not always pay for a bus driver so the task fell to Father Sidney Hall.[9]

For the sisters, stories abound about the dedication and zeal of Father Hall. He was originally from Sacred Heart parish and knew the city well. As the bus moved from Alkali Flat to Washington District, from Dos Rios to Bannon Street, sisters rode along as bus monitors. At the beginning of the 1960s, 99 out of 160 families whose children attended St. Joseph's were from Mexican famiies.[10] Another clustering of Mexican families gravitated toward the more agricultural area in Bryte and Broderick where the sisters worked in Holy Cross Parish School. Again, the importance of providing an excellent education was foremost in their ministry.

At this time there was no thought of bilingual education. The sisters believed that English proficiency was key to success for their students, and they did everything they could to encourage use of it both at school and at home. Even sisters of Mexican descent who were members of the community were not encouraged to speak their native language. Cultural celebrations treasured by the Mexican community such as the feast of Our Lady of Guadalupe or the celebration of *Las Posadas* were not part of the festal cycle of the community. The importance of fostering and honoring cultural diversity had not yet become an internalized value.

When Pope Pius XII died in 1958, there was a convergence of factors shaping the religious imagination of Catholic youth. The societal ferment for civil rights, the Vietnam War era, and the Kennedy factor for young Catholics all created the sense of a new time. This was a moment for social engagement. The world could be transformed into a "new creation." Stories of valor and dedication were lifted up for emulation. During the early 1960s, Dr. Thomas Dooley and his mission in Laos were highlighted as an example of the courageous work young disciples were all called to do. John F. Kennedy's words—"Ask not what your country can do for you, ask what you can do for your country"—were like kindling for the fires of service. The impact of public religious figures like Rev. Dr. Martin Luther King, Jr., and the Rosary Crusade of Father Patrick Peyton showed how the integrity of the gospel message could bring about transformation. A surge of young women entered religious life, numbers not seen before nor ones that would be sustained. The one thing they had in common was their desire to serve. The graduating class of Bishop Armstrong High School in 1962 saw thirteen women enter a variety of religious communities, including three who entered the Mercy community in Sacramento.

In 1957, the changed organization of Sacramento Catholic high schools had brought together students from both St. Joseph's and St. Francis High Schools. The generation of women that attended Bishop Armstrong High School now experienced the Franciscan Sisters and Mercy Sisters sharing the educational mission. There, the Mercy sisters strongly encouraged girls to follow the path of a religious vocation. Through the sodality of the Blessed Virgin Mary, spiritual development and acts of mercy were fostered. Through mentoring, "convent field trips," and relationships of warmth with sisters like Mary Loyola MacDonald, Mary Regina Armstrong, Ellen Philbin, and Mary DeSales Flynn, Armstrong girls were presented with the challenges of religious life. Sister Ellen Philbin, then called Sister Mary Gertrude, was particularly ardent in inviting her students to visit the Mercy novitiate, organizing overnight live-in experiences. For girls knowing hardly anything about the inner life of the convent, the live-in experience opened the blinds a little, but not much.

To understand how great a change Vatican II brought into the lives of the sisters, it is important to understand what "pre-Vatican" religious life was like.[11] The *Community's Customs and Guide* book of 1955 and minutes of superiors' meetings of the community give us an idea. While the apostolic works of the community were quite vigorous and demanding, the inner life was rather rigid, most regulated, and monastic in style.

The monastic element was not rooted in the practice of Catherine McAuley. It was more the consequence of the revision of Canon Law in 1917, which imposed characteristics of monastic life upon apostolic religious communities. The character and style of Apostolic Religious Life, the form of life adopted by Catherine McAuley, was not yet fully understood as a different mode of consecrated life. Apostolic communities like the Sisters of Mercy struggled to maintain the demands of active engagement in ministry outside the convent while being required to adopt monastic practices that were not consistent with that need. The result was a rather rigid form of life that was structured to keep the sisters separate from influences of the culture and society. That even extended to family influence.

Prior to Vatican II, young women entering the community did so with the realization that they would never return home again except, possibly, upon the death of a parent. This was true even if one's family lived nearby. Families were only able to come together on what was called "visiting Sunday," which took place once a month. For one hour, families could visit but only in the formal setting of the convent.

Sister Mary Mercy Longwich shared how difficult that kind of separation was for families. Her mother lived across the street from St. Joseph Academy but was not allowed to visit with Mary Mercy, even if they met in the school yard. Not to be completely thwarted, Mrs. Longwich and Sister Mary Mercy worked out a system of communication using the classroom blinds.[12] Separation from families was more than physical. Conversations about one's family members, familial customs or experiences were discouraged. Even religious occasions such as baptisms or weddings were not times when the separation could be breached. This would gradually change in the early 1960s.

The level of regulation seen in the religious life of the late 1950s is hard to imagine seventy years later. Whether a CEO of a hospital, school administrator, or a brand-new member, young and old sisters alike had to ask permission for a myriad of small things: to discard a worn-out piece of clothing, to make a doctor's or dentist appointment, or to go to school after hours to pick up something forgotten in their classroom. The customs book was full of directions about everyday actions even outlining how a sister should walk. Sisters were not to walk with "a gait to be too slow or too quick." There were to be no unnecessary movements, such as tossing the head or swinging the arms.[13] Movement was not the only thing addressed. The tone of one's voice, expressing one's opinion, and the prohibition on use of nicknames for each other were just a few of the topics addressed. The *Customs Book* even directs that there was to be no levity among them.[14]

One of the characteristics many people identified with pre-Vatican II religious life was the religious habit. It came to symbolize all they associated with religious sisters. For some, the habit symbolized holiness, charity, and a special relationship with God. For others, it was a catalyst to their memories of school days or hospital stays. For many, the habit created a sense of "otherworldliness"—women set apart and reminding them of God present with them. For sisters, the religious habit was a sacred garment. Prayers were said while putting on each piece of the vesture, and sisters kissed the garment before putting it on. Given all its multiple meanings, it is not surprising that the manner of dress was extensively detailed in the *Customs Book*. Even though Pope Pius XII had asked for the simplification of religious habits, not much had been done. Three full pages of the guide were given to how the veil was to be made, how the habit was to be pleated, and how it was to be worn. In the variety of changes in religious life engendered by Vatican II, nothing became more controversial or symbolic than the adaptation of religious dress.

The changes brought about by Vatican II were more than changes of dress, however. The most significant changes arose from how the Church saw its relationship with the world, its engagement with secular culture. Pre-Vatican religious life worked to limit the contact sisters had with the culture and society. In the *Customs Book* you find such cautions as: "The radio and television bring the Sisters into contact with the world and for this reason their use should be supervised by the superior."[15] "Because receiving and writing letters absorb time and may cause distraction," sisters were to limit their correspondence.[16] They were never to watch anything "worldly." No sister was ever to leave the convent grounds without permission.

Sister Mary St. Michael Myles characterizes the time as a period of strict adherence to policy. She reflects that younger sisters were always in fear of being sent home for the smallest fault.[17] Sister Eileen Mary O'Connor, who became a novice in 1956, shares that "Chapter of Faults" was still in practice in the community. The practice involved members asking the forgiveness of the community for any small infractions of rules. Sister Eileen Mary remembers that the discipline took place weekly before her novitiate director and monthly with the whole novitiate. Seen in the monastic tradition as a practice for fostering perfection and humility, it did not always succeed in that intent. Sr. Eileen Mary notes that the rationale for chapter of faults was never really explained to her.[18] Without understanding its solemn purpose, chapter of faults could devolve into a litany of small infractions such as slamming a door, being late for prayers, breaking a glass, or not properly cleaning one's area of responsibility.

Although separation from the "world" was engrained in the practices of the day, it was not part of the legacy handed down by religious founders who were drawn to serve those in need precisely because those founders were in touch with the society and culture of their times. The mindset came from ecclesial legislation or law. The *Customs Book* is very clear:

> The purpose of ecclesiastical legislation with regard to cloister and the relations of religious persons with the outside world is to protect religious institutes and their members from the injury which comes from free communication with seculars.[19]

Appealing to the opinions of spiritual writers and directors, the text goes on to say that interaction with seculars or outsiders is not only prejudicial to perfection but fills minds with worldly ideas, divides one's affections between God and creatures, and prevents religious from attaining close union with God.[20]

This perception of society and outsiders as a source of distraction at best, corruption at its extreme, meant that normal everyday interchange between the sisters and their societal counterparts was strictly regulated. The *Customs Book* indicates that there was control of both radios and TV usage. In the novitiate, access to newspapers was cut off although some folks, using old newspapers to cover the floor while polishing their shoes, took the occasion to read the headlines of the day. As a young sister, Sr. Mary St. Michael remembers that Sister Mary Lourdes Cook, convent librarian, cut out news stories that she felt were important and posted them for everyone to read.[21] Summing up the experience, Mary

St. Michael says: "It was terrible to be cut off."[22] As Sister Eileen Mary puts it: "We taught out of text books, not current events."[23] When the church articulated a totally different stance in the conciliar document, *The Church in the Modern World,* it challenged women religious, including the Sisters of Mercy in Sacramento, to reimagine how life was to be lived.

The vision articulated by the church at Vatican II had a profound impact upon the life of women religious because, being women of the church, they gave themselves wholeheartedly to its call to transformation. Bishop Rembert G. Weakland, O.S.B., in an article entitled "Religious Life in the U.S.—Understanding the Moment," identified three themes from Vatican II that were particularly powerful catalysts to changes in religious life. They were (1) a call to return to the foundational vision of their religious founders; (2) the recognition that all share in the mission of the church, religious and laity alike. Together, clergy, religious and laity are the People of God; and (3) reading the signs of the times, religious were to adjust their responses to meet the needs of their time and culture.[24] Heeding these three calls, women religious began their journey of transformation.

The impact upon the life of the community had moments of light and moments of shadow. Recognizing that all are called to the service of God's people and that religious life was not a higher state than lay life, waves of sisters left their religious communities. For the Sisters of Mercy in Sacramento, this dynamic of departure was rending. Between 1965 and 1975, over seventy women left the community, some very early in their religious life, others long professed. For a small community, the loss was overwhelming.

During these years, departures were often shrouded in secrecy. Sometimes there was no opportunity for sisters to say goodbye to women who shared their life. While the emotional toil was great, there was also a huge impact on the ministries of the sisters. Sister Mary St. Michael Myles notes that the "exodus" was disheartening not only because one lost friends and companions, but as a community, we lost a generation of good leaders for the mission.[25] The numbers of sisters available to staff schools and hospitals were significantly decreased.

Bishop Weakland, in speaking of this "exodus," remarks that many religious left communities because they believed they could better serve the church as active lay members. In his opinion, the Spirit had prepared these new ministers for service through their years in religious community.[26] The newly empowered laity were called upon to take up the mission as lay teachers and hospital managers. The change put in motion by Vatican II called the sisters to new levels of collaboration.

Experts in the field of change dynamics tell us that change brings fear and decreased trust. No matter how rigid or limiting the life style of pre-

Vatican II religious life was, it was familiar, predictable, and stable. Daily life was regulated by the *horarium* or schedule. Meals were always at the same time. There was a rhythm of life and time. The changes put in motion by Vatican II meant that apostolic religious life would now be structured around ministerial realities. Night meetings, once prohibited, would become common. It is not surprising that some sisters found this difficult. So, what sustained them and brought them through the changes? Most sisters who lived this transition say their faith, their prayer, their bonds of relationship within community, and a good sense of humor were the key factors in sustaining them through this challenging time.

Prayer was always core to Mercy life. In spite of the demands of ministry, sisters spent over twenty-two retreat days each year, days totally given over to prayer. Daily, every task was started with prayer whether entering a sick room or class room. In addition to daily office and meditation, the sisters had spiritual reading, extensive vocal prayers, and special devotions daily in May, June, October, and December.[27]

While maintaining its traditional commitment to prayer, the sisters changed the manner in which they prayed. Extensive vocal and communal prayer gave way to an emphasis on liturgical prayer, meditation on the Word of God and contemplative prayer. The small Office of the Blessed Virgin Mary, prayed in common since the founding of the order in 1831, was set aside in favor of the Church's *Liturgy of the Hours*. The sisters reclaimed their identity as apostolic contemplatives who, while giving themselves wholeheartedly in service to the people of God, strove to live in the presence of God at all times. True to the spirit of Catherine McAuley, they would remain centered in God. Only that would make this transformation possible.

Elected Superior in 1962, Mother Mary Teresita Durkin was charged with the responsibility for guiding renewal of the community. A woman of profound faith, she believed that all true renewal began with spiritual renewal and worked to deepen the spirituality of the community. She sought to bring the very best teachers of the times to Sacramento to help the sisters assimilate the theological and spiritual implications of their changing reality, teachers like Adrian Van Kaam from Duquesne University, Alan McCoy O.S.M., from the Franciscan Theological Seminary in Santa Barbara, California, and William Peters, S.J., known for his work on renewing the Ignatian Spiritual Exercises.

Mother Teresita saw the renewal of the community as an act of faith and fidelity. She wrote in March 1971, prior to the beginning of a special chapter of renewal:

For us, it is a ruling of the Church, that is to say, it is willed by God: this assures us beforehand that it carries with it His grace and that we ought to know how to accept it. The Special Chapter is a "bridge, it helps us to cross over, to pass through a stage." It recalls principles, opens doors, examines the past, fearlessly and honestly, so that our religious life may become ever more obviously the sacrament of Christ in the world.[28]

The speed with which the sisters integrated new understandings of religious life into their day to day lives is impressive especially in light how long depth-change takes to become normative. The chapter documents of 1968–1971 make this clear. The sisters fully embraced that path laid out for them by the church. As a result of their reflection, they wrote the following in their statement on religious life:

> As Sisters of Mercy entering a new age in the world of man [*sic.*] we are faced with the call to shape this mystery for our own time and in our own place. We can only properly respond to the challenge by transposing all the aspects of this mystery into our daily existence, so that who we are, and what we do, speaks, not of ourselves, but of Him "who set his heart on us and chose us, not because we were the greatest among his people, but because we were the least." (Deut. 7:7)[29]

The 1950s had been a time when religious communities focused on providing their sisters with the educational training needed for mission. In Auburn, that included a solid training in theology. This early preparation was essential in preparing the sisters for change. Sister Eileen Mary O'Connor gives us some perspective on how the sisters could make such a switch in perspective:

> We had priest teachers who opened us up to new theological views, priests like Rev. Charles O'Leary, Cornelius Higgins and Damian Lyons, O.S.F. Sister Mary Benignus Redmond, our director, really opened doors for us. Father Fergus McGuinness C.P. and T. Brendan O'Sullivan deepened those understandings. There was something about Vatican II that I just embraced. I could just eat whatever magazines I could read. It was like opening a door of fresh air.[30]

Father Gregory Staniszewski, C.P., was tapped to teach the Vatican II documents to all the sisters in formation.

The council's teaching on the People of God brought in more than "fresh air." It brought about changes in the notion of religious authority and in the understanding of shared mission. Where superiors might have worked from a hierarchical model prior to the council, post-Vatican II authority was more diffuse. Decisions were more a matter of communal reflection and discernment. Nowhere is this more evident than in what was called the extraordinary chapter of renewal in 1968. Mother Mary Teresita and her advisors called upon every sister in the community to take an active part in preparing for the chapter of renewal by working on what were termed "Position Papers." The work of the community as a whole, these papers formed the basis for decisions made on the renewal of the community.[31] The understanding that all People of God shared in the mission of Jesus brought about a new emphasis upon collaboration with persons who shared a common vision and who assumed their place as partners in ministry.

One of the unexpected outcomes of Vatican II was the rediscovery of Catherine McAuley, the Mercy founder. While early biographies of Catherine were published by Sr. Mary Vincent Harnett and Sr. Mary Austin Carroll, many sisters were not steeped in her story. They lived and breathed the Mercy charism because they absorbed it through the witness of their elder sisters in religious life. The memoirs of Catherine, written by the founding circle of Mercy women, were not yet accessible nor were her letters. The available books that preserved her teachings were basically lecture notes devoid of her humor. Directors of Mercy Charism retreats like Sr. Jeanette Noonan tell us that one of the most frequently heard comments after the retreat was "I never really knew Catherine. Thank you for making her come alive for me."[32] That same reality was echoed by both Sisters Mary St. Michael and Eileen O'Connor, who shared that learning about her was not a significant part of their formation.[33]

In the early years of renewal, Mercy historians like Sister Mary Ignatia Neumann, M. Bertrand Degnan, M. Joanna Regan, and Isabelle Keiss brought Catherine alive through their astute scholarship and deep spirituality. In 1969, Sister Mary Ignatia brought together a collection of Catherine's own letters, which fed the imagination and spirituality of Mercy women after the chapters of renewal. Through the works of these Mercy women, Catherine's sense of reading the signs of the time, her commitment to collaboration, her call to blend both the contemplative and active aspects of life, and her passionate love for persons who were poor, trust in providence and sense of bold initiatives sank deeper into the soul marrow of the sisters and shaped their decisions and service going forward.

The *Constitutions of the Sisters of Mercy in Auburn*, written by the sisters in 1978, was explicit in naming this reality:

We affirm that Mother McAuley's legacy to us is one of love and mercy expressed through service of the poor. This commitment we express in those apostolates to which Christ summons us and to which we are called by those in need.[34]

After naming the elements of spiritual renewal to which they were committed and the charity "by which faith expresses itself in love's steadfast fidelity," the document went on to state: "We affirm that such interior renewal is one with Mother McAuley's total giving of self in love to God to meet the needs of her time with courage and daring."[35] At every decision point in the future, the sisters would turn to the model of following the gospel embodied by Catherine McAuley. She was, in fact, their spirit mother.

A Time of Inner and Outer Change

Sister Eileen Mary O'Connor was surprised when her superior Sister Mary Magdalen Nagle asked her to take a ride into the country. It was an unexpected request. A somewhat new driver, Sister Eileen Mary remembers being very nervous as she drove the two-lane road taking them to Carmichael, site of the soon to be Mercy San Juan Hospital. The area where the hospital was to be built was undeveloped at the time. To Sister Eileen Mary, it seemed like being in the middle of nowhere, a spot with brambles, dirt, and two magnificent oak trees. Three years later, only the ancient oaks remained the same.[1]

While the diocese had done much to provide both educational outreach and parish centers, a major area of need was left unanswered. As Sacramento's population expanded and families flocked to the suburbs, there was once more an inadequate supply of hospital beds in the county. The Sacramento Regional Hospital Planning Committee had a vision of what it would take to supply this need. It would take a new regional hospital. The Sisters of Mercy responded by taking on the task of building a 215-bed facility in Carmichael. The decision moved the *Catholic Herald* to comment:

Not only the Catholic community, but the community at large, is witnessing first-hand the spirit of sacrifice which motivates members of the Order of Mercy, who daily practice one of the corporal works of Mercy, tending the sick. Knowing of the urgent need in the greater Sacramento Area for another general hospital, the Sisters of Mercy have elected to take on additional financial debt of great magnitude—two and a quarter million dollars—to assure the construction of the new Mercy San Juan Hospital.[2]

The article goes on to place that decision in the context of other projects undertaken by the Sisters at the time saying:

> This represents only one side of the coin of their financial obligations. For they have already pledged hundreds of thousands of dollars to provide a Mercy Nursing Home at 40th and H Streets, plus personally financing the additions to the Mercy Hospital in Redding, also maintained by the order.[3]

The boldness of this plan can only be understood in the light of the heavy investment in healthcare that the sisters already carried. In the mid-1950s, the sisters had taken on both the renovation of the Auburn motherhouse and the addition of an east wing at Mercy General. By 1965, the sisters were asked to send whatever monies they could to the motherhouse for, as the superiors' meeting minutes put it: "Our present debt plus our new obligations will mean that the Congregation will have a debt of about six million dollars."[4] The enormity of the debt was a direct result of responding to emerging needs of the people of Sacramento.

Charles W. Steding was selected to oversee the project. He was well-qualified, having served for twelve years as business manager for Mercy General Hospital and as a member of the Regional Hospital Planning Council. With the support of the sisters, grants from the federal government and a robust response to the fundraising drive lead by Richard W. Heldridge, the project moved forward. Mercy San Juan was to be an example of future healthcare. It followed a plan called the Freisen concept. Developed by Gordon A. Freisen, the intent was to return nurses primarily to the care of patients by installing automated devices. Headlines proclaimed, "Automation Will be King at New Mercy San Juan."[5] In the new automated world of healthcare, there would be no more trips to the pharmacy for patient medications or carrying supplies back and forth. Things were either built into rooms or provided through automation.[6]

Automation was not the only new aspect of the hospital. There was a focus on specialized medical care as well. In spite of all the innovations, the hospital did not have an easy start. Although the sisters had strong relational bonds with physicians, they underestimated the resistance that greets change. The emphasis on specialized care was not always aligned with the view of primary care physicians. To further complicate things, physicians with practices in Sacramento were not inclined to expand their practices to Carmichael. Sister Bridget McCarthy tells us that part of the context was a contrast between "high tech" and "high touch" healthcare. American River Hospital, also in the Carmichael area, was loved by the people because of its "high touch": spirit. It had built strong relationships with ambulance drivers, community members and its physicians.[7]

As a result, the early years of Mercy San Juan hospital were ones of struggle. Sister Mary St. Michael Myles remembers that at times there were more staff on duty than there were patients.[8] The situation was so precarious that the daily prayer intentions of the sisters sometimes included "patients for Mercy San Juan." The intent was not that people would get sick, only that if sick, they would come to the new hospital.[9]

A story from these years told by Sister Mary St. Michael provides insight into the situation. According to the story passed on to her, the struggle of the hospital to take root and thrive was so severe that board members from American River Hospital thought it might provide them with the possibility of acquiring the new hospital. When they approached the sisters about purchasing the hospital, Mother Mary Teresita Durkin's reply was: "Gentlemen, we will never think of selling this unless we cannot carry out the mission."[10] Mission always came first. It took almost five years for the hospital to thrive but thrive it did.

Building a new state-of-the art hospital was not the only healthcare project the sisters initiated during this time period. Another pressing need was to provide for Sacramento's aging population. In 1963, while involved in planning for Mercy San Juan Hospital, the sisters opened Mercy Nursing Home. Unlike Mercy San Juan, the new facility was at full capacity within a year. Part of the attraction for residents, in the opinion of Sister Mary Kevin Redmond, director of the home, was the chapel. "It's a source of consolation for the Catholics as well as the non-Catholics."[11]

Sister Mary Kevin emphasized a "homey" atmosphere. Friends brought homemade cupcakes, residents created various art projects and looked forward to visits from the future nurses, girls from Bishop Manogue High School. Sister Rosemarie Carvalho, then a student, remembers the times when Sister Mary Monica would drive the students over to the nursing home to decorate for big occasions like Thanksgiving or St. Patrick's. The small acts of kindness made a lasting impression.[12] All but six of the residents were permanent residents. Everyone knew everyone else, creating bonds of unity.

The needs of Redding were not forgotten. In spite of the struggle to finance Sacramento projects, the sisters undertook the task of expanding Mercy Redding. The urgency is seen in statistics. During 1966, over 700 patients had to be placed in "hall beds" due to lack of space. Projections indicated that the numbers would be even higher during the following year. Sister Mary Bernadine Schmidt, then hospital administrator, summed up the community perspective:

We have to provide for the needs of the area. If we aren't going to meet these needs, we have no business running a hospital. We would be failing in our responsibility not to go ahead with our Redding commitment in view of the severe shortage of hospital beds here at Mercy.[13]

Given the sisters' commitment to excellence of care, they saw no other option but to supply the need. After stops and starts, the necessary monies were raised to augment the monies contributed by the community. The new wing opened in July 1968, the last of the five major projects underway.

In the middle of these hospital projects, there was a little noticed event that happened, which had major consequences. In June 1965, Charles W. Steding and Robert F. Stephenson were appointed director and controller, respectively, of the five hospitals operated by the Sisters of Mercy in Northern California. The bringing together of the congregation's five hospitals marked the beginning of a path to more centralization of administration. Sister administrators in all five hospitals would now be accountable to a lay director in areas of overall business management. Collaboration with the laity and fostering lay leadership had taken its first step in becoming the norm within Mercy health care.[14]

When commenting on the change, Mother Mary Teresita Durkin shared that the rapid growth of all the various Mercy health care institutions and their constant need for monies to expand and modernize made it necessary to achieve greater efficiency and economy. "The only logical way this could be done, she said, was to place those operations which could be effectively centralized under one well-qualified person."[15] For the sisters, it was not about holding on to control. It was about identifying and using the best skills for the mission.

The $6 million debt that prompted Mother Mary Teresita's call for austerity was not completely caused by the need for new hospital projects. It was caused by the convergence of multiple major expansions. The three healthcare initiatives—Mercy San Juan Hospital, expanding Mercy Redding and opening Mercy Nursing Home—were not the only building initiatives taken on by the sisters. Two non-healthcare projects were also underway, expansion of the motherhouse in Auburn and building a new Mercy secondary school for the north area. It would take until 1968 for all these building projects to be realized.

An influx of new members caused a severe housing shortage at the motherhouse. A new novitiate wing was needed both for bedrooms and classrooms. Prior to 1960, the sisters annually had about five to six young women seek admission to the community, sometimes fewer and occasionally more. That began to change in 1960 when numbers significantly increased, reaching a peak in 1964 when nineteen new sisters entered in one year. The novitiate wing built in the 1950s was no longer sufficient. Bedrooms meant for one were shared, and even the office of the mother superior was converted into a bedroom. At one point, space for forty-two new members had to be found.

It was not just beds that were missing. Classroom and lab space were also needed. With the advent of the sister formation movement which stressed ministerial preparation prior to teaching or nursing, college education became a necessity. In speaking of the expansion, Mother Teresita said: "In each step we've become less a farm and more a school."[16] Mother Teresita was not kidding about being a "farm." The property had been the original Teagarden Ranch. At the time of the expansion the sisters raised beef calves until they were old enough for slaughter and cultivated a fruit orchard large enough to supply the needs of the convent and still have surplus to share. Vegetables and flowers completed the plantings. Earlier, the farm had raised lambs and chickens. The raising of sheep was short-lived since the novices tended to make pets of them, two having been nicknamed Cosmos and Damian. Chickens lasted longer. Sister Maureen Costelloe still remembers hours spent plucking feathers when it was time for them to move from farm plot to soup pot.[17]

The new addition doubled the size of the buildings even as numbers tripled. The addition provided a separate novitiate wing large enough to house forty sisters, multiple classrooms and a large community gathering room. In the main house, an up-to-date kitchen facility replaced the old kitchen, administrative offices were added and the old dining room was divided into two separate eating areas. A large library and gathering hall was also part of the expansion. The building was not without its disruptions. The *Annals* of the community note:

> We were in the middle of retreat at the 9:15 a.m. conference in the restful quiet of our lovely Chapel. Suddenly! Screeching! A dreadful noise! Father continued but his words fell on deaf ears for the most part. At the end of the hour and with some emotion and nostalgia, the retreatants silently viewed the trees which had been for so many years given TLC now leveled flat to the ground with one swift "push" of that mighty piece of equipment.[18]

Like all construction projects, noise and upheaval were part of the package. It would be months before the quiet, centering spirit of the campus could re-emerge. Completion of the buildings came by Thanksgiving. Sisters, home from college in the bay area, were pressed into service moving beds and furniture into what was to be called Marian Hall. Little did they know that no sister would ever take up residence in this new building. Between the years 1966–1968, forty-four sisters, mostly young, elected to leave the community. The numbers of those entering significantly lessened. A decision to experiment with a postulancy house in Sacramento, Roncalli House, meant that new members would no longer start out their religious lives in Auburn. There was no longer a housing shortage.

One additional building project claimed the attention of the sisters, building a high school to replace the old St. Joseph Academy. The 26-acre site for Mercy San Juan Hospital provided the possibility of building a new Mercy secondary high school for girls. It is hard to determine the exact reasons underlying the decision to build a new girls' high school in Carmichael. Quite possibly, the forced relinquishment of St. Joseph Academy necessitated by the diocesan reorganization of secondary education caused a deep regret in the hearts of the sisters. The philosophy of Mercy education was precious to them.

From the very beginning of their years in Sacramento, the sisters always sponsored their own school, creating a special environment for the flourishing of feminine talent. Sisters like Mother Mary Rita Bathurst urged that a new high school carrying the Mercy tradition be built. In Mother Rita's case, she even had a spot picked out, imagining a new Mercy high school on Rocky Ridge Road.[19] Not wishing to lose their link with the sisters, St. Joseph alumnae joined with the sisters in that hope for a new school.

Another reason for building Mercy High School was a desire to provide a Catholic high school for the growing numbers of young women attending Catholic elementary schools in north area parishes. There was a curious quiet in the press about the project. Even articles telling about the new Mercy San Juan Hospital gave no details about the school that would share its campus. In fact, there was little mention of the school at all. The doors of Mercy High School opened in 1966, welcoming a freshmen class of sixty girls. Since the school was built to accommodate 800, it was a small beginning.

From its start, the school faced challenges of sustainability. The establishment of the high school had not been part of the master developed by the Sacramento diocese in the early 1960s. Beginning in 1964, diocesan development drives focused on raising monies for new secondary high schools. The first of these, the new St. Francis High School opened in 1965 drawing girls from all over the area. The following year the drive focused on St. Pius X seminary while the third year included a plan for a second girls' school, Bishop Manogue High School. Mercy High was not part of the plan. It also was not alone in its struggles to make ends meet. The *Catholic Herald* carried stories of other schools working to remain viable including Jesuit High School.[20] Only diocesan financial support made it possible for diocesan high schools to prosper. Privately sponsored schools like Jesuit, Loretto, and Mercy did not have that safety net. They were dependent upon tuition and subsidies from the sponsoring religious community.

Mercy High grew slowly but was still unable to break even. As early as 1974, the sisters seriously considered closing the school. The community simply didn't have sufficient monies to subsidize it any longer. A number of alternatives were considered: 1) the diocese could assume the $750,000 debt; 2) the suggestion of Father George Schuster that the school merge with St. Francis could be accepted and the girls bused to St. Francis; and 3) the school could explore the possibility of going co-ed.[21] None of the options were feasible. Bishop Alton J. Bell directly intervened at the time by providing a $250,000 subsidy for the school. While enormously helpful, the subsidy did not resolve the problem but did postpone the final decision to close the school.

There was another challenge the sisters had to face, decreasing numbers of sister personnel to staff the high schools. Sister Rita Irene Esparza, a Mercy alumna, poignantly speaks of the situation:

> One of the perplexing issues I had was wondering why so many of the sisters left the community, such as Mary Fidelis Laskin, Annette Cummings, Margaret Hamilton, Mary Ligouri Sweeney, Mary Christine O'Hara, Gail Armstrong, Roberta Buford and Maureen Brennan. I think that is why I waited to enter until my early twenties.[22]

All the women mentioned were high school teachers.

The reasons for the school's struggle to thrive were multiple. Location was primary. It was close to Loretto High School which already was well established; the new St. Francis was located right off a major freeway route providing ease of access to downtown Sacramento for suburban commuters and the bus transportation in Carmichael at the time was limited. The school, while state of the art inside, had limited athletic fields in a time when women's sports were coming to the fore. Soccer fields, softball diamonds, and swimming pools were just as essential in girls' schools as they were in those that were co-ed or all boys. That was not possible on the Mercy campus.

By 1982, the sisters reluctantly decided to close Mercy High School and sell the campus to its sister ministry, Mercy San Juan Hospital. Sister Laura Ann Walton, then principal, explained:

> The congregation has poured close to $2 million into the school—$1.6 million in building it and the rest in maintaining it since them. Our

annual expenses are projected to go over $1 million by the year 1984–85 for 400 students. We cannot afford that.[23]

This was the first ministry the sisters closed through their own choice. For most, it was bittersweet.

Mercy High sisters had, in its sixteen years, forged strong bonds of relationship with their students. They had combined excellence of education with warmth and compassion. Most of all, they had shown that they were very human. Sister Rita Irene started her high school years at Mercy High in 1967, a member of its second class. In such a small school, friendships were lasting and classmates still remain connected today. Sister Rita shares:

> There were many memories of the sisters and lay teachers, but it was the sisters who had the most impact on me. I was able to connect with them and was very interested in their life and way of living. The sisters came to our dances and other events and made me feel special.[24]

The sisters were committed to have girls from all backgrounds and economic circumstances be a part of the student body. Sister Rita was one of many who took advantage of what was called a work study program, which helped defray the cost of tuition. This program brought her in close contact with Sister Mary Christine O'Hara, manager of the school bookstore. Rita shares that she was shocked to find sister listening to Giants' games while working. As Rita says: "She was just like me."

Rethinking the view of sisters was part of Catholic life during the early post-council years. As sisters took to heart the admonition of the church to embrace renewal, read the signs of the times, and re-appropriated the spirit of their foundresses, changes were bound to come. Mercy High School opened just as those major changes were coming to the sisters' community itself. Pre-dedication photos highlight one of the biggest changes. The traditional Mercy habit had given way to a new look, one which was considered more appropriate for the times.

The transition was not all that easy for women who had grown accustomed to dress in the dark without the use of mirrors. Sister Mary Philomene Gogarty remembers that she was very nervous when the big day of transition arrived. Her co-workers did not know about the change and she worried about what they would think.[25] In spite of apprehensions, a sense of eagerness is reflected in the memories written in the *Redding Annals*. They say:

> Finally, the word went out: every hook, eye and matching snaps were sewed on. The new habits were finally ready. This evening, Monsignor

O'Connor arrived to bless them! Spread out on a long table near the altar rail, seventeen could be counted. The assembled sisters responded to the two beautiful prayers. Following his appropriate homily, Monsignor asked for a preview since he was leaving for retreat on the following morning. Consequently, we proceeded to the community room where all awaited the appearance of designated models. Sister Mary Veronica represented the school sisters and Sister Mary Dolorita, the hospital sisters.[26]

By October 19, 1966, the sisters in their new habits made their first public appearance. In the words of the annalist, "We thought we all looked so 'well' and decided that the transition wasn't so difficult."

While some associated the original habit with the "holy sisters" image, it also concealed at times their identity as flesh and blood women. Though raised in a Catholic milieu and taught by women religious, Sister Rita remembers that she and her classmates were amazed when Sister Bridget Mary, frustrated by the student practice of rolling up their uniform skirts to shorten them, lifted up her own skirts to demonstrate the mandated length of their skirts. They just never expected to see her legs.[27] Their reaction is not surprising. Rules that required sisters never to be out at night, never to travel alone, or never to eat in public sometimes left the impression that they were women apart. The idea that they played tennis, went swimming, were ardent card players, or thoroughly enjoyed a good movie was not part of that image.

A story from before the habit change illustrates the dynamic. A few months prior to adopting the revised habit, two sisters attending the University of San Francisco finished their final exams and started to walk home. On the way, they detoured to the DeYoung Museum to treat themselves to a walk through its Asian art collection. As they moved through the museum, they realized that they were being followed by a group of school children. Wherever they went, the children followed. Soon, the two sisters found themselves in front of a samurai sword collection, surrounded by children. When the sisters started to talk with the students, they were asked: "Do you have ears?" or "Do you have feet?"[28] For children unfamiliar with sisters, the two seemed like space aliens.

It was not just their mode of dress that made people wonder about sisters. It was their whole lifestyle. Given the vision of religious life lifted up by Vatican II, sisters were challenged to explore the meaning of their vows in the current time and culture. This reflection and study would be the foundation for revised constitutions and rules. Between 1965 and 1968, Auburn sisters organized themselves into working groups that explored every part of their religious life. The climax of this work came to what was called a special chapter of renewal. There were three areas which needed to be articulated in ways that could be understood in the mid twentieth century: (1) the meaning of their vows especially consecrated celibacy; (2) the mission and charism of the community; and (3) the sisters' relationship to society.

For women thinking about entering religious life and for the people of God, it was vital information. The sisters set about articulating who they were and what they were. The answers that defined their essence were then captured in their foundational documents. Sister Mary Loyola MacDonald was missioned with the task of gathering that wisdom and bringing it together in a revised Constitutions, which was then submitted to Rome for approval.

This exploration and pondering went on during a time when the culture was experiencing the age of "free love." Sexuality was celebrated and many old restraints were rejected; yet, these women religious lived a life of strict celibacy. For those called to the religious life, it was a conscious choice, one which the woman called embraced with the whole of her being. It was deliberately countercultural. In the words of Catherine McAuley, their founder, the sisters affirmed: "Our hearts can always be in the same place, centered in God, for whom alone we go forward or stay back."[29]

In a time when the culture was moving to eliminate traditional taboos about sexuality, the sisters made clear their experience of celibate life. It was not just for the sake of new members that they made clear the inner nature of consecrated celibacy. It was important because Catholics and non-Catholics alike struggled to understand how vibrant young women could freely choose to follow a path that did not include marriage or children. Sometimes, even their own families questioned why their sister, daughter or aunt would live such a life. The revised Constitutions of 1978 brought together the important values and understandings that would guide the community going forward. In referring to the vow of consecrated celibacy, it said:

> This gift is freely and graciously given by God for the sake of the kingdom and demands of those who receive it a free, personal, and total dedication of their entire person to Christ. By her vow of consecrated chastity, a sister freely renounces marriage for the sake of the kingdom. She surrenders her whole person in undivided love to God and commits herself to living this consecration within community ... Consecrated chastity, embraced for the kingdom, leaves us free to further this Kingdom through service to others. This self-giving expressed in our apostolate, should spring from a love which is rich, deep, and truly human.[30]

Religious life was not to be lived as a negation of love, but as an alternate expression of love. As one sister put it:

> Our vow is not about what we give up but is about our living relationship with God, a relationship that shapes and reshapes our lives ... It, instead, impels us outward in love because of the love we have so freely received from God. Our vow is not a one-time commitment but, rather, one that we have to renew daily.[31]

This is not to say that sisters did not experience moments of regret about not having children or, at times, feel attracted to a co-worker or friend in a sexual way. That is part of being human. It does mean that while naming and claiming those feelings, their actions and decisions are shaped by their life-long vows. Claiming God as their center and first love combined with the love and support of their community made their lives rich and their vowed commitment strong. With those two supports, they could fully embrace the celibate path.

Their way of life was to be one of love flowing out in service. The community affirmed other aspects of their life:

> Mother McAuley's legacy to us is one of love and mercy expressed through service of the poor: this commitment we will continue to express in those apostolates to which the Church summons us and to which we are called by those in need.[32]

The sisters committed themselves to address the cultural evils of their time. "We affirm that we will vigorously oppose racial, religious, or cultural discrimination in any form."[33] Later in the same document, we find another insight into how the sisters saw their call to service: "Our service is marked by respect for the sacredness, dignity and inviolability of the individual."[34] It was this vision that was to guide and illumine subsequent choices about the forms of ministry they would undertake.

Reading the signs of the times brought about other significant changes. Prior to the chapter of renewal, most Sacramento sisters were engaged in either education or healthcare. They ministered within institutions that the community either sponsored or administered. New members presumed they would be assigned to these works based on needs of the community.

Looking at the needs of the time meant a new type of social engagement for the sisters. Accustomed to limited public engagement, the sisters began to publicly support social causes that were important to them. Sometimes this support took the form of their presence and participation in demonstrations for justice and memorials events. The first indication of this type of action is found in the *Annals of Our Lady of Mercy* in Auburn. It reports that on March 21, 1965, Mother Mary Rita Bathurst along with Sisters Mary Christopher Brannigan, Mary Philip Moniz, and Mary Pierre Cummings all attended such a demonstration on the state capitol steps in support of the marchers at Selma.[35]

Other Sisters of Mercy across the county joined in these efforts. By June 1965, the Sisters of Mercy of the Union issued a public statement condemning racism and committing themselves to work for its elimination. It was not surprising then in April 1968 to see several sisters represent the community at the march and memorial Mass for Rev. Dr. Martin Luther King, Jr., held at the Cathedral of the Blessed Sacrament. Not everyone was happy with the visibility and voice that sisters brought to social issues. In fact, a survey of Catholics in 1968 revealed that 57 percent of Catholics did not believe that clergy or religious should be involved in political or social issues, remarkable since papal teachings on the dignity and rights of persons were the seedbed for their actions.[36] According to the polling, the majority of respondents felt that clergy and religious should primarily be devoted to promoting spiritual comfort.

Much of the work for social justice went on quietly in classrooms and board rooms. One example of this work was highlighted by the *Catholic Herald* in January 1975. It focused on the Christian social action class at Mercy High School taught by Sister Maura Power. The class blended study of the church's social teachings with first-hand experience of service. Some students studied California Rural Legal Assistance while others left campus to volunteer at facilities serving children with intellectual disabilities, convalescent homes or tutored at area schools. The goal of the program was to be aware of human need in the Sacramento community and then give of one's time and service to meet these needs.[37] It foreshadowed the current model of community service programs prevalent in all Catholic high schools.

The struggle of farm workers for living wages and better conditions was another cause in which various sisters participated. Among the most active sisters were Sister Maria Padilla, Sisters Maria Campos, and Sister Michelle Gorman. Their presence was an example of the sisters' maxim: "Where one is present, all are present." The social justice activities of the sisters were not limited to the areas of immigrant rights and racism, however. They were also engaged in opposing violence, especially nuclear arms and the death penalty.

In 1982, the sisters' stance against nuclear weapons brought them into direct conflict with the federal government. It was over a program called the Civilian Military Contingency Hospital System, which the government wished to implement to provide medical support for future major conflict outside the United States. It was predicated on the possibility of nuclear war. The sisters declined the request that their hospitals, now seven in number, participate in the initiative.[38] In explaining the reasons for their decision, the sisters shared that they had undertaken a three-month process of research and education. The pastoral letter of Archbishop John Quinn, studied by the sisters, was a factor in the final decision.

Bishop Quinn had noted that the proposed system was based on the false idea that there could be an effective medical response to the catastrophe of nuclear war. In the opinion of the bishop such an event would irrevocably alter our ecological system, genetic structures for generation to come as well as break down our social systems.[39] Sister Kathleen Dunne, superior of the community at the time, said that although she anticipated some criticism of the stand taken by the sisters, if the statement made others aware of the gravity of the build-up of nuclear arms, it had achieved its purpose. From the perspective of time, these years were ones in which the sisters embraced the prophetic role of women religious, that role which identifies the gap between the practices of contemporary society and the vision of God's reign of peace and justice. There was to be no turning back from this call.

Collaboration as a Way of Life: 1978–1991

Mother Catherine McAuley wrote to Mother Frances Warde: "This is your life, joys and sorrows mingled, one succeeding the other."[1] Such was the reality confronting the sisters during the 1980s. It began with the closing of St. Joseph's Convent at 9th and G Street. Ten years earlier, the opening of Bishop Manogue High School resulted in the closure of St. Joseph's Academy and St. Joseph Elementary School, a Cathedral parish school that shared the same campus also closed. Finances led to the closure of the latter. Now the buildings, with the exception of the convent, were empty and the diocese was greatly in need of money.

Over the years, the sisters had ceded much of the St. Joseph's property to the diocese in return for monies to make necessary renovations. In 1953, Mother Mary Barbara Ley, in the name of the community, had signed an agreement with the diocese that "at some future date a check for the price finally agreed upon at the time of the negotiation would be given to the Sisters of Mercy."[2, 3] That time had come.

The need to relocate was not an unwelcome idea. Over the years, the neighborhood around the convent had changed. The neighborhood now included some houses of prostitution and all the dynamics that such activities bring with it. Aware of that reality, the sisters thought it prudent to exchange their red sanctuary lamp for a clear one. The old caution of never traveling alone proved wise during this time. Once, as two younger sisters returned around midnight after chaperoning a school dance, they no sooner made it inside the house than a huge racket started outside. Alarmed by the noise, they went to call the police only to discover it was the police making all the noise. Entering the convent, they had literally passed by an escaped prisoner hiding in their bushes. Spotlights, dogs, and bullhorns were most effective in alerting them to how close they had come to danger. More than once, police officers would be called to the convent in response to an attempted burglary or persons seeking help after muggings.

By 1977, the diocese was anxious to sell the property and met with the Mercy community leadership. After finalizing the conditions and terms of the sale, a buyer was quickly found for the property. Mother Mary Teresita Durkin and her council had agreed in 1973 to accept 25 percent of the net sale price for the property along with being provided with a convent for the sisters in residence at St. Joseph's while teaching at Manogue. At the time of the sale, no convent was ready for the sisters. In the memorandum, it was noted that if the sisters had to leave St. Joseph's Convent on short notice, efforts would be made to temporarily relocate them in other Mercy convents around the city.

Short notice was exactly what happened. St. Joseph's Academy was a site with rich history, and fearful that it could be declared a historical landmark, diocesan leadership felt an urgency to have the buildings demolished at the earliest possible date. It was to be demolished in June 1978. Moving out of the convent at St. Joseph's was very challenging. The diocese set the earliest possible date for the sisters' exit from the convent, just a few days after classes closed for the year at Bishop Manogue.

With so little time available, the salvaging of valuable convent assets started while the sisters were still in residence. Every day, upon returning from school, the sisters looked to see what was gone this time. It could be anything, sometimes bookcases, sometimes special doors, even the chapel reredos.[4] It was like having one's home dismantled around you. Finally, all was complete and the convent abandoned. On the very night the sisters left, the convent was burglarized and anything that could be salvaged was taken.

Lacking a new convent, the community did its best to keep the Manogue sisters together. Eventually, St. Robert Convent was selected as a temporary housing option. All the Manogue sister faculty converged upon St. Robert convent resulting in very cramped quarters. Two sisters moved into make-do bedrooms, one a converted storage closet without windows, the other the house study/workroom. The diocese never provided the housing promised for the sisters. In hindsight, the rush seemed both unnecessary and ironic since nothing was ever built on the St. Joseph's site. Today, the former site of St. Joseph Academy is now a parking lot for jurors on duty at the County Courthouse. It is fittingly called the "St. Joseph's Jury Parking Lot."

Balancing the sadness of leaving the St. Joseph's property was the joy in a major hospital expansion at Mercy General. Mercy General had not upgraded its facility since the major expansion of 1954. Twenty years in hospital time spells "over-due." In response to that need, a $24 million long-range building project was initiated in 1978.[5] It is significant that the project was focused on medical services, not additional beds. It was part of Mercy's commitment to providing excellence in care. The new core building included a new X-ray department, intensive care unit, clinical lab, and central supply area. It also would provide much needed parking. Sister Mary Celestine Dyer put it succinctly: "Our objective is to provide a high level of care and professional excellence in an atmosphere of Christian compassion."[6] She went on to highlight the extent of the preplanning process noting that over 1,000 persons had been engaged in the planning process. Doctor William Tucker put it another way: "Today we are building more than a new core building, we are really building a new 'care' building."[7]

No building project avoids disruption and this project was no exception. In speaking of all the putting up and tearing down, the project manager C.C. Merrick said "What this adds up to is NOISE, DIRT, and DISRUPTION. While still allowing the work to proceed, each will be kept to a minimum."[8] That was easier said than done.

The hospital purchased various homes that adjoined the hospital property. The houses were demolished to make room for much needed parking. Even the fifty-year-old convent was not exempt. That too had to be torn down to make way for new buildings. The former home of Dr. and Mrs. Gandolph Prisinzano on 41st Street was purchased by the sisters to replace the convent. It was the reverse of the St. Joseph experience for the first four sisters moving into their new home. The new house was being renovated around them. All available spaces were used for makeshift bedrooms while a new wing was added on to the house.[9] In the process, some of the doors and the reredos from St. Joseph's were able to find a home at what would be called Mercy Convent, Sacramento.

By April 1981, all was completed. *The Sacramento Bee* commented on the new hospital addition, saying: "There is nothing homey about the environment of the addition: Its endless array of electronic equipment gives it a science-fiction feel."[10] Homey or not, the new facility allowed the hospital to pursue its goal of medical excellence.

A special aspect of the new addition was its name, the Sister Mary Peter Pavilion. For many Sacramentans, Sister Mary Peter Carew represented the face of healing and mercy. Before her retirement in 1968, she had spent forty years in hospital administration. Stories about her are legendary: stories about her praying for sufficient money to cover payroll and having the needed monies arrive just in time, stories about her way of challenging physicians and staff alike to be compassionate to those who were poor.

No task was too small or lowly for Sister Mary Peter. Sister Mary Virginia Sullivan, assigned to the hospital kitchen, fondly recalls being overloaded with peaches to peel for the evening meal. Sister Mary Peter passed through the kitchen and seeing her plight, stopped and joined her in the peeling. In Mary Virginia's memory, she was "Someone who connected with everyone, had a word for everyone."[11]

Naming the new building in Mary Peter's honor was a way of honoring the past at a time when healthcare was rapidly changing. Economies of scale, federal regulations, contractual demands, and rapid advances in new medical technology all converged to demand a more formalized, centralized approach to hospital affairs. The strong family ethos personified by Sister Mary Peter was cherished but had to be transformed to meet the realities of the time. Sister Kathleen Dunne summed what was at the heart of that transformation: "Mercy—Compassion—is the only reason for sponsoring health-care services such as we have here."[12] New ways of organizing had to be found so that high tech and high touch could stay together.

Changing realities called for new skills. By 1979, the sisters moved to adopt a more participative and collaborative form of decision-making, one that called for listening, consultation, animated dialogue, and consensus building. Community leadership engaged the Center for Planned Change from St. Louis to facilitate the process of learning such skills. It was a unique model. Four sisters were to be selected from the whole to serve as a "Renewal Team." They were to be as diverse as possible in age, backgrounds, personalities, and experience. The four entrusted with this task were Sisters Rosemarie Carvalho, Mary Carmel Donoghue, Mary Raymond Holzworth, and Hannah Mary O'Donoghue. Diverse they were. Sister Rosemarie suggests that the idea was: "If we can do this, anyone can do this."[13]

The "this" was an ongoing stance of listening, authentic sharing, mutual respect, and consensus building. Open discussions surfaced unvoiced conflicts in local communities, some rooted in differing visions of religious life, some just normal clashes of personalities. Three areas were identified in which the sisters needed greater skills: problem-solving, listening, and decision-making.[14] Sister Hannah Mary O'Donoghue, an original team member, feels a process for acquiring such skills was absolutely necessary. "We needed it basically because it provided an opportunity for us to communicate with each other. Prior to that we were not in the habit of discussing things with each other. It was all about communication."[15] Years of silence did not foster great communication skills.

For two years, the community engaged in what was called a "corporate reflection inventory" (C.R.I.) on every aspect of their lives. It was not easy.

Some sisters suggested that C.R.I. was about crying. Through the process, long buried hurts, disappointments. and resentments were allowed to surface and be set down. Sister Rosemarie reflects: "No matter how hard the process was, it brought the community a long way."[16]

The work of the renewal team laid the groundwork for one of the most important tasks of the sisters during this time, setting the future direction for mission and ministry. As the sisters convened for the chapter of 1982, they knew there were hard challenges to address. Needs had grown but members had decreased. There were not enough sisters to respond to the various requests for their presence. It was necessary to answer the core question: "Where are we called to serve today?" Sister Maura Power, the newly elected superior of the community, laid out the challenge in her opening address to the chapter body:

> When we, the Delegates, drew up our Mission Statement, did we realize what we said? I quote: "we recognize that we have been entrusted with authority to set a direction for the future in keeping with the vision and charism of Mercy. The Prophetic responsibility we bear urges us to revitalization of our Mercy mission to the Community, the Church, and the World." We have stated what our task is: let us go to it, being mindful that the decisions we make, and the direction we set will not affect only the next four years in the life of this Congregation but will lead to its re-founding and re-vitalization in the Church in the Sacramento diocese.[17]

Ministry took center stage in the discussions of the chapter. By the chapter's conclusion, the delegates had affirmed the direction hospital leaders had taken in bringing the community's hospitals together into a new structure; called for the establishment of a congregational foundation to support the work of all community ministries; directed that an in-depth study be undertaken of all apostolic works, especially education; voted to move forward with the closure of Mercy High School, Carmichael; provided for an initial study of a Mercy Association for laity; and committed the community to participation in the national movement to adopt a Core Constitution for all Mercy sisters.[18] These decisions were all the culmination of sharing, study, prayer and consultations that had occurred prior to the chapter. The delegates had acted on Sister Maura's admonition: "Let us go to it."

The chapter's call for a study of the community's apostolic works was immediately put into motion. Sister Kathleen Horgan, appointed to chair the Apostolic Study task force, led a three-year study utilizing surveys, data collecting, and interviews with significant civic, political, and activist leaders. With the assistance of Sister Marilee Howard, all the materials were collated and analyzed. Some findings were surprising to the sisters. Although the study found strong affirmation of the high esteem and respect the sisters had in the Sacramento community, a significant number of interviewees acknowledged knowing little about the sisters themselves, only about their presence in healthcare or education. The words "low profile" were frequently used. The comment was often partnered with a desire for the sisters to tell their story more effectively. In a nutshell, the sisters had a visibility problem.

The responses from the civic community surfaced challenges as well, particularly in regard to Sacramento's minority populations where their presence was seen as lacking. Interviewees like Pastor Royal Blue of the North Valley Baptist Church in Redding called for sisters to "always be for the people," while others like Ray T. Brophy, an influential statewide leader in education, worried about the danger of overextension.[19] LeRoy Chatfield, later director of Loaves and Fishes, asked the sisters to think about their impact on women:

> This is the age of women. The religious woman has the unique opportunity to be a healthy role model for other Christian women by her place in the church. This includes involvement in all aspects of church ministry.[20]

From a church perspective, Bishop William Levada, later made a cardinal, challenged the sisters to keep a balance between traditional and new ministry. Of particular importance to him was retreat work. He saw the role of sisters within the context of spiritual growth and outreach to those who were poor. Other voices raised multiple concerns. There were perceived needs for the elderly, the homeless, and those who were economically poor as well as a desire to have the sisters continue what they were doing. Among the sisters themselves, there was a sense of wanting clarity about where God was calling them at this moment in time. When you cannot do everything, what do you choose to do? Many people would be impacted by their decisions. The Apostolic Study determined that in 1982 alone, the sisters through their ministries impacted directly or indirectly 440,980 persons.[21]

By 1984, the sisters came together around the path they would take. Recognizing reduced numbers of sisters for leadership in schools and hospitals as well as new urgencies arising at the time, the sisters voted on February 13, 1984, to "expand their ministries through collaboration."[22] The expansion would not only touch the education and healthcare ministries, but would include expanding into new ministries. The summary report of the Apostolic Study states:

This decision was influenced by the affirmation of the Mission given by the laity and clergy, by the increasing needs as evidenced in the study of the environment, and by the Sisters' faith and desire to continue to serve.[23]

Committed to the path of collaboration, the sisters would now seek new opportunities to partner with others. It would no longer be what can we do but, rather, what can we do with others?

Throughout the three years of study, other developments were underway. The needs identified in the study stretched beyond classroom and hospital. Sister Kathleen Horgan shared: "What I remember is that at the time there was a sense that we should go out and serve the materially poor."[24] With limited financial resources, the sisters needed to find a way to support such ministries. That need was heightened by the realization that, in 1981, there was insufficient income to cover the operating costs of the community. Monies that might have been available for such ministries or for releasing a sister to work without compensation in ministries serving the poor were seriously diminished. Another way of funding such efforts had to be found.

In January 1981, Corarelli Associates, a consultant group working with the sisters, was asked to explore the feasibility of establishing a congregational foundation. The purpose of the foundation would be three-fold: (1) to support, maintain and develop the services and programs consistent with the sisters' mission of service to the poor, sick and uneducated; (2) to respond to the needs of local communities served by the sisters, thereby widening the base of partners sharing the works of mercy; and (3) to develop resources required for sustaining the mission in healthcare, education and social services.[25]

This would be a change for the sisters. Since 1954, the hospitals had relied on the efforts of Mercy Foundation, but that was limited to raising monies for the hospitals. What was now being envisioned was a foundation that would serve all ministries. Jack Diepenbrock, community legal advisor at the time, sees this as a decision of high significance. The increasing pressures from healthcare systems meant that hospital foundations were expected to focus intensively on healthcare need alone. Mercy Foundation, as a congregational foundation, would be protected from such future pressures and thereby provide more comprehensive funding for all the works of mercy.[26]

In the meanwhile, the sisters initiated a Sisters of Mercy Development Fund and appointed Sister Bridget Mary Flynn to be its director. Sister Bridget Mary had a great passion for the undertaking. Having been principal at Mercy High School, she knew first-hand how essential philanthropy was in sustaining the works of the sisters. She worked tirelessly tapping into the wisdom of an advisory board of civic leaders, donors and partners. With minimal staff, Sister Bridget Mary managed in her first year to build a program, obtained over $11,000 in donations, and worked up plans for a marquee event that would be not only a fundraiser, but an awareness-raiser for the sisters.

Sister Bridget Mary and her committee thought big, setting a goal of raising $10 million in five years. There was discussion of hosting a city-wide gala event featuring Pavorotti or another headliner of similar stature. No such event came to pass. While Sister Bridget Mary was enthusiastic about her task, she made clear to community leadership that she would only make a three-year commitment to the task before returning to education. She strongly encouraged the congregational leadership team to pursue exploring the option of transitioning the hospital foundation to a congregational foundation.

By March 1981, the general council called for a study committee to be formed involving representatives from the board of governors of Mercy Hospital Foundation as well as representatives from the Auburn, Folsom, Redding, and Roseville areas. Getting hospital foundations' buy-in was critical because the change would expand their fundraising focus and make them directly accountable to the sisters, not to hospital leadership. It called for re-visioning and reimaging. By February 1982, the study, chaired by Oleta Lambert, was underway. It had to deal with such thorny issues as structure, local identity, broadening the base of financial support, staffing, and timeline.

A key concern was how to determine the priorities of need when it came to capital expenses. Larry Garcia, a Mercy Foundation Board member, reflects that there was always a struggle to balance priorities for funding. Expenses for the foundation were paid by the healthcare system which expected primary focus to be on the needs of the hospitals. Other ministries focusing on directly responding to peoples' basic needs provided board members with compelling cases for funding. It was hard to prioritize where funds should be allotted.[27]

The transition was not a rapid one. Each issue had to be examined in the light of goals and broader implications. By March 1984, the sisters were ready to appoint the first chairperson of the foundation as well as its first board of directors. Shaping the new undertaking would be: Steve Thomas, Chairperson, Russ Baldo, Bill Beaty, Sandra Cook, Jack Diepenbrock, Harry Gashoff, Oleta Lambert, and Bill Schopfer. Sister Kathleen Dunne, Sister Mary Celestine Dyer, Sister Bridget Mary Flynn, and Sister Maura Power comprised the sister board members. Mr. William Schopfer was appointed the new system's first executive director.

The future that was to come would exceed the imaginings of the sisters who labored to make the change a reality. The foundation was not just about fundraising. It was also about mission and relationships. Over time it would be a magnet for those looking to make a difference. Mike Genovese, a long-time foundation board member, captured his experience of working with the sisters in this way:

> Watching the sisters in their steadfast commitment is such a great example for everyone in this Sacramento community ... the selfless example of what they do from Cristo Rey High School, the Spanos Center at Mercy Hospital or Sister Libby Fernandez and her work with the homeless. It all has a meaningful and immediate impact.[28]

Throughout the 1980s, plans for ministry were examined through the lens of "What can we do better together?" Healthcare was the first ministry that came under review. Re-organizing had already begun in 1965 when the sisters appointed Charles W. Steding to direct all operations of the Mercy hospitals. Changes in healthcare brought about by federal programs like Medicare, as well as the demands of technology, had combined to create an environment in which the stand-alone hospital was at a disadvantage.

The impact of Medicare upon Catholic healthcare nationally cannot be underestimated. By paying hospital costs for those who earlier were given free care, Medicare dramatically increased hospital's profit margins. Some would say that, "as a result, the voluntary sector of the health care system increasingly came under question—and often under attack—for the economic benefit it derived from the altered health care market."[29] The notion of charity was clouded, and religious communities struggled to reconcile their mission-driven ministries with marketplace reality.

A second factor experienced throughout Catholic healthcare was the changing face of leadership. In 1965, only 3 percent of hospital administrators were laity. By 1985, that percentage had grown to 70 percent.[30] How would the mission and charism of the community be handed on to the new generations of lay Mercy leaders?

Reading the signs of the time, religious communities looked at how they could better organize to maintain the healing ministry of Christ with better structures and fiscal practices while maintaining a vibrant sense of mission and charism. In September 1980, prior to the Apostolic Study, the sisters initiated an in-depth study of their healthcare ministry. The study was prompted by a desire to expand the process of renewal and adaptation from the life of the community to institutions and works sponsored by the sisters. The result of the study was the establishment of Mercy Health Care Organization (MHCO).

Sister Maura Power attributes the success of the transition to the work and vision of Sister Eileen Barrett, the president and executive officer of

MHCO, and Jack Diepenbrock, the congregational legal advisor. In her opinion, both were instrumental in bringing about the change.[31] Speaking at the congregational chapter on July 5, 1982, Sister Eileen identified the factors which led the sisters to establish MHCO. She identified it as a response to the church's call to renew ministries as well as religious life. It addressed a concern about the ability of the sisters to experience and influence the institutions as tangible expressions of the mission.

Sisters questioned the emerging "big business" character of healthcare. They worried about the demands placed upon community leaders due to the increased complexity of the apostolate and were distrustful of the increasing government regulations and enhanced competition. For them, there were risks arising from becoming "too big."[32] Those were formidable concerns. What Sister Eileen asked of the chapter was approval to move forward with the vision and structures proposed for the new healthcare system. The chapter responded by approving the mission statement, purposes, goals, and values of the organization by a unanimous vote.

Change can bring in its wake fears, lessening of trust, and a sense of loss as well as excitement and expectation. The amount of change experienced by the sisters during these years was huge, yet they found the courage and boldness to continue reshaping their future. Trust in the guidance of the Holy Spirit, confidence in each other, and reliance upon lay partners to help them read the signs of the times fed that boldness. The sisters in Sacramento were not alone in their efforts to restructure their ministries. Increased conversations among the various Mercy communities across the country led the sisters to join with the Sisters of Mercy in Burlingame to explore what might be best for their California healthcare ministries.

Like the sisters in Sacramento, the community in Burlingame had created a system for their five hospitals and care center. Sister Terese Marie Perry, president of the Burlingame community, was convinced that there should not be two Mercy health care systems in California. Sister Maura Power remembers that their conversations were part of a national trend; in fact, in 1979, the Omaha Mercy community, part of the Union of the Sisters of Mercy of the Americas, had incorporated their eighteen medical facilities into one system. St. Elizabeth's Hospital in Red Bluff was part of that system.

The conversations between the Auburn and Burlingame sisters as well as with the leaders of their respective healthcare systems began in 1983. Shared history, common values and mission, and investment in the healing work of mercy joined the two communities in a common purpose. In March 1986, Larry Garcia presented to the leadership of both communities a range of options for coming together. Larry remembers: "They rushed to the option of total merger. That was a really bold step."[33]

Sister Terese Marie attributes the idea to Sister Mary Michael Murphy, who spontaneously declared: "Oh for heaven's sake, let's just merge!"[34] So it was. Larry commented that much still had to be worked out, however.

Two difficult decisions facing the group were where to locate the office of a shared system and whether the new system would be open to other religious communities that wished to join. While Sister Terese Marie favored an exclusively Mercy system, Doug Bruce, president of MHCO, advocated for a co-sponsored system. Ultimately, it was decided that the new system would welcome other religious communities. The name selected grew out of that decision. It was to be called Catholic Healthcare West (CHW).

Talks continued for three years, addressing all the necessary legal and organizational issues. Finally, in March 1986, the two communities signed a letter of intent to merge their two not-for-profit health care systems, forming the largest California-based Catholic health system. It would include nine hospitals with more than 3,000 acute care beds; four skilled nursing facilities; an extended care facility; two residences for the elderly; and a wide variety of ambulatory, diagnostic and treatment centers.[35]

What remained was determining where it would have its administrative center. That decision was left to last and resolved itself when, honoring the historical roots of Mercy in California, Sister Maura Power suggested that San Francisco become the administrative center for the new system.[36] It would now be the responsibility of CHW and its sponsoring religious congregations to pass on the values and legacy of Mercy healthcare to subsequent leaders.

Not all the undertakings flowing from the decision to expand through collaboration worked as well as those in the health care field. In particular, efforts in education proved challenging. As early as 1974, there were signs that the community was running low on sister principals. Sister Eileen Enright remembers Mother Teresita Durkin telling her that if she did not accept the principalship of St. Joseph Elementary School, Auburn, the sisters would have to give up the school.[37] At the time, Sister Eileen had neither administrative experience nor administrative training. What she did have was a natural gift for educational leadership. Such was the case for others during these years. The community recognized the problem of decreasing numbers of sisters trained for educational leadership. Though stretched too thin, it was most reluctant to relinquish leadership in schools they had come to feel were "Mercy Schools." Longtime relationships were involved as well as rich history.

Sister Kathleen Horgan, chair of the apostolic study, noted: "The strategy for the future is to share the Mercy philosophy with others—laity, clergy, or other religious—who then become partners with the sisters in their services to the needy."[38] Knowing that the numbers of available sisters for administration was continuing to decrease, the sisters developed a model of collaboration through which parochial or diocesan schools could partner with the sisters once a lay principal was put in place. To accomplish the goal, a Mercy education and parish ministries system was set up. Member ministries would be formed in the mission and philosophy of the community and be able to tap into needed services such as mentoring and coordinating or other needed assistance. A key element was the oversight that the schools would be provided through the Mercy coordinator of education.[39]

It was a great model for serving schools that were sponsored by the community, but there was one huge difficulty. There was a distinct difference between a sponsored school *v.* one that was staffed by Mercy sisters. In the former, the community holds responsibility for the school's philosophy, mission, fiscal well-being, and direction. In a staffed school, such areas are under the direction of the diocese, though influenced by the sisters. None of the schools currently staffed by the sisters was community sponsored. All were diocesan or parochial schools where authority rested with the pastor and diocesan school department. The sisters could suggest but had no power to require anything.

The model was first implemented at St. Rose, Roseville, and proved successful for some years, but it was the only success. From the perspective of time, it is evident that the sisters struggled with the reality of having to withdraw from cherished ministries. This model tried to keep a linkage to those traditional parishes, but it came at a time when pastors still had the last say about their schools. New principals sometimes lacked a strong bond with the Mercy heritage, and some saw the system itself as "in competition" with the diocesan school department.[40]

The story of two schools vividly paints a picture of the challenges and the disappointments faced by the sisters. The first school, Holy Cross, West Sacramento, had been opened by the parish in the 1960s. The parish was both culturally rich and economically impoverished. Voluntarily, the Sisters of Mercy had subsidized the school through waiving or reducing the religious stipend for sisters. Sister Rosemarie Carvalho remembers that families were often so poor, they bartered in exchange for tuition. When she began at Holy Cross, there were only ninety-seven students. Experiencing the struggle first-hand, the Sisters of Mercy recommended that the school be closed and transformed into an early education center. The answer was no. When the community could no longer supply a sister principal to serve at Holy Cross, the sisters put in place a "service" model to assist the school.[41]

For the next ten years, Holy Cross School continued with a lay principal. The school was heavily subsidized by the diocese, something that happened only on a limited basis during the Mercy community's administrative tenure. Sisters Mary Dolores Wagner and Mary O'Meara, devoted to Holy Cross families, remained on staff. Sister Mary Dolores comments that she thoroughly enjoyed working with the first lay principal, Dominic Puglisi.[42] After the gap of ten years, Holy Cross once again had a Mercy principal when Sister Jane Golden assumed that responsibility in 1999. Ultimately though, economics won out and the school was closed by 2010.

A second painful episode was the closure of Bishop Manogue High School. Sister Eileen Enright remembers that in 1989, Christian Brothers High School had reached a crisis. School administrators wished to relocate the school to Natomas in hopes that the new location would stem a trend of decreasing school enrollment. At the same time, Bishop Manogue High School was experiencing a gradual decrease in enrollment. The contributing factors for Bishop Manogue's situation were easily identifiable.

The school was highly ethnically mixed. Over 51 percent of the students were from black, Mexican, Mexican-American, and southeast Asian families. It was not an academically elite school in that it did not limit itself to exclusively providing a top-level academic track. It also provided special support for students struggling with English proficiency or who had transferred in from schools which failed to supply adequate educational support. Some parents could not see how both realities could exist in the same school. A pattern of "white flight" set in for some families. As early as 1981, a parent shared with the then principal: "We are not going to send our younger daughter to you, Sister. There are too many of those people in the school."[43] While aware of the reality of "white flight," the school department chose not to act on establishing boundaries to ensure more economically and ethnically diverse student populations in both St. Francis and Bishop Manogue High Schools.

A second factor leading to a decrease in enrollment was the increased emphasis on women's athletics brought about by implementation of Title 9, which significantly enhanced women's sports programming. Manogue was not built with girls' sports in mind. It had no regulation outdoor playing fields, no swimming pool, only a really good volleyball/basketball court. It was not a recipe for ongoing success.

By diocesan decision, Bishop Manogue High School was closed in June 1990. Students were given the opportunity to enroll at the now co-educational Christian Brothers, or at St. Francis. Manogue and Christian Brothers may have come together but it was not a merger. There was no plan for shared governance or shared charism. Perhaps even more telling was the retention of the Christian Brothers' name. For all purposes, Mercy secondary education had come to an end in Sacramento, at least for a time.

Embracing a New Identity, Starting New Initiatives

While deeply immersed in reorganizing and re-visioning their ministries, the Sisters of Mercy were thrust into new relationships, new opportunities, and new structures when they became a founding community of the Sisters of Mercy of the Americas in 1991. This was not a sudden decision. Sisters of Mercy had traditionally remained separate foundations. Catherine McAuley had initiated that custom. As soon as a community could be self-sustaining, it would become autonomous. It remained that way until 1929 when the Union of the Sisters of Mercy was formed. The Union presented a new model for coming together, one which gathered diverse groups from all over the country and wove them into a single unit. At the time, the Sisters of Mercy in Sacramento were adamantly in favor of independence. Now, seventy years later, the question was once more before them.

The impetus for unifying had two main roots—shared charism and revitalization of the mission. In 1981, Sisters of Mercy worldwide had joined together in celebrating the 150th anniversary of the founding of the order. The celebration ignited Catherine McAuley studies, formed new connections among the various Mercy communities, and sowed seeds for future conversations around becoming one. The Sisters of Mercy throughout the world also shared a common task. As a result of Vatican II, all Mercy communities were asked to revise their rule and constitutions in the light of contemporary understandings of religious life and the realities of today's world. Once more, the question emerged, "Can we do this better together?"

In the United States, Sister Helen Amos of Baltimore suggested that the task of revising the Constitutions be a shared one. The vehicle for this project was Mercy Federation, a loose association of Mercy Congregations which had been gathering together since 1965. After the Federation meeting in 1980, Sister Helen and a group of twenty sisters set themselves to the task of writing a Core Constitution that could be accepted by all the eighteen autonomous Mercy congregations of the U.S. It was a formidable task. Initially, the group focused on just thirty paragraphs, which captured common values, charism, and vision. Anything that was unique or a legal piece was left to the various communities to supply. By June 1981, it was ready. Now it was time for distribution.

The Auburn Sisters of Mercy did not participate directly in this process. Instead, throughout the early stages, they were represented by Sister Mary Celeste Rouleau of Burlingame. While interested in the process, the Auburn sisters felt no urgency or pressing need to actively engage in the constitutions project since the revision of their own Constitutions was well underway. While the general council sent a letter to Rome in August, 1981 saying that we were involved in the process, it noted that it would be up to the 1982 chapter to make the final decision.[1] That timeline was overly optimistic for their final decision was not made until 1986.

The official introduction of the Core Constitutions to the Mercy communities was a celebrative one. Over 1,800 sisters from the various Mercy congregations came to Pittsburgh for the U.S. celebration of the order's 150th anniversary. After an explanatory presentation by Sister Helen Amos, the sisters stood and received the Core Constitutions from one of the eighteen superiors of the U.S. Mercy congregations. It was a memorable moment for Sister Doris Gottemoeller, RSM, who reflects: "The symbolism was powerful ... Receiving one's Core Constitution from any one of the superiors signaled that, at some deep level, we were already one."[2]

The Core Constitutions effort was not the only project underway. Since its inception, the projects and undertakings of the federation had grown and its structure was no longer suited to meet the need. Just as work on the Core Constitutions started, the Federation appointed a task force to examine "alternative structures" for the Federation itself.[3] By September 1981, a Mercy Futures task force was formed to explore how the congregations could be united under a common governance structure. It not only had to imagine a new governing structure, it also had to find a way to have 7,000 Sisters of Mercy support such a change. Among those 7,000 sisters were the 120 sisters of the Auburn community.

The two processes—the Core Constitutions and Mercy Futures—moved along side by side. What is less documented was the inner journey that Sisters of Mercy in Sacramento had to make, going from the familiarity of a small, intimate group of sisters with a strong common focus to a large, international, and diverse congregation. A full spectrum of emotions arose:

fear, anger, resistance, delight, uncertainty, grief, and excitement. Sister Susan McCarthy, community president at the time, reflects that there was "resistance and trepidation and lots of unknowns that we had to live into. We were quite independent in those days."[4]

What might initially have been seen as a three-or-four-year process turned into a decade-long journey to unity. Along the way, there were multiple consultations with members, dialogues with Church leaders, planning groups, updates, and rituals. In order to foster personal relationships, vacation houses from the eighteen communities would now be open to any member of the whole. A group of artists and writers were asked to design a ritual called the "Grand Right and Left," an event during which art pieces representing all the eighteen communities would move around the country. Each community contributed an artistic rendering to the collection and selected one to keep as a symbol of their interweaving. At the time, Auburn had not been greatly engaged in the process.

When word came that the "Dance" was arriving soon, Sister Eileen Mary O'Connor was asked to create Auburn's contribution. Reflecting back on that experience, Sister Eileen Mary shares that, "A quotation of Catherine McAuley came to me, the one about 'God can bend and change, form and reform any of His creatures to fit them for the purposes He designs."[5] Sister Eileen Mary was teaching pottery at the time and had a collection of photographs tracing the stages of creating a vessel. Blending her photography with Catherine's quotation, she created Auburn's contribution to the ritual. The sisters in Auburn selected from the collection a handmade quilt made by the Cedar Rapids sisters. It hangs in the chapel narthex in Auburn as a silent testament to being one in Mercy. Sister Eileen shares that: "Ever since that time when I meet a Cedar Rapids sister I always say: 'We have your quilt!' I always think about them when I pass by."[6]

A major step forward in the process of becoming an institute was taken by the Auburn sisters on June 27, 1986, when their chapter adopted the Core Constitutions as their official constitutions. The sisters also chose to participate in Mercy Futures. The resistance and trepidation earlier identified by Sister Susan had not totally disappeared, but the sisters were ready to go together into the unknown. Still, it would take another five years. This time, the delay was not on the part of the sisters. It was on the part of Vatican authorities who wanted to be absolutely sure that the rights of each individual sister were honored.

Every one of the 7,000 Mercy Sisters needed to either give or withhold her support for coming together as one. When a straw vote had been taken in 1985, the vote was 5,683 in support, 1,714 opposed. The church would not proceed until the exact steps were outlined concerning the futures of those who did not wish to join the new institute.[7] As the process moved along, church authorities called for a three-step process of approving the new institute. First there would be a straw vote, then a chapter vote, and finally each sister would be asked to affirm her support and willingness to be part of the institute. Sister Maura Power once described the Sisters of Mercy of Auburn as "a very cohesive group, geographically close with a strong local identity."[8] The cohesive nature of the community nurtured a sense of being in this process together. It also helped to overcome the anxieties about losing their local identity and bonds of relationship. Delegates to the special chapter of 1988 voted unanimously to join the Institute. Now they only had to wait to see if all the other groups would do the same.

The desire for all to be one was palpable throughout the community. No one wanted to leave anyone behind or to experience a rending of relationships. Prayers were ardently lifted up as each chapter met and as the day came when sisters would have to indicate their personal assent. To say no would result in leaving the community or transferring to a different one. No one wanted their friend or sister to do that. While rejoicing that all Auburn sisters elected to join the new Institute, everyone shared the grief of the Portland, Maine, sisters when a small group withdrew and formed a new diocesan community. There was great relief when the Mercies in Merion, Philadelphia, and those in Plainfield, New Jersey, ultimately voted to move forward.

In anticipation of approval by Rome, a transition administrative group (TAG) was formed. Their job was to prepare for the founding event and the first Institute chapter. The next months were spent shaping and reshaping the way in which all this would be done. There were a visioning process, inter-congregational meetings, and new interest group networks being formed. Excitement was growing as the Founding Event on July 20, 1991, approached. At the 1990 chapter in Auburn, five delegates and two alternates to the first Institute chapter were elected. They were joined by ten additional sisters. Special T-shirts were made identifying them as Auburn Mercies. Plans were made for everyone at home to join the event in spirit.

The day finally arrived. Sister Sheila Browne relates:

> I still get chills when I think of Buffalo. I'll never forget the feeling of the doors opening and 3000 sisters pouring into the space, Sister Amy Hoey proclaiming, "We are sisters of mercy" and signing the document. There was such hope because we were part of a bigger group with opportunity for common voice and more resources. It was a moment that will be in my brain forever.[9]

Sister Susan McCarthy has similar memories. "I remember the opening of the doors, the level of excitement which was enough to blow the roof off … I remember the proclamation of the Founding Document, etched in my memory." Never would the words be forgotten:

> We are Sisters of Mercy,
>
> We gather this day, knowing that our bonds are rooted in God, and that we strengthen and enable one another for mission.
>
> We remember our heritage, the many gifts of life we have received from God, through Jesus, Catherine and the women of Mercy who have gone before us
>
> We believe that the life of our community is a vibrant sign of the gospel; we believe that the presence of the church is made visible in this world through our service to the poor, sick and ignorant.
>
> We women of faith, remember our heritage and celebrate our community.
>
> We, women of Mercy, have discovered a new relationship among us, and we pray that the bonds we formalize today will endure, will enliven us, and will serve our church and touch our world. We affirm this moment; we proclaim this reality; and we found this Institute of the Sisters of Mercy of the Americas on this 20th day of July, 1991. In witness whereto, we sign our names.[10]

For Susan, "becoming Institute was great!"[11] What was left was to live into the new reality and a new name. The Sisters of Mercy of Auburn would now be called the Auburn regional community of the Sisters of Mercy of the Americas. There would be another change as well. The Sisters of Mercy in Auburn has always used the initials "S. M." to identify their congregation. Going forward, they would join with other Mercy communities is using RSM.

One of the concerns that surfaced during the formation of the Institute was that of forming relationships. How would 7,000 sisters get to know one another? Decisions would now be made by sisters you did not really know. Sister Susan McCarthy puts it this way: "The reality was that decisions were no longer made locally. That was a huge change for us and the sisters felt once removed from leadership."[12] Changing that reality meant building relationships.

Even before its beginnings in 1991, leaders looked for ways to bring sisters together. Mercy Communicators met together before the founding event in Buffalo. Sister Anna Marie Sliman, Auburn's communicator, represented the sisters. Telling the story was vital and the focus of the meeting was how to share the experience and message of the first chapter.

It would take excellent communication to bond the groups together. One topic addressed by the communicators was Mercy Image. This latter project aimed at presenting to the public the face of the Sisters of Mercy today. Sister Rita Irene Esparza was among the six sisters selected to image the Institute and draw attention to its works. With message and image identified, the process of forming a unified identity began.

To accomplish the purpose for which the Institute was founded depended on building trust, confidence, and shared vision. That vision was made clear in the direction statement adopted by the first Institute chapter:

> Animated by the Gospel and Catherine McAuley's passion for the poor, we, the Sisters of Mercy of the Americas, are impelled to commit our lives and resources to act in solidarity with:
> the economically poor of the world, especially women and children;
> women seeking fullness of life and equality in church and society; and
> one another as we embrace our multicultural and international reality.
> This commitment will impel us to
> develop and act from a multicultural and international perspective;
> speak with a corporate voice;
> work for systemic change;
> practice nonviolence;
> act in harmony and interdependence with all creation; and
> call ourselves to continual conversion in our lifestyle and ministries. [13, 14]

No time was lost in organizing to confront the justice issues identified in the direction statement. By March 1992, the Institute leadership team proposed an Institute justice structure that would be led by five full-time area justice coordinators. The western justice area was comprised of the Auburn, Burlingame, and Omaha communities.[15] Nineteen Auburn sisters attended its first conference. Among the topics explored were strategies for addressing specific justice issues, getting to understand more about our sisters in the Pacific and Latin American/Caribbean areas, identification of an area project in which all would take part, and listening to the stories of those who had been touched by our ministries.

Advocacy was identified as a key area where coming together as one could give new power to voice. Corporate stances such as the one's taken by the sisters prior to becoming Institute would be now have a national and international voice. Catholic Healthcare West already had adopted a policy of socially responsible investing. That meant that no monies would be invested in companies whose policies violated social justice teachings or which harmed those who were poor. This practice grew as Mercy communities and healthcare systems joined their monies together through Mercy Investment Services. Shareholder resolutions became a new vehicle through which sisters could influence social practices. Another avenue for advocacy was found in the office of Mercy Global Concerns, which holds non-governmental organization (NGO) status at the United Nations. Here, Mercy could bring the voice of the voiceless to the global arena.

While the justice team worked to keep sisters informed about the justice issues of the day, the Auburn regional community worked to develop ministries that addressed those issues and focused on the underserved. Wishing to do maximum good with the means they had available, the sisters used their monies to establish a Fund for the Poor. Instead of giving food or money to those who knocked on the convent door, they gave monthly funds to groups like the Salvation Army so that such charity would be maximized. Monies were also given to the diocesan social concerns office as well as Cathedral parish's outreach to the downtown poor.[16]

Providing food and basic necessities through Loaves and Fishes was an on-going commitment of the Sisters of Mercy. The origin of Loaves and Fishes rests with Chris and Dan Delany. They moved to Sacramento in 1983 at a time when there was a growing need to feed the hungry. The Delanys responded to that need. The website of Loaves and Fishes puts it this way:

> What started as a simple midday meal for Loaves and Fishes in 1983 grew to include breakfast, showers, laundry, a school for homeless children, mental health counseling, legal advice, on-site resources from community partners, and much more.[17]

From its beginnings, the Sisters of Mercy along with other faith-based communities in Sacramento, joined them in that effort. The first step was to commit to a "Mercy Day" for feeding the hungry. Once a month, sisters would join with their benefactors and coworkers in providing the midday meal at the Loaves and Fishes dining room. Mercy chili casserole was the specialty of the day. Soon, junior high students from schools taught by the sisters joined in the work.

Hands-on-engagement with those who are in need leads to identifying other needs. That was what happened. After serving at the dining room for a period time, Sister Laura Ann Walton recognized that a significant number of women and children were among the hungry. That led to the opening of Maryhouse, a daytime shelter for women and children. The absence of access to healthcare was also identified and soon Mercy Hospital partnered with Sacramento County to open a free clinic for the impoverished. Among those ministering at the clinic were Sisters Joan O'Connor, Mary Glenda Shaw, and Mercy Associate Suzi Ettin.

As services expanded, the need for staff did as well. Mercy Volunteer Corps, sponsored by the Sisters of Mercy, began to supply staff for the ministry. The Corps was established in Sacramento in the mid-1990s. The volunteers are usually young adults, live in a community, share resources, and pray together. Captured by the passion to be of service to those in need, the volunteers give themselves in direct service to the economically disadvantaged, receiving only a small living stipend for their work.

Sister Libby Fernandez, known throughout Sacramento for her advocacy for the homeless, first came to Loaves and Fishes as a social worker, working at Genesis, a counselling program for the chronically homeless. When speaking of her experience Sister Libby, who became executive director of Loaves and Fishes in 2006, says:

> I was drawn by the works of Mercy with the homeless. Loaves and Fishes was an experience of this. I was inspired by the direct services of sisters and mercy associates at Loaves and Fishes. Our ministries become involved in all this. We are a major support group for the ministry. We are one of the first five groups: Catholic workers, Sisters of Mercy, Holy Spirit Parish, St. Vincent de Paul and Poverty Resistance. Sister Laura Ann was instrumental in linking the sisters to the ministry and developing what it was about. Mercy Clinic came in 1985; Maryhouse 1986; Genesis 2006, Mercy Foundation came on as a support in 1985 and continues its support today.[18]

Women's Wisdom Project was another example of the new ministries taken on by the sisters. Its purpose was to use the Arts as a tool for transformation and healing, aiding women in cycling out of poverty and despair.[19] Mercy Associate Dorothy Smith points out that Sister Laura Ann had the vision of something beyond the first step:

> Laura Ann said years ago, people get to the point where they take the next step. She wanted to provide a safe place to heal through the creative arts so they would be empowered enough to ask for what they needed for that next step.[20]

Working with women who were recently homeless, sometimes abused or addicted, most with very low self-esteem, staff and volunteers helped each participant to find the beauty within herself and express that beauty through painting, pottery or poetry. A studio was rented and provided all the needed materials for creative process, a child-care area, plus a gallery where art was displayed and sold. Support for the women was sometimes just a matter of presence. Dorothy Smith remembers vividly the impact it made upon her when Sister Mary Mercy Longwich, then aged, took the city bus to the project's art show just to support the women's efforts.[21]

The women's growth in confidence and self-esteem led many to seek better employment as well as improved living conditions. The program supported this by providing a skills enhancement and life planning component. So successful was the transformative process offered through Women's Wisdom that it received an award for its visionary work from the Social Work Honor Society of California State University, Sacramento.[22] Within its first two years of operation, over $10,000 worth of art was sold at Women's Wisdom events. After a number of years of independent operation, the Women's Wisdom project was absorbed into the Sacramento Food Bank.

It was not only the homeless who needed food, support, and opportunity to create new lives. There were also refugee families, many of which settled in the West Sacramento area. Sister Cora Salazar, ESL teacher and immigrant herself, was recruited by the Washington Unified School District to teach in an educational program serving forty adults of Southeast Asia origin. Out of this experience, "families in self help" (FISH) was born. A federal grant allowed her to set up a community-based literacy program that operated out of an apartment in a public housing complex. Sr. Cora estimates that 1,000 Asian refugees lived there.[23]

The program soon grew beyond literacy to include sewing classes and community gardens. A skill-based curriculum became the heart of the program, assisting students to hone culinary and sewing skills they already possessed. That led to the next step which was the development of a "cottage industry" where clothing could be made and sold. Participants were successful in winning contracts with the school district for farm produce and school uniforms. Business skills and self-sufficiency were the end product. Julie Hoskins, a bi-lingual specialist with the district describes it this way: "She's [Sister Cora] providing them the forum and they've grabbed on and run with it."[24] Cyndi Thompson is even more expressive: "[Sister Cora] has such energy and commitment and it's contagious. She is the lifeblood of West Sacramento's concern for Southeast Asian refugees and has been an inspiration to me."[25]

Reaching out to new areas of need and efforts to address issues of social justice was not limited to starting new ministries. With the founding of the Institute, the Auburn regional community became part of a congregation that spanned eleven countries and one territory, many of whose people suffered extreme poverty. Individual sisters, responding to the direction statement, sought to deepen their understanding of global poverty while providing direct service to those who were trapped in situations of dire need.

As early as 1968, the community encouraged sisters to think about serving in South America. During pre-Institute years Sister Michelle Gorman had participated in the "global awareness through education" (GATE) program in Mexico City and subsequently joined with Sister Maria Campos and Laurie Eckhert in volunteering with the Burlingame sisters in Tijuana.

Sister Maria Campos was one of the first to embrace the call to serve in South America. She was invited to work with the Mercy foundation in Peru. Her initial experience was not promising. Sister Maria tells it this way:

> I wanted to serve the poorest of the poor. It was a really volatile time, during the time of the Shining Path. Within my first three days in Lima, we were arrested. Five young people had committed vandalism and were killed but one escaped. That one was a woman and they took the sisters at gunpoint. I thought "they can't kill us we are Americans but what about the others?" The guard tore the papers out of my hands but when I could I continued. They told us never to travel without our original permission to travel. We agreed to everything and, after four hours, they let us out. I was there about three or four months during which Bishop Romero was assassinated.[26]

After four months, Sister Maria returned to the United States but returned a few years later to serve in Peru's Altiplano with Sister Rosemarie Carvalho.

Peru was not the only one of the Institute's international foundations to have Auburn sisters serve within them. For Sister Anne Chester, her experience began in Jamaica with participation in "Bridging the Gap," an immersion study designed and directed by Sister Teresa Lowe Ching, RSM. After completing the program, she went on to help in Plaisance, Guyana, at St. John Bosco Boys' Home. While there, she not only worked in the school but went with sisters to Mahica Leprosarium, assisted in the library of St. Joseph Hospital in Georgetown and helped with planning the 100th anniversary of the sisters' arrival in Guyana. It became very plain that sisters were called upon to do a plethora of activities. Returning home by way of Jamaica, Sister Anne was asked to consider serving as interim principal at Mount St. Joseph Preparatory School in Mandeville, Jamaica.

Serving in Jamaica also meant doing a little of everything. At St. John Bosco school in Mandeville, an elementary and trade school, she even organized a training manual for butchering. Sister Anne shares that her time in Jamaica was very impactful:

> I had not experienced the stark contrast between rich and poor as deeply as in Jamaica. Though Guyana was poor, it did not have the 'mansions built next to shacks' that was so much part of the Jamaican town.[27]

Like Sister Maria Campos in Peru, she had to become accustomed to seeing soldiers patrolling streets and guarding malls due to political violence. Such things did not deter her returning to Jamaica a second time to assist as coordinator of mission integration in Mercy schools. Later Sister Frances Walshe took up the challenge of a foreign mission when she answered a call to minister in Uganda. For over ten years, Sister Frances, trained in counseling, has responded to Uganda's need for counsellors to work with trauma victims.

While most sisters were not able to devote themselves to missionary service outside the United States, all were called to be involved in serving those who were poor here or abroad. One could work at refugee camps in Campeche, Mexico, or support the women's co-op by marketing their goods like Sister Maria Campos. Others could work with farm worker families in the migrant camps, like Sister Maria Padilla. Every sister was encouraged to walk with those who were economically poor.

Commitment to those who were poor did not demand youth. Five of Auburn's elder sisters—Sisters Mary Mercy Longwich, Margaret Helena Mullin, Mary Camillus Murphy, Mary Christopher Brannigan, and Mary Eileen Brannigan—provided vivid examples of what could be done. Long before Loaves and Fishes was established, Sister Mary Mercy boiled dozens of hard-boiled eggs weekly and drafted other sisters to assist her in making sandwiches for Sacramento's homeless community. The sandwiches would then be taken by Sister Mary Mercy to those who were homeless.

Sisters Mary Christopher and Eileen set up their own little cottage industry, crafting all sorts of knitted goods and baked goods that were sold to raise monies for Mercy's Fund for the Poor. Sisters Margaret Helena and Mary Camillus, both in their nineties, responded to a plea for help from Mrs. Joan Haan, a Mercy associate and former vice principal of Bishop Manogue, then working in Kenya. Flooding had destroyed the village's Catholic school and funds were needed to rebuild. Together, the two sisters knitted and crafted enough goods for a sale and raffle. The goods, together with their persuasive way of selling raffle tickets, resulted in providing sufficient funding to rebuild the destroyed school.

In spite of staffing fewer schools, the sisters' passion for education never wavered. In the Mercy tradition, education had always been the doorway to dignity of life. People denied education through poverty or oppression were denied the means of achieving their full potential. That was an injustice. Young people raised in environments of serious poverty were often forced to attend schools lacking adequate resources. They were, in fact, educationally deprived. Other students who experienced such conditions as attention deficit disorders or other learning difficulties also found themselves lacking the resources to succeed. Recognizing this reality, the sisters approved a plan to set up an educational resource center to provided support and services for those who needed them.

Initially, Mercy Education Resource Center (MERC) was to address the needs of students who were educationally challenged or had a learning disability, new immigrants seeking ESL assistance, and support for religious educators. Sister Anne Sekul was tapped to lead the effort. Sister Anne was well suited for the task for she had twenty-one years of experience in education serving in secondary education, as an elementary school principal and finally, trained as an educational psychologist. Sister Anne summed up the impetus for the undertaking:

A group of sisters were looking for a way to carry on their founder Catherine McAuley's mission to teach and the center seemed a perfect match. We're working with children who appear not to be able to learn in a regular classroom. We're here for children, all children.[28]

Key partners joined in the effort. Sister Mary Lorraine Mullin from Burlingame created the tutoring component while Dr. William Merz from California State University oversaw counseling interns. Jackie Merz joined the effort, providing counseling services. Sister Rosemarie Carvalho directed ESL learning while Sister Jean Marie Gorman provided childcare for the children of Sister Rosemarie's students. Through a unique blend of counseling, psycho-educational assessment, tutoring, adaptive learning techniques, and ESL classes, the center was able to assist students succeed within their school settings. Sister Anne notes:

The whole purpose is not entirely just to keep the child in school but to keep them from academic and societal failure, to help make them more successful. Sometimes my job as a teacher is not to make a genius or a college-bound child but a kid that has spirit, belief, faith and knows how to be happy.[29]

When MERC first began in 1992, few Catholic schools had on site counselors or specialized resource teachers. MERC showed that such resources were essential if all children were going to be successful. This was especially true in schools where families often did not have the economic resources to obtain outside assistance.

The challenge of providing educational opportunity to adolescents whose families could not afford tuitions cost for Catholic secondary education was not lost upon Bishop William Wiegand, bishop of Sacramento. He was anxious to find a way for young adults from poorer families to access an excellent Catholic secondary education. The strong desire to provide such educational opportunity converged with the desires of the Sacramento sisters. Father John Foley, S.J., provided the blueprint. In 1996, he started a new type of high school, Cristo Rey High Schools, which blended academics and work. Attending a Cristo Rey High School, "a school that works," meant economically disadvantaged youth could receive academic formation four days a week while participating in corporate job training on the fifth day. Through partnerships with over 120 Sacramento area businesses, including law firms, hospitals, government entities, and small businesses, students worked five full days per month, providing entry-level skills to their employers. The money they earned through this work was applied directly to the cost of their education.

Initially Bishop Weigand consulted with Jesuit Provincial John Previtt S.J. and Father John McGarry, S.J., then principal of Jesuit High School. Such an undertaking would take a lot of support both from donors and the business community. By 2004, then Jesuit Provincial Thomas Smolich authorized a feasibility study to determine if a Cristo Rey High School could survive in the Sacramento environment. The study indicated high interest but what made the endeavor possible was the collaboration of the Sisters of Mercy, California Jesuit Province and Notre Dame de Mur Sisters, all of which agreed to share sponsorship of the school.[30] Sister Michelle Gorman remembers the beginning:

> Because the Cristo Rey model blended so well with our charism, there was little need for a long and arduous discernment about our accepting the invitation to be co-sponsors. It was rather humorous when a lawyer and a Jesuit were sent to our Regional Leadership Team to extend the invitation. The pros and cons were laid out with judicial persuasion and legal precision. I had to bite my tongue to keep from shouting, "Enough already. We're in."[31]

Once more, the Sisters of Mercy were engaged in a treasured ministry—secondary education. Sister Sheila Browne put it this way: "It was a recommitment to our education ministry again especially to those who would not have such an education. It was taking on a new ministry and the vision was a match for us."[32]

The school was first housed at the vacant St. Peter's Elementary School. It was very much a make-do situation. Not only were the buildings not designed for secondary education, the grounds were difficult to secure. With the help of Mercy Foundation, a search began for an appropriate new site for the school. That search ended in 2014 when the school moved into a renovated office complex which is their new home. The success of the school is enormous with 100 percent of its first five graduating classes being accepted by colleges or universities.

Educational and Social Justice spheres were not the only areas which experienced growth during the post Institute years. Beginning in 1991, the healthcare system entered into a period of growth and expansion. Mercy American River Hospital was the first to enter the new Catholic Healthcare West system. Methodist Hospital in south Sacramento joined next, the first community hospital to do so. In the north state, St. Elizabeth Community Hospital in Red Bluff united with the system. Soon, both Woodland Healthcare and Sierra Nevada Memorial Hospital, Grass Valley, were counted among CHW entities. A new hospital, Mercy Folsom, was built for the Folsom community, opening in 1989. Other small hospitals like Modoc hospital were also stabilized and sustained by CHW until other options were put in place for health care in their areas. Adding six new hospitals in the North State area created a new corporate culture.

With fewer sisters to maintain Mercy presence, the question of passing on mission and values was critical. William Cox, CEO of the Alliance for Catholic Health Care, wrote of one of the greatest challenges facing religious communities that sponsored hospital systems:

> Catholic health care is authentic when its members provide care, develop healthier communities, and act as advocates for others out of an intentional commitment to the healing mission of the church. The central reality of that commitment is a ministry that others, when they encounter it as community, experience as a revelation of life's deepest truths—about human dignity, community, success, power, growth, sacrifice, love, suffering, debility and death. People go forth from this experience more healed, more whole, more able to love and hope.[33]

For Cox, such a health care milieu could only be sustained by leadership formation in mission. It was now up to Mercy leaders like Sister Bridget McCarthy, executive vice president of Catholic Healthcare West, Northern California region, to see that emerging leaders within CHW were formed in that mindset. Mission formation was done in formal and informal ways such as the way questions were asked of board members, staff, and site administrators. Sister Bridget says:

We had a mission and were mission driven. All decisions were based on that mission and vision which we received from our early sisters whose commitment was to meet the needs of the community.[34]

Still, there was worry that the pressure of external factors upon Catholic health systems would threaten the very culture of Catholic health care. Responding to market pressures, CHW followed the industry trend toward mergers, acquisitions, updating facilities, or building new ones. In 1999, Mercy Hospitals in Sacramento and the Northstate posted a $3 million loss with the whole of CHW losing $82 million.[35] Such realities were ripe for downsizing, cutbacks, and cost-cutting measures. To fulfill its mission, there had to be a viable margin.

As CHW expanded, the visibility and presence of sisters was diluted. That diminishment plus the cost-cutting realities of the business climate caused some people to see the hospitals as corporations rather than ministries. Some lost trust in leadership and looked to unions as a way of guaranteeing workers' rights. The path to unionization was not easy for anyone. Hard ethical issues had to be faced by the hospitals. Father Michael Place, president of the Catholic Healthcare Association, pointed to the dilemma: "You often can find yourself in a position where you are at a competitive disadvantage when you act in accordance with your conscience."[36]

Sister Marilee Howard, director of ethics and justice for Catholic Healthcare West, affirmed that Mercy would rather its workers remain independent and maintain a direct relationship with Mercy management. That relationship, Sister Marilee noted, was characterized by guiding principles and values such as dignity, care for the poor, stewardship.[37] While the system preferred to work directly with its staff, Sister Clare Marie Dalton, vice-president for mission integration at Mercy Hospital, summed up Mercy's position: "Let me assure you that whatever you decide and whatever the final vote is, the outcome of the election will be respected by the Sisters of Mercy."[38]

The conflict was not solely over unionization. It was partly over how that election would take place. Mercy leadership strongly objected to a vote that was not a secret ballot. They wanted one that was protective of the right to choose without the possibility of pressure. The modality of voting proposed by the union did not provide that protection. Union organizers accused hospital administration of unfair tactics while some employees protested visits to their homes by union organizers.

Sister Sheila Browne, president of the community during this period, shares that it was a difficult time. For those sisters who saw the desire for unions as a sign of decreased trust, it was painful. Sisters felt that they had always reverenced their employees and done whatever they could for their well-being. Tactics of organizers were more painful. Sister Sheila recalls:

> The picketing was really tough. We were on our way to Sacred Heart. Union supporters with bull horns outside our house were calling out "Mercy, Mercy go away." It brought me back to the early days in San Francisco.[39]

Ultimately, the situation was resolved but there was no instant healing. The fractured relationships had to be rebuilt over time.

Mercy General brought the sisters both sorrow and joy. The aging hospital faced a critical dilemma. Updated seismic requirements put in place by the state of California after the Loma Prieta earthquake of 1989 meant major renovations were needed. The top-ranking cardiac care program needed a facility to match its reputation. Plans for a new $150 million hospital were given impetus through a $15 million donation from the Alex G. Spanos family. The new building would provide a state-of-the-art cardiac care facility and 228 new hospital beds. There was only one major hitch: the five-story heart center was projected to be in close proximity to Sacred Heart Elementary School, and Sacred Heart parents were adamant that the hospital plan not go forward.

Although the hospital offered options for mitigation and even to relocate the school, all proposals were declined. Two ministries—Sacred Heart School and Mercy Hospital—were pitted against each other. Only when the hospital agreed to build a $15 million state-of-the-art school for the parish did the project go forward. The city elected to limit further growth at the hospital site and required the plan to include a public plaza.

Strong feelings were generated on both sides of the conflict. Some felt it was unjust to require Mercy to fully fund a new school while others saw that requirement as a just request for the benefit of all. When all negotiations were completed and the project approved, Monsignor Robert Walton, pastor of Sacred Heart parish, said he appreciated "all parties who put so much time and effort into creating something truly workable for the hospital, school and community as a whole."[40] Future generations were the true winners. A much-needed new hospital was built, a new school replaced the one built in 1939, and twenty new apartments replaced housing demolished for the project. It had taken two years—years of disappointment and sadness for the sisters caught between two of their cherished ministries.

New Horizons, New Needs

Becoming the Institute of the Sisters of Mercy of the Americas sparked new ways of visioning and new modes of reaching out, creating new supportive relationships with sisters across the United States and the world. It was a time of expansion and energy. Sisters, long associated with institutions, began to move into new areas. The cohesive visibility of strong institutions gave way to a more defused presence. Changes in religious dress along with a more diverse ministry brought about a diminished public profile.

John Kelly, owner of KCRA Channel 3, wanted to change that profile and he had just the person to lead the process, top anchorman Stan Atkinson. Stan relates that John Kelly called him into his office and said: "We need to do something for the sisters, and to make them more visible in the community."[1] Stan notes that in John Kelly's mind, it was about creating a wider vision, about telling the stories of what the sisters were really able to do—in other words, to create an opportunity to showcase their ministries and works. To do this, Kelly encouraged Stan to become part of the Mercy Foundation Board.

Atkinson forged a partnership between KCRA and Mercy Foundation, the philanthropic vehicle of the sisters. The next steps were to imagine an event and gather folks that could bring it to life. What would such an event look like? Mary Beth Marks and Val Nichols came up with the idea of designing something sports minded. Watt Gray, then sports anchor for KCRA, joined the effort by organizing Sacramento media personalities to competitively play against Hollywood celebrities in tennis matches and a softball game. The Mercy all-star weekend was being born.

The event took place over three days, Friday night softball between Walt's Media Mis-Hits and Hollywood celebrities, a Saturday tennis tournament, and a concluding gala on Saturday night. Sunday was reserved for showing off Sacramento to the celebrity guests. Walt observes: "It was the stand-out entertainment event of the time, more of a publicity event than a fundraising event. It was primarily one of fun and people getting to know Mercy."[2]

For eleven years, the all-star weekend, first held in 1992, highlighted the work of the Sisters of Mercy for the city and its environs. Sharon Margetts, the first chairperson of the event, describes the aim of the all-star weekend as "putting a spotlight on the various works" as well as fundraising.[3] It is hard to estimate the overall impact of the weekend from the perspective of mission. Each year for ten days, KCRA newscasts carried four-or-five-minute pieces about the ministries that were the recipients of that year's event. A longer merged program was structured to help raise funds. It was a win-win undertaking that raised over $2 million for the designated ministries and KCRA received high media ratings.[4] Since media personalities from all the news channels and many radio stations were participating, there was lots of coverage.

The all-star weekend was marked by a spirit of inclusivity. Events were planned in such a way that everyone in the Sacramento area could participate. The Friday evening softball game, with a ticket price of only $3, was geared to families. The Saturday tennis matches between celebrities, patrons, and even sisters were the same price with the evening gala driving the fundraising. Sharon Margetts enlisted Patrice Coyle, Diane Grenz, and Pam Shubert, among others, to design gala events to remember.

Recipients of monies raised were also expansive, including both Mercy ministries and other charities that served the economically poor. The scope of the grants had a wide range, including such efforts as: Mercy Education Resource Center's outreach to the Boys and Girls Club, White Rock Clinic, St. Francis Terrace's after school program, Mercy Clinic at Loaves and Fishes, Elder Friends, and Medicine for the Poor.

Even though numbers of sisters were decreasing during the 1980s and '90s, advocacy and grant allocations significantly increased. Mercy Foundation was a main channel for these monies. There were yearly grants made available through the program allocations component of its structure. During the years 1991 through 2008, the foundation distributed over $8,000,000 in grant monies. Again, these grants were given not only to Mercy ministries, but to others groups that shared the same vision: Mustard Seed School, AIDS ministry, Folsom Family Clinic, and Genesis Counseling Services among others. Still, there was more. Diocesan agencies received assistance through Mercy Healthcare grants. Those monies were focused on domestic violence awareness, efforts to enroll Latina children in health insurance programs, and other diocesan social programs.[5]

Areas in the northern part of the Sacramento diocese were not left out of the process. Mercy Foundation North oversaw the distribution of yearly CHW community benefit grants, which in 1999 included such needs as the crisis intervention program of the Siskiyou Child Care Council, Shasta County's Women Refuge Center, and Home Help for Hispanic Mothers in Tehama County. In Sacramento, Mercy Hospital's community benefit grants between 1990 and 2004 went to 105 different social, healthcare, or educational programs.

Reading the signs of the times led the sisters to unexpected places. As early as 1980, Sister Mary Monica Burns tells us that the Sisters of Mercy had become aware of an acute need for affordable housing in Sacramento. Homelessness was emerging as a serious issue for the city.[6] Similar situations were happening across the country. The Sisters of Mercy in Omaha were among the first to respond, establishing Mercy Housing, Inc. It was the beginning of a ministry that would change the lives of many families, including those in the Sacramento area.

Mercy's Omaha regional community drafted Sister Terese Tracy RSM to be the leader of the housing initiative. For the next six years she worked to develop a multi-phased housing ministry, Mercy Housing, Inc., which provided both shelter and supportive services. The Sisters of Mercy in Sacramento became one of its sponsoring communities in 1988 when Sister Lillian Murphy, RSM, then CEO of Mercy Housing, invited the Omaha, Burlingame, and Auburn communities to sponsor Mercy Housing California. Sister Mary Monica Burns championed the efforts in Sacramento while Sister Diane Clyne led the efforts in San Francisco.

Jane Graf, former CEO of Mercy Housing California, speaking of Sisters Diane and Mary Monica, shares that "Neither had any experience in housing. They did what was almost impossible, pulling it off because it was such an important thing to do. It was tough going but they were fearless, especially Monica."[7] Sister Mary Monica was passionate about improving the plight of economically disadvantaged families, and after years in educational leadership and congregational service, she went to Denver to intern in housing development. Returning to Sacramento, she set to work.

Dorothy Smith, an original board member of Mercy Housing California, relates that the first project was a collaboration with the diocese of Sacramento. With minimal advance preparation for parishioners, the diocese told the folks at St. Francis parish that they were giving property adjoining the school and church for affordable housing.[8] Resistance soared. Sister Mary Monica had to win over everyone so that the project could go forward. Jane Graf tells us:

Monica was a force. When she started working on St. Francis Terrace she had street smarts and really worked at making transactions happen. Nothing was impossible to her. She made herself vulnerable and everyone who worked with Monica loved her. Every minute was busy; no task too inconsequential. She would go on every site visit, becoming a construction expert. She was always helpful. There was nothing she couldn't do.[9]

To gain acceptance of the housing project took a lot of effort. Sister Libby Fernandez puts it this way:

When plans for St. Francis Terrace started Monica had a lot of problems, "Not in my backyard" based. She had to work really hard to win the support of the neighbors. She really listened to the associations and upscaled the project design.[10]

Mediator-led listening sessions brought folks together. Two persons, representing every perspective, were brought in and they stayed with the conversation until compromise was achieved.

Finally, in 1993, construction on St. Francis Terrace started. The need for affordable housing was so great that 300 applications were received for the forty-eight apartments being built. Mercy Housing brought a new model of housing development to Sacramento. It was more than apartments. Mercy Management Services brought a supportive services model to the undertaking. Families could tap into afterschool programs, job skills training, and parenting skills. At the time, Sister Mary Monica summed up the approach: "We feel you can't have a housing project without having program services for the residents if we're going to help them improve their lives, and in some cases get off welfare."[11]

Along the way, Sister Mary Monica experienced what many social reformers and advocates face. Dorothy Smith sums up Sister's experience: "Political groups did not treat her well. In the face of rudeness, she was most gracious."[12] Winning over public agencies demanded more than graciousness, however. It required results. Mercy Housing provided such results. Not only did St. Francis Terrace prove to be an asset to its neighborhood, but Mercy Housing's renovation and management of a large apartment complex on Duchow Way in Folsom transformed the complex from one plagued by crime and drugs to one providing security, safety, and new hope. Bert Smith, Redevelopment Director for the city of Folsom says: "[The fact] that we able to pursue our combined of goals of reducing crime, improving the quality of housing and the quality of life—there's a minor miracle involved."[13]

Since its inception, Mercy Housing California has grown to over 10,000 units serving over 20,000 residents. The ministry expanded beyond the city to include rural areas such as Live Oak, special needs housing like Colonia San Martin in Sacramento, and other projects including Quinn Cottages, a transitional village for the homeless. Dorothy Smith attributes the success of the ministry to its way of approaching things:

> Mercy housing sustains what it builds. It makes sure it works for the people it is supposed to benefit. Because we had supportive services and the complex won't be sold, it is about stabilizing the housing for people. We build a community with no thought of profit. In quality and fulfillment of the mission, we get it done.[14]

Mercy Housing did not limit its work to affordable housing for families. It also provided housing for seniors and for persons with special needs. Shortages in affordable senior housing existed in Sacramento, Folsom, and Auburn. A collaboration among CHW, Mercy Housing, and the sisters allowed that need to be addressed. In Folsom, through a donation of land from CHW, Mercy Housing was able to respond to senior housing needs. In Sacramento, Russell Manor, a much-needed senior housing complex, was built in South Sacramento. This was Sister Mary Monica's final undertaking before her sudden death in 1996.

The housing shortage for seniors in Auburn was long standing. In the late 1980s, the sisters were approached by a group of developers and asked to collaborate in what was called the Auburn Palms Housing Project. Developers asked the community to give a portion of the convent property to the group for the purpose of building senior housing. At the time, after much exploration and consultation with the community as a whole, the proposal was declined. The need did not go away, however. The sisters remained mindful of the need and in 2013 were able to lease (for 100 years at $1) a portion of their campus to Mercy Housing for McAuley Meadows, a complex of fifty senior housing apartments. The complex was opened in the summer of 2014, and, like Russell Manor, had a long waiting list of those hoping to live there.

Looking backwards over the long history of Sisters of Mercy, one can see an enduring concern for the elderly, especially those who were infirm. One of Mother Mary Baptist Russell's great hopes was to build a home for the aged. That same concern was within the hearts of the Sisters of Mercy in Sacramento. After building Mater Misericordiae Hospital in 1897, the sisters converted Ridge Home into a residence for the old. When the hospital moved to 40th and J Streets, the sisters took the elderly residents with them to the new site. In the early 1990s, Sacramento still lacked adequate housing for frail seniors. Though Mercy Housing was providing new housing options for independent seniors, there remained a need for those who needed assistance in daily living.

Claire McMahon, a generous donor, helped to respond to that need. She had a desire to build a senior housing facility for Sacramento. Upon her death, monies were left to the Sacramento Diocese to bring her dream to reality. When, after five years, no progress had been made on the project, Jess Wilson brought together the executors of the estate with Mercy Hospital leaders. With the facilitation and support of Monsignor Albert O'Connor, the process of planning began.

Mercy Hospital took the lead in developing the new facility. It would be a 118-apartment complex for independent and assisted-living seniors. Sister Mary Carmel Donoghue was its first director. Called Mercy McMahon Terrace, it was a welcome addition to the East Sacramento neighborhood, and many of Sacred Heart parish's older parishioners were among its first residents. In blessing the new residence, Bishop Francis J. Quinn prayed: "May this be a place of love and hospitality, two very special qualities of our Divine Lord. Above all may this be a happy place, a place of celebration."[15] Almost twenty years later, in 2007, upon completing his ministry with the Indian peoples in the Southwest, Bishop Quinn returned to Sacramento and himself became a resident of Mercy McMahon Terrace.

The needs of senior citizens in the Redding area were not forgotten. For fifty years, the services of Golden Umbrella have provided the elderly citizens of Shasta County an opportunity for socialization, assistance, and opportunities to serve their community. It began with a Project Find Grant. The idea was simple: seek out the friendless, isolated, needy, and disabled senior citizens in Shasta Country and implement action to help them.[16] Golden Umbrella provided a wide span of activities including the Golden Umbrella Raindrops Band; a diabetic food buyers' club; a foster grandparent program; quilting, arts, and crafts; and adult day care. The program was so successful that it outgrew its original gathering spot and opened a new facility on Pine Street in Redding.

For thirty years, the group thrived, but space was always a challenge. Not owning a building, the organization was always at the mercy of their landlords. At times, Golden Umbrella was forced to relocate due to space constraints or because the buildings were sold by their owners. Golden Umbrella affiliated with Catholic Healthcare West North State in 1997, and by 1999, it was clear a new facility was needed. Mercy Foundation North undertook the task of helping the group to raise $1.5 million needed for building their own permanent home. Catholic Healthcare West supplied land for the facility on property which was also the site of Shasta

Senior Nutrition. A major donation from the William E. Baker family allowed the new building to include space for the areas' first dedicated day care for Alzheimer patients.[17] Services provided by Golden Umbrella included an adult day care program; a weekday adult day healthcare program; Project Match, which brought together elderly living in their homes with adult companions; foster grandparent and senior companion programs; and a link to other services for Shasta County seniors.[18]

While the sisters tried to respond to the needs of frail and economically struggling senior citizens, they found themselves facing a housing crisis. As the senior members of the community grew increasingly frail, it became apparent that the Auburn convent was not adequately meeting the needs of older sisters. While smaller renovations to provide needed infirmary rooms and better care for the elderly had taken place over the years, more changes had to be made.

The needs of the sisters' convent in Auburn had evolved over the years. When the campus was purchased in the 1940s, it was seen as a house of formation for young sisters. Fifty years later, it had slowly become a residence for older sisters who had devoted their lives to service of God's people but were no longer able to engage in active ministry. Sister Michelle Gorman explains that part of the call of sisters today is the way in which they live their lives: "We want to model for the world how to grow old gracefully and how to take care of elderly people."[19]

Recognizing that the Auburn convent was a special place—a sacred place where sisters would live out their final years—meant that it had to provide all the things needed to maintain quality of life. Spiritual needs came first with the renovation the community chapel. In 2001, it was redesigned to bring it into harmony with modern liturgical practice and symbolism. While retaining original elements such as the stained-glass windows, the marble floor, and the reredos, skylights were used to bring in new light and seating became more flexible to accommodate those in wheelchairs. Reflecting on the redesign, Sister Katherine Doyle noted that every change was rooted in meaning. The skylights were just one example: "Mercy always reaches out to the world. We want to have a visual connection between the place of our prayer and the world beyond."[20] Two etched crystal glass screens, designed by Sister Eileen Mary O'Connor, separate the reservation chapel and the main celebration area, completing the design.

Planning and implementing the renovation of the chapel was relatively simple. Renovating the house, a more complex task, required a great deal more time and planning. The whole undertaking started with a suggestion to install an elevator since the stairs were very difficult for older sisters to manage, and all the bedrooms were upstairs. The cost was so high that it prompted the leadership team to call for a thorough study of the sisters' needs and possible options to meet those needs. They tapped Franc Blackbird of Blackbird Associates to conduct the study.

Speaking with *Catholic Herald* reporter Nancy Westlund, Sister Katherine Doyle noted: "When we took a look at the whole campus, one of the things we discovered was that the only room in the entire place being used for what it was originally meant for was the chapel."[21] The community gathering room, called the "Fireplace Room," was a good example. It originally was the convent chapel, then transitioned to the community library and was now a living room. The community dining room was made into administrative offices.

Sister Sheila Browne, community president at the time, considers the renovation that ensued one of the best things that she guided.[22] It was a huge undertaking which took almost three years to complete. The overall plan was rooted in three values—practicality, beauty, and safety. The old novitiate building was partially demolished to open up space for emergency vehicles to access both the convent and the retreat center. The residence for sisters living in Auburn was transferred to one side of the building instead of being split into two parts. Renovated rooms in the infirmary were designed with medical care in mind. Outside, fire hydrants and new roadways were put in place.

The cost of infrastructure improvements, a new elevator, and provisions for medical support exceeded what the sisters could finance on their own. Mercy Foundation Sacramento and Mercy Foundation North launched the "A Promise Kept" campaign to help with the funding. The fundraising effort coincided with the three-year celebration of the presence of Sisters of Mercy in California. In many ways, it was a tangible mode through which the wider civic community said "Thank you" to the sisters for their years of service. To know that their home would carry them forward into the future was a great gift for the sisters. Sister Eileen Mary O'Connor summed up the convent's significance, saying: "This is where we were born into religious life."[23] For many sisters, it would also be the place where they passed into eternity.

The sisters in Auburn had long seen their campus as a resource for the people of God, something to be shared. By 1992, it had become a spiritual refuge for those seeking God and an incubator for forming lay ministers. This was not a foreseen development. It evolved over time. At the beginning of the 1970s, the sisters found themselves with Marian Hall, a brand-new building intended as a new novitiate. When construction ended in 1967, the large numbers of new members had diminished, and there was no need for the new wing.

Mother Mary Teresita Durkin saw that the empty building could become a resource, a spiritual oasis, for people of faith. Mary Teresita invited William Peter, S.J., to come to Auburn and provide a training program in spiritual formation for religious leaders. The two-month program, dubbed the "Auburn Experience" by Vatican Congregation of Religious, was steeped in the tradition of St. Ignatius of Loyola's Spiritual Exercises. By 1977, over 150 sisters from all over the world had participated. In the beginning, little was said publicly about the retreat experience. It was known primarily to major superiors and novitiate directors of religious congregations.

For Father Peters, the program was not a class but an experience, an experience of God bubbling up through God's initiative. For most, it was a profound time. One participant put it this way:

This was not an ascetical exercise designed to pressure you into anything. God was speaking, especially through our praying with Scripture, His word to us. This was clearly His work, indeed. Above all it was a time of peace, of God's nearness, of gradually coming to stand in the light, of deepening union with God.[24]

The sisters' concerns did not stop with prayer and spirituality. Prior to the establishment of the diocesan lay ministry program, Sister Mary Teresita was instrumental in bringing together a team of teachers to design and present a program of lay formation. She was convinced that the renewal of the church called for by Vatican II would only grow out of the spiritual renewal of its people. Sisters Mary Loyola MacDonald, Joan Marie Fagerskog, Maura Power, and Katherine Doyle were among the instructors along with Frs. T. Brendan O'Sullivan and Vincent O'Reilly. The program transitioned to diocese sponsorship in 1986, but the sisters' efforts to bring solid adult education did not end.

Within two years after the closure of Auburn's ministry formation program, Sister Mary Loyola MacDonald organized a scripture institute to respond to the desire for greater knowledge of the Bible. Fathers Daniel Looney and Vincent O'Reilly joined with Sister Mary Loyola and her team of sisters in bringing the institute to fruition. This program was also transitioned to the Diocesan Office of Lay Ministry, although it continued to gather at Mercy Center. Going full circle, in 1993, Sister Anita Minihane assumed responsibility for that office, once more bringing the energies of Mercy to that task.

Between 1970 and 1990, it became evident that the spiritual hungers of society were becoming more urgent and pressing. The more frenetic society became, the more people longed for a place of quiet and solitude in which to find peace and renewal. In May 1992, the Sisters of Mercy responded to that longing by opening Marian Retreat Center, later renamed Mercy Center Auburn. It provided a home to lay ministry formation as well as "a place of hospitality for those seeking food for the spirit and a time of reflection."[25] The center welcomed seekers of all traditions as well as groups that were aligned with the sisters' values.

Colleen Gregg, Mercy Center's director, relates that many individuals come to the retreat center for days of spiritual renewal, "just breathing in the spirit of God as experienced in nature, art, reading walking or silence."[26] In addition to group and individual retreats, the center offers days of solitude; oasis days; presentations on theological, biblical, and spiritual topics; and the opportunity for spiritual direction.

Over the decade of the 1990s, the ministries of retreat work and spiritual direction multiplied within Mercy communities across the country. The same was true for the Auburn community. There was a special desire to support the spiritual hungers of women. Through Mercy Center's programs and through spiritual direction, women were given the freedom to explore the shape of the feminine path to God. Colleen points out: "Women hunger to find a deeper connection with God amid life's business demands, to grow toward authenticity and wholeness. Mercy can provide opportunities to integrate faith, work, home, life."[27]

The transitioning of sisters into the ministry of spiritual direction was only one of the transitions which took place during the 1990s. Sisters moved out of the classroom and into parish life. Recognizing that not all families could afford Catholic education, sisters like Hannah Mary O'Donoghue, Maura Power, Ellen Philbin, Anne McCrohan, Mary Celine Heneghan, Cora Salazar, Eileen Mary O'Connor, and Mary Juliana Clancy all moved into parishes where they dealt directly with the faith needs of adults and children. Sister Juliana tells us:

> While the ministry of education in a Catholic school may be the ideal setting for faith formation, parish ministry reaches a larger community through catechesis, including the Rite of Christian Initiation.[28]

Sisters found that parish ministry allowed them to touch the lives of people from all sectors of life. In a special way, they were able to respond directly to those who were economically in need. The direction statement of the Institute of the Sisters of Mercy had asked sisters to stand in solidarity with the economically poor of the world, especially women and children; women seeking fullness of life and equality in church and society; and one another as we embrace our multicultural and international reality.[29]

Parish ministry allowed sisters to actively work to address all three of those areas. Welcoming new immigrants, preparing worship experiences expressive of diverse cultures, and hosting prayer and faith-sharing opportunities for parish women were ways of making a profound difference.

As parish reality changed, some sisters were called to be parish stewards. For the Sacramento Diocese, it was a new role instituted to meet the pastoral and spiritual needs of parishes with no resident pastor. Sister Nancy McInerney was one of the first women in the Sacramento Diocese called to such a role. Bishop Richard J. Garcia presented her with the symbols of her responsibilities during her installation. Her tasks included leadership, administration, evangelization, catechesis, worship, spirituality, and the spiritual and corporal works of mercy.[30]

Sister Nancy was entrusted with responsibility for both St. John's parish in Dunsmuir and St. Joseph's in McCloud. It was not a small task, but was one for which she was well seasoned. In 1977, Sister Nancy had helped forge new ground for sisters when she left teaching for parish work. With a Master's degree in religious education, she worked in a variety of parishes including Holy Family, Citrus Heights, St. Joseph's, Elk Grove, and St. Catherine's in Vallejo. It was in the latter parish that she gained valuable experience as a pastoral associate.

Joining Sister Nancy in the ministry of pastoral steward was Sister Anne Chester, appointed as a pastoral steward to minister to the parishes of Sacred Heart in Fort Jones and St. Joseph in Yreka. In addition to the two main parish communities, Sister Anne was also responsible for four mission churches. Like Sister Nancy, she brought a deep richness to her work. She had not only served as a pastoral associate at St. Anthony's in Winters, but also at St. Joseph's in Elk Grove. Sister Anne brought another expertise to her assignment. She had been director of the research and planning office of the diocese during the 1980s and was instrumental in the development of the diocesan pastoral plan. She saw her role as one of empowerment. "It's freeing. I feel like I can do many things. It's like having a new lease on life. I never expected to have this opportunity at this stage of my life."[31]

While Sisters Anne and Nancy were pathfinders in their roles of parish stewards, Sisters Marita Cunningham and Mary Padilla led the way into diocesan-wide ministry. Both were vitally concerned about the formation of lay catechists and in the early 1970s joined the staff of the religious education department. They moved throughout the diocese bringing needed formation programs to both city and rural parishes. Sister Maria Padilla was particularly influential in supporting programs for the Spanish speaking and in working with families in migrant camps. In the camps, she began coordinating religious education program for their residents, often with resistance from farm owners who wish to bar religious workers from the camps. Sister Maria's fluency in Spanish and her experiential knowledge of the culture brought constant demands upon her wisdom and expertise.

Increased needs in the Sacramento Diocese brought new requests for sisters to meet those needs. By the mid-1980s, Mercy sisters were found serving in the Catholic school department, office of youth and young adult ministry, department of Catholic faith formation, marriage tribunal, office of research and planning, RENEW, office of evangelization, vicar for religious, vocation office, and office of lay ministry formation and chancellor. Such presence is reflective of the strong bonds of relationship and spirit of collaboration which has marked the 150 year partnership of the Diocesan Church and the Sisters of Mercy in Sacramento.

Concern for how the needs of the mission would be tended into the future caused the sisters to reflect on the charism of Catherine McAuley and the teaching of Vatican II regarding mission. That reflection brought the sisters to new understandings about how the Mercy mission flourishes. It was a simple insight but one with broad implications. The Sisters of Mercy are not the exclusive holders of the charism of Mercy. Fueled by that conviction, and recognizing the importance of their partners in ministry, sisters in healthcare and education had provided formation for mission for those working in their sponsored ministries. Now they wished to go further.

The sisters began to explore ways in which they could support others who are called to live the Mercy mission, join with them in supportive relationships, and provide grounding in the spirituality of Mercy. The process, begun in 1984, came to fruition in 1992 with the sisters joined other Mercy regions in the formation of the Mercy Association. Tied to the community through bonds of prayer, friendship, and mission, Mercy Associates bring mercy to their everyday experiences at home, work, or society. Like the sisters, they are called to make the works of mercy the "business of their lives."

The first group of Mercy Associates set the pattern. All had been active in the works of mercy prior to their commitment but wanted more. The prospective Mercy Associates wanted an animating and supportive relationship with the sisters that would help sustain their own call to bring Mercy to the world. The first Mercy Associates were Joan Haan, Pam Butts, Myrtle and Nick Knickerbocker, Barbara Ghattas, Mary Hogarty, Karolyn Spring, and Marie Sheahan Brown. Among the many works they would take up were advocacy for justice, visiting the shut-in, working at Loaves and Fishes, and assisting where needed at the retreat center. As the numbers of sisters decreased, those actively engaged in the mission of mercy through Mercy Association or through partnerships in mission expanded to meet new challenges and new needs. Today, there are over 3,100 active Mercy Associates across the Institute, all carrying out the works of mercy.

Crossing the River of Fire

The energies placed in motion by the creation of the Institute of the Sisters of Mercy of the Americas were palpable in the aftermath. Ministries were started. Sisters entered new fields of engagement and planning took place for an unknown future. Part of an international institute, the Auburn sisters were now engaged in a larger conversation about what would be good for the whole, not just beneficial for the sisters in Sacramento. They had to expand their horizon to enfold the Institute as a whole.

One of the biggest tasks of the Institute leadership was building relationships among all the Institute's members. Going from a community of less than 100 sisters to an Institute numbering over 7,000 was formidable for Sacramento's small community. The "getting to know you" process started by uniting with other regional communities around task and mission for that was a natural starting point. Clusters of Mercy communities around the country formed collaborative teams in areas of vocations, justice, and life development.

Getting together had never been a problem for the Sacramento sisters because all the members of the community were within a reasonable driving distance from Auburn. Jubilees, funerals, professions, and community meetings were all times when everyone gathered. That would now begin to change. Auburn gatherings had to be planned around the schedules of Institute leaders who had to travel from Silver Spring, MD, to attend regional gatherings The spontaneity of gathering for consultation diminished. As members of the community began to serve on Institute committees and task forces, they became "frequent flyers." One area that exemplified the changing connections was vocation ministry. Prior to 1990, the Auburn vocation minister primarily functioned within the

Sacramento Diocese. Reaching out to parishes usually involved a short trip or, if meeting in the Redding area, an overnight journey.

As the new Institute evolved, vocation work was divided into various geographical teams. Auburn became part of the Mercy new membership team: West/Midwest. This team would serve eight regions, encompassing thirty-seven states. The 168-mile journey to Redding, which sometimes seemed long in pre-institute days, paled by comparison. Sister Michelle Gorman was part of the first new membership team and reflected on her discernment experience:

> Throughout the whole process, there was an awareness that our interconnectedness as Sisters of Mercy transcends our individual fears and feelings of inadequacy. We have enough goodwill, experience and talent to bring to life this dream that has been emerging for several years.[1]

That dream, one of union and solidarity, was also the focus for other groups. One collaboration working to bring everyone together was Mercy Institute life development (MILD). During the early years of Institute, MILD designed and implemented a wide variety of communal experiences, bringing sisters together from across regions. Mercy Charism retreats, a Constitutions study process, "Journey to Wholeness" retreats, and shared faith guides were just a few of the processes developed. Mercy Center Auburn played a big role in supporting these initiatives. Sisters from throughout the country came to Auburn to take part in Charism retreats as well as Journey to Wholeness, a formative experience through which sisters met and formed new friendships.

One of the outgrowths of these collaborations was a decision to take a year of relationship building between the St. Louis and Auburn communities. At the beginning of the Institute, the two groups had been prayer partners, but now they came together more intentionally. They did not start from scratch. The Sisters of Mercy in St. Louis had always supported and welcomed Auburn sisters who pursued advanced degrees at St. Louis University or George Washington University or participated in the IRF program for religious formators. New friendships had been formed through the emerging committees and task forces. Throughout the time of relationship-building, planners brought together sisters in various age groups. Silver, golden, and diamond jubilarians got together for special retreats and shared their experiences of religious life. Both leadership teams spent time together imagining the future.

One only has to reflect on one's own experience to recognize what a huge amount of energy was demanded of members. Sisters not only had to invest time and energy into the expansion of their ministries but also had to be fully invested in the internal changes of the community. Letting go of familiar ways of doing things, reorganizing policies and practices, and living into the unknown took faith, courage, and stamina.

The preparation process for the 1999 chapter was called Pathways to the Future. Everyone was asked to reflect on what was best for the Mercy mission. What was God asking of the Institute? Sister Mary Waskowiak was the Institute leadership team's liaison for the Pathways project. Sister Mary called the members of the Institute to look at their current reality. That included statistics. When the Institute was formed in 1991, there were 7,300 members; membership in 1996 showed that 1,190 sisters had either died or departed the community in that five-year span. Mary pointed out:

> The numbers and ages of our sisters have definite implications for where we are going as a community. These issues press us to examine questions like what ministries will be available for our older sisters. The challenge of our current reality may prove to be both rich and complex.[2]

Janet Baker, a member of the planning committee for Pathways, identified the heart of the challenge: "It is key that the Pathways project be grounded in our faith so that the paths we uncover come from efforts born of a contemplative reflection on who we are and who we are called to become."[3]

In the middle of this, sisters were asked to give their time and attention to processes that were meant to build a common identity of sisters of the Institute. Recognizing the need for common vision, the Institute invited everyone to participate in opening worlds of mercy, a three-year theological reflection process. Exploring such issues as multiculturalism, racism, earth and women in the church, Opening Worlds of Mercy prepared the sisters to identify the critical concerns of the Institute which would be formalized by the chapter of 2005.

As Pathways evolved, it became clear that the path forward would involve a restructuring of governance functions. Was it practical for the Institute to have twenty-five regions? Twenty-five separate leadership teams? Twenty-five different agendas? The answer to the questions was, "No." That "No" propelled the whole to a momentous decision, that of re-imagining and re-structuring the Institute. On December 12, 2002, the institute leadership team sent a letter to all sisters articulating a new direction. The Institute would organize its infrastructure to intensify its focus on mission and sisterhood.[4] Now, re-imagining had become reality.

Moving from twenty-five separate regions to six asked for change on every level of Mercy life. Sponsorship of ministries, staffing, leadership, vocation ministry, and finances all had to be realigned. The big question for Auburn sisters was realigned with whom? Selecting your partners in the new larger communities was up to the regions to decide. With only two Mercy communities west of the Rockies, it was not easy. While Mercy Burlingame and Mercy Auburn were natural partners, they were really too small to constitute a separate community. There had to be more.

Initially, it was thought that the St. Louis sisters might be a possibility, but long-standing links of history and geography moved them in a different direction. Mercy Omaha was the most likely third partner having shared historical relationships with both Auburn and Burlingame, but their sisters stretched across the country to Michigan, Missouri and dotted the Mid-West. For months, discussions continued and still there was no final decision. The clock was ticking. In May 2004, the leadership teams from across the Institute gathered in Miami. Results from all the consultations showed consensus around key elements of Mercy life going forward. It was now time to identify who would constitute the six provisional areas of the Institute. The meeting was to begin May 3, and Auburn was still uncertain where it belonged. Sister Sheila Browne explains some of the difficulty:

> On the leadership level we were meeting as eight in a collaborative in justice and formation. Losing that group was hard. Every region had a group but us. For our own region there was fear of losing some of the intimacy we had and our identity as who we were. It was a journey into the unknown.[5]

The decision on how to form the West-Midwest area was made only the day before the meetings began. As all the leadership teams joined together, their decisions were ritualized through the action of crossing a symbolic river of fire which stretched across the room. There would be no turning back. Auburn joined with the Mercy communities of Burlingame, Cedar Rapids, Chicago, Detroit, and Omaha to form the West-Midwest Community. Sister Sheila put it simply: "Crossing the river of fire was a hard transition."[6] By September, the West-Midwest community would create a logo for the area, develop a secure web site, select prayer partners and establish circle groups."[7] It was to be full steam ahead.

With the work of creating reimagined communities as background music, the Auburn sisters poured their creative energies and zest into another undertaking, the celebration of 150 years of Mercy presence in California. In the middle of reorganizing themselves and stewarding new ministries, the celebration of the 150th anniversary of the arrival of the Sisters of Mercy's in San Francisco and their expansion to Sacramento would be a moment of great joy. Memory gives birth to thankfulness; thankfulness begets praise. Looking back over their years in California brought the California sisters a renewed sense of shared history and identity. The Sacramento Mercies were one with the San Francisco sisters for their first thirty years. Reflection on that reality prompted the sisters to plan one unified celebration with two key moments spanning the years 2004–2007. What they did, they would do together.

Festivities began with a focus on those who were poor. The Auburn and Burlingame Mercy communities joined together in a public act of mercy donating $1,000,000 to Mercy Housing for affordable housing initiatives. In presenting the gift, Sister Sheila Browne noted that it was in the Mercy tradition of providing safe havens and homes. "We are convinced that 'the Act of Mercy' we are making today, will make a difference in communities in the future."[8]

To continue making a difference into the future, it was vital that the mission, vision, and spirit of the Sisters of Mercy be shared with the wider community. For a community accustomed to staying in the background, this was an unusual focus. It began with retelling their shared community story to each other. Storytelling gatherings were held in Auburn and Burlingame, providing an opportunity to build stronger relationships. A joint committee of Auburn and Burlingame sisters planned all the early events as well as a three-year calendar for the celebration. Dramatic storytelling brought life to the early sisters, telling their stories, hopes, and dreams. Storytelling for the public was provided through the creation of media materials shared in sponsored ministries and through public media. Everything was focused on celebrating what had been, while pointing to the future. The San Francisco moment of the celebration culminated with a Eucharistic liturgy at St. Mary's Cathedral.

In 2005, the celebrative activities moved to Sacramento. The storytelling continued in new forms. Historical walking tours of Mercy ministries in the downtown area were hosted, and a pilgrimage to the historical roots of the community in Ireland took place. The pilgrimage made a lasting impression upon its participants. Sharon Margetts shares: "I knew nothing about sisters. The history is stunning and the fact that I got to go to Ireland with the sisters, I discovered all that."[9]

While Mercy Foundation members were hard at work on the Promises Kept campaign to renovate the Auburn convent, they also took the lead in organizing the various events held during the final year of celebration. Sacramento had a tradition of "Gold Rush Days," which honored the gold rush roots of the city. It took place in Old Town, the part of the city that has recreated 1850s Sacramento. Historical restoration has preserved such things as the Eagle Theater, cobblestone streets and school house. During

Gold Rush Days 2007, sister volunteers, garbed in the original wool habit, re-enacted the community's arrival by boat on October 2, 1857, A series of historical vignettes were performed by sisters at the Eagle Theater, while other sisters met with families and interested visitors at the school house. Sister Michelle Gorman shared that the purpose of the theatrical presentation was to "share the joys of the Sisters of Mercy" and to show appreciation for "the sacrifices of people who lived difficult lives."[10]

Sacramento's museums joined in telling the Mercy story. Just as the sisters started their celebration in 2004, the California Museum opened a new exhibit focusing on the contribution of women to the state. Sisters like Mary Padilla, Hannah Mary O'Donoghue, and many Mercy nursing sisters were included in the photographic display. The lives and accomplishments of the sisters were on exhibit at the Discovery Museum in Old Town, the main Sacramento Library, and the Folsom Historical Museum.

In a way, the celebration provided an immersion in the Mercy story. At a gala event, held at Sacramento's Memorial Auditorium, that story was put in a dramatic musical format seen through the eyes of Mother Mary Baptist herself. Kerry Wood, Mercy Foundation's liaison for the event, attributes the success of the gala to the women who worked to make it happen. "Working with the gala committee, Patrice Coyle, Diane Grentz, Sharon Margetts, etc. was so inspiring. They worked so hard."[11]

The culmination of the 150th celebration was held on September 29, 2007. It began with a liturgy of Thanksgiving at the Cathedral of the Blessed Sacrament where a stained-glass window had been dedicated to the Sisters of Mercy. Father Paul Crowley, S.J., homilist for the Mass, noted:

> No lofty missionaries from enlightened Europe, these women were immigrants serving immigrants, aliens in a strange land. [They] were women on a mission and in doing the work of the Gospel, works of mercy, they were also proclaiming Jesus Christ. For them nothing could be more important. The two goals were linked through mercy: entering the worlds of the poor and serving Jesus.[12]

While the culminating liturgy was rich and joyous, there was one more event that left a lasting impression upon all those involved in its execution and fulfillment. Recognizing that the land where the state capitol is located was originally owned by the sisters, a plaque had earlier been installed on the grounds to mark that reality. Due to a security breach, that historical marker was now partially hidden by the new security entrance. Kerry Wood took on the task of changing that. Kerry tells us:

It took about three years to bring to fruition. It was an issue of visibility. Several months earlier Ruth Coelho, a skilled sculptress, had moved next door. Inspired by the Baptist book, we had conversations about what would it take to make a statue. We had to learn how to work everything through the system. We were working on lifting the moratorium on statues. We had to get a senator to author a bill to support the proposal and we had to look for funding. Bill Hunt was one who was a champion of the cause.[13]

Not everyone was excited about the idea. In fact, both the assembly and the historic commission turned down the proposal because they did not want another statue on the grounds.

The impasse was resolved when Chief Senate Sergeant of Arms Tony Beard, Jr., having the authority to authorize what could be placed within 50 yards of the security entrance, approved the replacement of the original plaque by the new memorial statue of Mother Baptist and the works of mercy. Perseverance and providence combined to make it happen. The memorial to the sisters was unveiled and dedicated immediately after the anniversary Mass.

One last surprise remained. After the dedication of the memorial, sisters and friends returned to the cathedral for a light reception. Bishop William Weigand, speaking for the diocese as a whole, announced that the assembly room on the lower level of the cathedral was to be renamed the Cathedral Mercy Memorial Hall. In addition, $25,000 would be given to Cristo Rey High School for student scholarships, the stained-glass window donated to the cathedral by the healthcare system would be dedicated to the sisters, and a special papal blessing was given to the community. To say that the anniversary celebration was unforgettable would be an understatement.

The excitement and joy of the 150th celebration was a prelude for saying goodbye. As the sisters rejoiced in their past and present, they were also keenly aware that a major change was just around the corner. It was a change that asked them to set down their Auburn identity but not its spirit or its works. In just a short while, they would join with their sisters to create a new future and a new identity, that of the Sisters of Mercy, West-Midwest. Behind the scenes, everything was already in transition for the change. All that remained was the unfolding.

The Sisters of Mercy of Auburn ceased to exist as a separate unit on July 1, 2008. While there was a sense of loss, there was also constancy—a constancy of mission, relationship, and mercy. The sisters would go into their future with the same vigor, faith, and determination that characterized their heritage. A song composed for one of their final assemblies put it simply: "We are crossing the threshold of hope, no turning back, no turning back."

Enduring Wisdom, Abiding Mercy

The sisters in Sacramento did not turn back as they became part of the Sisters of Mercy West Midwest. They continued doing what they always did. They discovered new ways of responding to need around them, continuing to advocate for justice and human dignity. Though now older and smaller, the sisters continued to live faithful lives. Today, they stand as living paradigms of the lessons passed down to them by the women of mercy who went before them. Sister Susan McCarthy sums it up this way:

> I would say that we are standing on the shoulders of the women who went before us. We don't always see what we are contributing until we look behind us. The sisters who went before us often did so at great personal sacrifice. Hopefully, we are doing the same, but clarity will come as the journey continues.[1]

The story of the Sisters of Mercy's lives and works can be experienced in many ways. One can simply enjoy the story or one can be challenged to emulate the courage and dedication of its main characters. One's curiosity can be stirred or one can find the story touching something within their own spirit. The story can be mined for inspiration, information, and paradigms upon which a future might be built. Jane Graf, working side by side with sisters at Mercy Housing California, points to the power of this story:

> They are quiet giants. I think the work that the sisters do and their role in the community have been amazing, an untold story. It is an eyeopener when you start to learn their history. When you think about their

individual stories and their willingness to take risk. The value of how they make decisions is so important. They are in it for the long term and so the way in which they make decisions is invaluable. There are so many things that teach what makes good leadership. It is a secret in a way. Watching how they get things done, with so much humility, is an enormous learning. There is a depth and breadth of the wisdom they have from collective learning.[2]

As we began this study of the Sisters of Mercy in Sacramento, we asked: "How was it possible for a small circle of women to make such a lasting impact upon a whole city? Do their lives give us insights to guide our actions in the present moment?" The answer is found in the story itself. Embedded within the history of the sisters are the vision and values that were instrumental in making them a lasting part of Sacramento's history. Kerry Wood, chief marketing officer for the Sacramento Region Community Foundation, shares:

Sacramento would be very different if the sisters hadn't laid the foundation of service to the poor and those in need. The city we see today is stronger because the sisters were one of the pioneer groups in this region. They had a strong base of compassion and did so many things. We wouldn't have the solid foundation and model for others without them.[3]

The sisters' beliefs and values converged to provide paradigms of action as vital today for those wishing to make a difference in their communities as they were for the sisters. For civic leaders or church leaders, social activists or social service agencies, small faith communities or community action groups, these paradigms give light for the way. They are seven in number:

*Our mission is our North Star
*All persons possess the right to human dignity, are worthy of respect, and deserving of compassion
*You achieve most when you empower persons to be their best selves.
*Where one is, all are present
*Mission is expanded through Collaboration
*It is all God's work, not our own
*Let our lives speak

These were key understandings guiding the choices and actions of the Sisters of Mercy, past and present. By vigorous adherence to these principles, the sisters were able to triumph over natural disasters, fiscal crises, scarcity of members, and political circumstances that threatened their ability to carry out the mission of mercy. Examining each of the paradigms separately allows us to understand the inner dynamism that flowed out in service to those who were poor, sick, or ignorant.

Mission Is Our North Star

The clarity with which the sisters saw their mission was evident from their beginning. In correspondence with Monsignor Gallagher, Mother Francis made explicit what would and what would not be in harmony with their mission.[4] Her clarity about what the mission demanded was so strong that, fearing it would be compromised, she almost turned down the California foundation. In a public appeal for support carried by the *San Francisco Evening Bulletin* on August 4, 1856, you find the mission of the community clearly outlined: instruction of the ignorant, rich or poor, old or young regardless of creed, country, age or condition; care of the sick; protection of unemployed women of good character; care of the orphan; and protection of the poor outcast. That is what they were to be about and that is exactly what they did.

Throughout their history, the sisters strongly resisted attempts to subvert that mission or attempts by ecclesial leaders to interpret that mission and charism. Sr. Bridget McCarthy said it best:

> We had a mission and were mission driven. All decisions were based on that mission and vision which we received from our early sisters whose commitment was to meet the needs of the community.[5]

Holding true to that commitment meant that Sacramentans could count on them. It provided an integrity of word and deed. When crisis loomed, Sacramentans knew that the sisters would not draw back or abandon those in need.

The sisters saw themselves as stewards of a mission entrusted to Catherine McAuley at the beginning of the order. The charism or special call of the Sisters of Mercy was to make the mercy of God present in their time and circumstances. It took the form of education, healing, and outreach to those in need, especially the poor. The seriousness with which the sisters regarded their charism was seen in the Apostolic Study undertaken after Vatican II. Its intent was to listen and respond to where God wanted them to be in the present time. For any organization or faith community, this paradigm is essential. It is the foundation upon which persons build their trust, relationship, and hope in the word and works of the group.

Every Person Possesses the Right to Human Dignity, Is Worthy of Respect, and Deserving of Compassion

The Sisters of Mercy held everyone who came their way in reverence and compassion. They made no distinctions based on religion, ethnicity, economic status, race, or "worthiness". No one was excluded from the arms of their compassion. This reverence and inclusivity were expressed through the quality of hospitality. No one was turned away from their care. The *San Francisco Call Bulletin* got it right when it said: "the saint and the sinner, the pure and the defiled, the godly and ungodly pass side by side through the open door of the Sisters' Hospital."[6]

This same inclusivity was found in their schools. An examination of the early school register of St. Joseph's Academy lists students from a variety of religious traditions as well as ethnic identities. Both schools and hospitals served persons from all economic strata. The conviction that everyone deserved your best impelled the sisters to provide excellence in both education and healthcare. They kept up with the latest breakthroughs in medicine as well as advances in the field of education. This was not done to remain competitive or for status, but because those served deserved nothing less. Their institutions were not to be havens for those who could afford them. For the sisters, making their services available to those without material means was an essential part of their charism.

Jail ministry was another mode through which the sisters witnessed to the inclusivity of their mission. The prisoner was a social outcast. In their visitation of the jail, the sisters would visit with those who were condemned to death, encourage those who wished to change, and assure the prisoner of God's forgiveness and mercy. This ministry was carried on in more recent times by Sisters Kathleen McCarthy and Mary Padilla.

Merciful action arising from the belief in the dignity of every person provides a powerful paradigm for persons wishing to make a difference in contemporary society. Such a belief moves one to embody a stance of hospitality to all, excellence in service, and utmost reverence in relationships. It shows us that compassion is not earned. It was available to everyone but forced upon no one. That unqualified acceptance allowed persons to share their stories with the sisters as the first step toward their healing, helped them to be vulnerable enough to seek help knowing that it would be given without judgment.

You Achieve Most When You Empower Persons to be Their Best Selves

The sisters left an example of loving persons into growth. Their willingness to accept others as they were, allowed that person the freedom to grow at her/his own rate and in one's own way. The context within which the order was founded highlighted that insight. The Sisters of Mercy started in Ireland at a time when many persons were deprived of the opportunity to be educated and were unable to freely express their religious beliefs or to pursue economic equity. Catherine McAuley knew, first-hand, what such deprivation did to persons especially women. In her *Rule of the Sisters of Mercy*, Catherine wrote: "The Sisters shall feel convinced that no work of charity can be more productive of good to society, or more conducive to the happiness of the poor than the careful instruction of women ..."[7]

When the sisters arrived in California, they found that women, especially those without economic security, were easily exploited. Without education or employable skills, women were condemned to bleak futures. The sisters sought to change that picture by providing young women with the best education possible. To ensure self-sufficiency, they included in St. Joseph's curriculum commercial education and helped to place their students in businesses throughout the city. In the nursing school, they sometimes encountered young women with generous hearts but no elementary school education. To allow them to grow personally and professionally, the sisters provided sufficient educational formation for them to succeed and earn their nursing degrees.

It was not just school learning that the sisters provided. The sisters instilled confidence in their students through public presentations, mentoring their staging of fairs and fundraising, and submitting their writings for publication. Recognizing the vital importance of education, the sisters opened a "normal school" at the academy to train generations of public-school educators. During particularly hard times, they opened an employment office, actively seeking jobs for their students or for any women in need of a job.

The role the sisters played in the empowerment of women is noted by Sacramento historian Steven Avella:

A unique group of Catholic women, religious sisters (or Nuns), made a powerful impact on Sacramento. Their various services—health care, education, and child care—were critical to the civic project. There is an added dimension to their work and presence in Sacramento that is worth noting. Not only did sisters provide critical social services, but they also represented a significant instance of female autonomy and agency that was remarkable in the nineteenth and early twentieth centuries.[8]

Avella goes on to describe St. Joseph's as "female-centered space." It was designed for women, by women, and looked to provide students with the tools for reaching their full potential. The sisters showed their students that women were capable of leadership in business, education, health care, and societal affairs. Training their students in social consciousness, the sisters mentored women to become advocates for a more civil and just society.

The support services provided to residents by Mercy Housing California is another example of the belief that you have to go beyond providing basic needs. People need the tools with which to better their lives and transition to permanent housing, stable employment, and a living environment where their families can grow. This paradigm of empowerment for full potential is vital for our society today. Dependency upon benevolence might provide for the present moment but does not build a future of hope. Agencies and social services can unwittingly prolong the cycle of poverty if they do not challenge their clients to grow.

Where One Is Present, All Are Present

There is a maxim within the Mercy community that is evident in the lives of the Sisters of Mercy in Sacramento: Where one is present, all are present. This points to the strong bond of community among them. They were united in how they chose to express their fidelity to God, united in their dedication to serve those in need. Together, they decided how they would express that service at any given time. This bond of community was rooted in pattern of Christ Jesus as interpreted through the Mercy charism passed on to them by Catherine McAuley.

The *Constitutions of the Sisters of Mercy* emphasizes this by stating that the sisters are to "live together in affection and mutual respect."[9] This oneness of spirit and life made it possible for them to take risks. They knew they were in it together and would share equally in the success or the hardship involved. Again, their *Constitutions* affirms the belief: "Community strengthens us for mission."[10] No matter how difficult the situation, sisters could be confident that they were being held in prayer and support by their sisters.

Two practices confirm this strong paradigm. The first is the practice of "missioning" sisters to their work. In the early years, sisters would either receive a formal note sending them in the name of the community to their ministry or would have their assignment formally posted for all to see. As time and practice evolved, that way of being sent in the name of the community changed to a ritual missioning ceremony in which every sister, having received the permission of the community to serve in a particular place and capacity, was sent or missioned to that work of mercy.

Community thrived when it tapped into the gifts of its members. Each sister contributed to the whole for the sake of the whole. Those missioned to leadership within the community knew that it was a temporary call. Larry Garcia noted that this dynamic was important to understand:

> One needs to understand how the sisters manage themselves. The one who answers the phone at a ministry can be the leader next time around. It is an egalitarian model and changed leadership regularly.[11]

A second practice was the manner through which the sisters came together in chapter, a formal time of gathering for decision-making, allowing them to act as one. They came together to decide such things as who would be accepted into the community, whether they would take on a new ministry, what prayers they would say, and how they would share life together. In these times of communal decision-making, the sisters sought to read the signs of the times and discern where God was calling them in the present moment. The decision to close Mercy High School is an example of a decision made together after much discussion and prayer.

In reviewing the history of the sisters across their 165 years in Sacramento, one is struck by the absence of focus on individual sisters. Apart from the occasional obituary that tells something of an individual sister's story, most references relate to the community as a whole. No sister was seen apart from the whole of which she was part. Some sisters did draw more publicity because of their works. Larry Garcia notes that the community "had some colorful and powerful personalities that shaped what the sisters could do," sisters like Mary Peter Carew, Mary Teresita Durkin, Mary Monica Burns, and Libby Fernandez among others.[12]

Witnessing to the reality of one community, united in mind and heart, allowed the sisters to show that divisions and differences could be overcome by respect, acceptance, and single-heartedness. The sisters learned from the experiences of other Mercy foundations that where such community was lacking, the mission failed. The importance of this learning cannot be underestimated. No entity can succeed if it is rife with division or enmity.

Living together, praying together, and sharing all things in common taught the sisters the reality of interconnectedness. What one sister did or did not do impacted the whole community. Living this reality sensitized the sisters to the interconnectedness of society and creation itself. Sometimes, this was graphically experienced as in the case of Sacramento's raising of the downtown streets. That project brought great good to one area of the city but caused harm to the area of the city in which the sisters dwelt. While being among those harmed in this case, sometimes the sisters themselves had to adjust their decisions in light of the common good. Negotiation with surrounding neighbors when expansion of hospital facilities came about were sometimes painful reminders of that interconnectedness.

The lived experience of community taught the sisters another truth. The whole is only as healthy and strong as its weakest member. They knew what it was to have weak and vulnerable members, how such instances make demands upon resources and upon the human spirit. Out of that truth, the sisters understood that the same was true for society. To thrive, a society must address critical needs such as housing, health care, food insecurity, and violence, as society is only as strong and healthy as its most vulnerable members. For civic leaders, church leaders, and the public in general, that insight provides much fodder for reflection. When the paradigm of community and interconnectedness is embraced, it has profound consequences upon society.

Mission Is Expanded Through Collaboration

One of the remarkable aspects of the works of the Sisters of Mercy in Sacramento is that they were always ones of partnership. The sisters consistently went where they were invited. Their major partner was the wider church community and its ecclesial leaders. The sisters did not accept invitations to serve where such collaboration was lacking or where their own charism and autonomy would be thwarted. Coming at the request of Bishop Alemany, the sisters depended on the Sacramento citizens to assist them in establishing their ministry in the city. The bishop depended on the sisters to help him carry out his ministry. For the Catholic church in Sacramento, that collaboration was essential for its growth. For almost fifty years, the Sisters of Mercy were the only women religious in the city.

Some undertakings were the result of requests arising from Sacramento's citizens. This was particularly evident in the area of health care. Intervention from persons like Drs. Parkinson and Huntington resulted in the Mater Misericordiae Hospital and Nursing School. The hospital only succeeded because of the vital partnership between sisters and doctors. The Nursing School was a thoroughly collaborative effort with doctors contributing their time as instructors. Later hospitals were built or expanded only with the understanding that the civic community would partner with the sisters in raising the needed monies.

The sisters joined with partners who shared a common goal or vision. They did not require that they be Catholic. As their works served all peoples, persons from other religious denomination or no church affiliation were willing to support the sisters in times of need. Mother Mary Gertrude King was quick to enlist St. Joseph alumnae to join in the sisters' efforts to improve the quality of education they could provide. For better or worse, the sisters sought guidance from leaders of commercial enterprises when making real estate or business decisions.

The sisters' understanding of collaboration evolved over time. In the beginning, it expressed itself through a pattern of responding to a request for assistance, seeking support, and tapping into the wisdom of persons outside the community. Only when they moved to the establishment of the Nursing School did this pattern change. While St. Joseph Academy did employ lay staff, there is no indication that such staff members had significant influence in decision making. It is Mater Misericordiae Nursing School that first places a lay woman, Miss Louise Igo, in charge of a whole program. She was an important partner with the sisters, entrusted with the shaping of the curriculum, working with physicians and oversight of the nursing students.

Throughout their history, the sisters called together boards and advisory groups to assist them in their ministries. The boards were given a strong role in decision-making. Examples of this collaborative stance are seen in the process used by the sisters to establish Mercy Health Care Organization as well as the transition of Mercy Hospital Foundation to Mercy Foundation, a congregational foundation. All participants continued in dialogue until members were agreed upon a direction.

The appointment of Charles Steding over the unified departments of the Mercy Hospitals marks the third level of collaborative action. This was the first time a layman was placed in authority over sister administrators. The sisters had given over direction and authority for part of the works to someone outside the community. It was a natural progression.

As young sisters, new members were taught that they were "to work to make yourself dispensable." When others could do the work, the sisters could turn over that work to them and move on to the next greatest need. That could not happen without a commitment to form persons for leadership and to collaborate with them in the work of mercy. The acme of collaboration was expressed through the Apostolic Study of 1978. The decision of the sisters to expand the mission through collaboration crystalized their belief that they did not own the charism or the works. They were meant to be shared with others of like vision and values.

Like those previously mentioned, the paradigm of collaboration was, and is, essential to the success of those engaged in the works of mercy. While a group might have great success initially, long term success depends upon the utilization of a wide variety of gifts and viewpoints. No group can be solo operators, but is most effective when partnering with others of like vision.

Larry Garcia sees this spirit of collaboration as vital to the ongoing work of the sisters today as their numbers decrease. Where collaboration is a high value, it provides an opportunity to continually widen the circle of partners. Larry says: "You have to enlist others. Offer them the next thing in their lives. You have to show them, 'Here is a way to contribute.'"[13]

It Is All God's Work, Not Our Own

In examining the history of the Sisters of Mercy in Sacramento, one discovers a pattern of silence about themselves. Last names were rarely used, and they often simply signed their works with "a Sister of Mercy." While consistently highlighting the accomplishments and proficiencies of their students or the excellence of their hospitals, little is said about the sisters themselves. There is an absence of ego concerns. At first this seems puzzling, but the more one explores the story, the more one discovers that for the sisters the work is not claimed as their own. It is all God's work. In an editorial written by Bishop William Weigand for the 150th anniversary of the Sisters in Sacramento, he calls attention to that stance. He quotes Catherine McAuley's words: "It is for God we serve the poor and not for thanks ... bestowing ourselves most freely and relying with unhesitating confidence on the mercy of God."[14]

The sisters saw themselves as responding to the call of God to serve God's people. The conviction that what they were doing was a response to God's desire, allowed boldness in response. Debt could be risked. Sisters could freely accept service in the face of contagious diseases as they did with cholera epidemics or the 1918 flu pandemic. Hardships could be endured. This could happen because there was a selflessness permeating their lives and works. No work was taken on for public acclaim or individual glory. They embraced the maxim of Catherine McAuley:

We have one solid comfort amidst this little tripping about: our hearts can always be in the same place, centered in God—for whom alone we go forward—or stay back. Oh, may He look on us with love and pity, and then we shall be able to do anything He wishes us to do—no matter how difficult to accomplish—or painful to our feelings[15]

While not calling attention to themselves in times of success, neither did the sisters publicly defend themselves in times of attack. They declined to say anything about the vandalism of the convent property by a member of the A.P.A. Mother Mary Baptist modeled the practice of "public silence" in the early years in San Francisco when the sisters were frequently under attack in the press. The reserve that marked the lives of the sisters could be a bit frustrating to their friends. Mike Genovese notes: "You are so modest about what you've done and do. It would be great to find a way to 'toot your horn'."[16]

Catherine McAuley was once called the Sister of Divine Providence because of her great dependence upon God. Indeed, it was the practice of the sisters to pray the litany of Divine Providence before starting a new foundation. They relied upon God to provide what was needed, nothing in excess, just enough. This was a gospel-based belief rooted in such texts as the lilies of the field from Matthew's Gospel.[17] It reflected their understanding of the words of Gamaliel from Acts 5:39: "If this be from God, you will not be able to overthrow them."

For persons of faith, this is a critical paradigm. Works taken on for the people of God are rooted in faith and trust. It is all about God and God's desires for humankind. When ego concerns take center focus, the work loses its energy and clarity of purpose. Even for persons who are not religiously motivated, the work only maintains its energy and power when it is focused upon those who are in need, focused upon its mission. Focus on the giver always drains that energy and dilutes the focus.

Let Our Lives Speak

The final major paradigm arising from the lives of the Sisters of Mercy is, "Let our lives speak." Embedded within the Mercy tradition is a strong conviction that the strongest witness you can proclaim is the witness of one's life. Words have to be matched by deeds. This paradigm was expressed through the qualities of presence, constancy, love, and relationality. As their lives reflected their commitment to justice and compassion, persons grew to expect them to speak out for the outcast. Walt Gray puts it this way:

When it comes to taking stands about issues of injustice such as trafficking or homelessness, there is an expectation that the sisters are going to be "all-in" on those issues. It is woven into their DNA, that they will challenge.[18]

For people who worked with the sisters or came to know them well, the authenticity that characterized their lives stood out. Kerry Wood reflects on that:

> Sometimes people who didn't know the sisters would view them as angelic but they were real people with families, selfless, value based, shrewd business women—approachable and caring for community.[19]

For Sharon Margetts, the witness is the legacy of the sisters' works:

> I'd like people to understand that the sisters are involved with so many things, things like Cristo Ray High School or Sr. Michelle's serving as chaplain for the State Senate. To understand the endurance of the sisters from 1857 and what they set out to do. How entwined they are with the community. Think about how many people have been helped through the Mercy health ministry. Think about how much the homeless have been helped through Loaves and Fishes and the benefits brought by the whole education ministry. There would have been a gaping hole if the sisters were not here.[20]

The civic engagement in the jubilee celebrations of the Sisters of Mercy as well as the grandeur and joy of the events hosted in honor of the sisters testify to the truth that their lives spoke. They spoke of hope, compassion, and enduring relationships. All faith communities, ecclesial groups, or social agencies must face that test. Do they witness in deeds or just in words? When lives speak, incredible works can be accomplished. The history of the Sisters of Mercy in Sacramento affirms that truth. Their lives show us that when works flow from the abundance of love, persons and communities can be transformed. The Sisters of Mercy enflesh the mercy of God in the present moment. That is what they have done since their arrival in Sacramento in 1857.

It is hard to summarize exactly what the Sisters of Mercy have meant for the people of Sacramento. Perhaps Father Paul Crowley, S.J., comes closest in his homily for the 150th anniversary Mass of the Sisters of Mercy in Sacramento. Father Paul asked those gathered to consider the contributions of the sisters over time:

> The mission of today's Mercy Sisters rests on the shoulders of these pioneer women who lived Gospel discipleship. The church needed such women then, desperately; the church needs such women and men now, even more desperately. Let us say it plainly: These were powerful women, women whose power rested in their unshakable faith in God, in the urgency of the Gospel's call, and in what God could accomplish through them. That is why they succeeded.[21]

Endnotes

List of Abbreviations

SOMA-MHC: Sisters of Mercy of the Americas, Mercy Heritage Center Belmont,
   North Carolina
SOMA-AC: Auburn Community Collection
SOMA- AR: Auburn Community Collection, held at Auburn Repository
SOMA-BC: Burlingame Community Collection (typescript)

Chapter 1

1 McGloin, J. B., *San Francisco, The Story of a City* (San Rafael, CA: Presidio
   Press, 1978), p. 33.
2 Avella, S., *Sacramento and the Catholic Church Shaping a Capital City* (Reno,
   NV, University of Nevada Press, 2008), p. 15.
3 McGloin, J. B., *California's First Archbishop the Life of Joseph Sadoc Alemany,
   O.P. 1814–1888* (New York: Herder and Herder, 1966), p. 74. All rights
   reserved. Used with permission of the Crossroad Publishing Company, www.
   crossroadpublishing.com.
4 McGloin, 1966, *op. cit.*, p. 15.
5 Portions of this chapter are adapted from *Like a Tree by Running Waters, the
   Life of Mother Mary Baptist Russell, Pioneer Sister of Mercy*, Chapters 3 and
   4 (Nevada City, CA.: Blue Dolphin Press, 2004) previously published by the
   author.
6 Gallagher, T., *Paddy's Lament* (New York: Harcourt Brace Jovanovich, 1982),
   pp. 204–206.
7 Gallagher, *Ibid.*, pp. 210–211.
8 Vaughn, A., "Bonnets by the Bay" in *The Academy Scrapbook*, Vol. III, No. 2
   (October 1952), p. 66.
9 *Ibid.*, p. 67.
10 *Ibid.*, p. 68.

11 Cloister refers to the practice of women religious being confined to their convents as well as the exclusion of outsiders from all designated areas of the convents considered enclosed. It was mandated by the church.

12 Butler, A. M., *Across God's Frontier: Catholic Sisters in the American West, 1850-1920* (Chapel Hill, NC: University of North Carolina Press, 2012), p. 44.

13 *Annals of the Sisters of Mercy, 1854–1886*, SOMA-BC, pp. 10–11.

14 *Ibid.*

15 *Ibid.*, p. 15.

16 *Ibid.*, pp. 22–23.

17 Russell, M., *Mother Mary Baptist Russell* (Dublin: Apostleship of Prayer, 1902), p. 55.

18 Sullivan, M. C., *The Correspondence of Catherine McAuley 1818–1841* (Baltimore, MD: Catholic University Press, 2004), p. 70, letter 104.

19 *Annals*, Presentation Archives, San Francisco (PASF) pp. 16–17.

20 Ibid.

21 *Annals of the Sisters of Mercy*, p. 25.

22 Carroll, M. A., *Leaves from the Annals of the Sisters of Mercy* (New York: Catholic Publication Society Co., 1889), Vol. 3, p. 473.

23 *Ibid.*, p. 474.

24 *Ibid.*

25 This term refers to a very small vessel that could usually navigate in shallow waters. Here the waters were so shallow that even such a boat or raft could not be used.

26 Carroll, *op. cit.*, pp. 474–475.

Chapter 2

1 Doyle, K., *Like a Tree by Running Water: The Story of Mary Baptist Russell, California's First Sister of Mercy* (Nevada City, CA: Blue Dolphin Publishing, 2004), pp. 60–61.

2 *Annals of the Sisters of Mercy*, SOMA-BC, RG2. Series 2.1-Box 19, pp. 10-12.

3 Sullivan, Mary C. RSM., "Catherine McAuley and the Care of the Sick, "*The MAST Journal*, Vol. 6 (Spring, 1996), p. 11.

4 A workhouse at this time in Ireland was a place where indigent persons were confined and required to work in return for food and shelter.

5 Doyle, *op. cit.*, p. 81.

6 *Ibid.*, p. 121.

7 *Alta California*, April 9, 1855.

8 McArdle, M. A., *California's Pioneer Sister of Mercy* (Fresno, CA: Academy Library Guild, 1954), pp. 39–40.

9 *Annals of the Sisters of Mercy*, pp. 33–34.

10 Doyle, *op. cit.*, p. 88.

11 Butler, *Across God's Frontier*, p. 118.

12 Doyle, *op. cit.*, p. 88.

13 Dobie, C. C., *San Francisco Pageant* (New York: DD Appleton-Century Company, 1939), p. 126.

14 Nativists were persons who embraced a policy of favoring native inhabitants as opposed to immigrants. In particular they were opposed to Irish Catholics during this period.

15 Doyle, *op. cit.*, pp. 89–90.

16 Starr, K., *Americans and the California Dream 1850–1915* (New York: Oxford University Press, 1973), p. 94.
17 *Annals of the Sisters of Mercy*, pp. 24–26.
18 Carroll, *Leaves from the Annals of the Sisters of Mercy*, p. 497.
19 *Annals of the Sisters of Mercy*, pp. 88–89.
20 McGloin *California's First Archbishop the Life of Joseph Sadoc Alemany*, p. 160.
21 Trimbe, P. C., *Riverboats of Northern California* (Charleston, SC: Arcadia Publishing, 2011), p. 9.
22 Doyle, *op. cit.*, p. 137.
23 Kennelly, M. B., Typescript: *Sacramento Annals*, SOMA-AC, RG1, Box 7,350.10, p. 3.
24 *Annals of the Sisters of Mercy*, p. 123.
25 Morgan, M. E., *Mercy Generation to Generation* (San Francisco, CA: Fearon Publishers, 1957), p. 90.
26 *Sacramento Bee* (published as THE DAILY BEE) "Local News, Sisters of Charity," September 30, 1857, p. 3.

Chapter 3

1 Lord, M. S., *A Sacramento Saga* (Sacramento Chamber of Commerce, Sacramento, 1946), p. 3.
2 *Ibid.*
3 Holden, W. M., *Sacramento* (Fair Oaks, CA: Two Rivers Publishing Co., 1988), p. 162.
4 *Annals of the Sisters of Mercy,* p. 135.
5 King, G., *Early History of the Sisters of Mercy in Sacramento*, unpublished manuscript, SOMA-AC, Box 7, 1.350.10, pp. 1–2.
6 Doyle, *Like a Tree by Running Water*, p. 215
7 *Ibid.*
8 Butler, *Across God's Frontier*, p. 142.
9 Doyle, *op. cit.*, p. 215.
10 Doyle, *op. cit.*, pp. 205–206.
11 Doyle, *op. cit.* p. 210.
12 Doyle, *op. cit.* p. 201.
13 *Annals of the Sisters of Mercy*, p. 116.
14 *Annals of the Sister of Mercy*, p. 115.
15 King, *op. cit.*, p. 3.
16 Carroll, *Leaves from the Annals of the Sisters of Mercy*, Vol. 4, pp. 32–33.
17 *Ibid.*
18 *Ibid.*
19 *Ibid.*
20 *Ibid.*
21 Jones, R., *Memories, Men and Medicine a History of Medicine in Sacramento, California* (Sacramento, CA: Sacramento Society for Medical Improvement, 1950), p. 457.
22 *Sacramento Bee*, "Local News: Stop the Nuisance," July 26, 1860, p. 3.
23 Stapp, C. A., *Disaster & Triumphant: Sacramento Women, Gold Rush through the Civil War* (Sacramento, California: Cheryl Anne Stapp, 2012), p. 183.

24 *The Sacramento Daily Union,* "City Intelligence-Drainage"
    February 10, 1866, p. 3.

Chapter 4

1 Annals are an official record of the religious community written by either
   persons of the time or collected by later members of the community using
   records of the period.
2 Doyle, *Like a Tree by Running Water,* pp. 73–74.
3 *Annals of the Sisters of Mercy,* p. 116.
4 *Ibid.*
5 *Annals of the Sisters of Mercy,* SOMA-BC, RG2. Series 2.1-Box 19, Vol. 2,
   pp. 158–159.
6 *Annals of the Sisters of Mercy,* Vol. 1, p. 250.
7 Avella, S., *Sacramento and the Catholic Church Shaping a Capital City* (Reno,
   Nv.: University of Nevada Press, 2008), p. 77.
8 Doyle, *op. cit.,* p. 200.
9 McArdle, M. A., Collection of talks on early founders, unpublished manuscript,
   SOMA-AR, Box 1.
10 *Sacramento Daily Union,* "St. Joseph's Academy—Annual Commencement,"
   July 2, 1880, p. 3.
11 Burlingame Community Obituaries, Sr. Genevieve McCue, SOMA-BS, IV.1,
   Box 13.
12 *Annals of the Sisters of Mercy,* Vol. 1, p. 323.
13 *Ibid.,* p. 330.
14 *Annals of the Sisters of Mercy,* p. 422.
15 *The Sacramento Bee* (published as THE DAILY BEE), "Local News-St.
   Joseph's," Sacramento, California, May 20, 1865, p. 3.
16 *The Sacramento Daily Union,* "Senate," Jan. 31, 1868, p. 1.
17 *Sacramento Bee* (published as THE DAILY BEE), "Local News—Fair and
   Festival," Sacramento, California, Oct. 28, 1868, p. 3.
18 *Annals of the Sisters of Mercy,* p. 383.
19 *Sacramento Daily Union,* "City Intelligence-Drainage,"
   Feb. 10, 1866. p. 3.
20 *Sacramento Bee* (published as THE DAILY BEE), Sacramento, California, Nov.
   9, 1861; May 19, 1864; April 8, 1881 and *Sacramento Daily Union,*
   June 17, 1865.
21 *Sacramento Bee* (published as THE DAILY BEE), "Local News—Vernon House
   Hospital," Sacramento, California Sept. 7, 1864, p. 3.
22 *Sacramento Bee* (published as THE DAILY BEE), "Local News," Sacramento,
   California October 13, 1865, p. 3.
23 *Annals of the Sisters of Mercy,* p. 523.
24 *Ibid.,* pp. 542–3.
25 A "normal school" was one a two-year school for training chiefly elementary
   teachers.
26 *Sacramento Bee* (published as THE DAILY BEE), "Commencement at St.
   Joseph's Academy," Sacramento, California July 1, 1880, p. 3.

Chapter 5

1   Avella, S., *The Diocese of Sacramento a Journey of Faith* (Ireland: Booklink, 2006), p. 25.
2   *Ibid.*, pp. 32–33.
3   *Annals of the Sisters of Mercy*, Vol. 2, p. 45.
4   The Children of Mary were a religious society of ordinary people who committed themselves to service and daily prayer.
5   *Annals of the Sisters of Mercy*, SOMA-AC, RG 1, 1.350, p. 63.
6   King, *Early History of the Sisters of Mercy in Sacramento*, p. 6.
7   *Sacramento Bee* (published as The Bee), "In A Good Cause, a Fair and Festival to Aid the Sisters of Mercy," Nov. 4, 1889, p. 3.
8   *Sacramento Bee* (published as The Bee), "Sisters of Mercy—The Convent Buildings to be Renovated," Oct. 13, 1891, p. 3.
9   *Sacramento Daily Union*, "Their Convent Grounds and School to be Improved," October 13, 1891, p. 6
10 *Sacramento Bee*, Oct. 13, 1891, *op. cit.*, p. 3.
11 *Ibid.*
12 *Sacramento Bee* (published as The Bee), "Progressing Well—The Subscriptions In Aid of the Sisters' Convent," Oct. 26, 1891, p. 2.
13 *Sacramento Bee* (published as The Bee), "A Great Lift, Senator Stanford's Check for Five Thousand," April 13, 1892, p. 1.
14 Apnosa is not a term in use today. It seems like there was a type of pulmonary distress which caused Sister Mary Dolores to stop breathing.
15 *Sacramento Bee* (published as The Bee), "A Sister's Death. She Expired Yesterday at St. Joseph's Convent," Sept. 3, 1891, p. 2.
16 Jones, R., unpublished lecture notes on History of Mercy Hospital, 1949, SOMA-AC, RG 1, Box 54, 3.400.4.36, p. 3.
17 Ibid., p. 5.
18 *Sacramento Daily Union*, "The Sisters' New Hospital," Nov. 27, 1896, p. 3.
19 *Sacramento Bee* (published as The Bee), "A Home for the Infirm," Sacramento, California, Nov. 25, 1896, p. 1.
20 *Ibid.*
21 Jones, R., unpublished lecture notes on History of the Nursing School, SOMA-AC, RG1. 3.400.3.48, p. 1.
22 *Sacramento Bee*, "Diplomas for New Nurses," March 30, 1900, p. 2.
23 Chapter is the word used by religious communities when they come together as a whole or as an elected representative body to make decisions about significant issues. When the community came together to accept a new member that meeting would be an example of a chapter.
24 Sisters of Mercy of Auburn, Chapter minutes, Jan. 1893, SOMA-AC, RG III, Box 3, 1.1887.
25 *Sacramento Bee* (published as The Bee), "Reliable Help, Families Will be Supplied by the Sisters of Mercy," August 14, 1894, p. 1.
26 *Sacramento Bee* (published as The Bee), "Local News—Murderous Assault," Nov.19 1869, p. 3.
27 *Sacramento Bee* (published as The Bee), March 16, 1883, p. 3. March 15, 1883, p. 3, May 30, 1873, p. 3.
28 *Sacramento Bee* (published as The Bee), "A Dastardly Deed Done Under the Cover of Night," Oct. 2, 1894, p. 1.
29 *Ibid.*

30 *Sacramento Bee* (published as The Bee), "Notes," Oct. 6, 1894, p. 4.

31 *Sacramento Bee* (published as The Bee), "She Was a Good Woman,"
Feb. 3, 1897, p. 5.

32 McClatchy, C. K., "Death of Mother Mary Vincent at St. Joseph's Academy
To-Day," *Sacramento Bee* (published as The Saturday Bee), April 30, 1902, p. 8.

33 *Sacramento Bee* (published as The Bee), "A Saintly Woman is Laid to Rest,"
May 2, 1902, p. 3.

34 *Sacramento Bee* (published as The Evening Bee), "To Honor Sisters of Mercy,"
August 26, 1907, p. 5.

Chapter 6

1 Jones, *Memories, Men and Medicine a History of Medicine in Sacramento,
California*, pp. 462–465.

2 Howell, J. D., "Early Clinical Use of the X-ray," *Transactions of the American
Clinical and Climatological Association*, 2016, Vol. 127, pp. 341–349.

3 *Sacramento Union*, "Hospitals Here as Good as in the East,"
November 29, 1909, p. 2.

4 Jones, *op. cit.*, pp. 463–464.

5 *Sacramento Union*, "Hospitals in City Have All Latest Appliances,"
Jan. 1, 1913, p. 26.

6 *Ibid.*

7 *The Sacramento Bee* (published as The Evening Bee), "Rider Finds Use for
Funds," Feb. 27, 1908, p. 4.

8 *The Sacramento Bee,* "Small Pox Causes the Academy to Close,"
Jan 27, 1910, p. 14.

9 Barry, J. M., *The Great Influenza, the Epic Story of the Deadliest Plague in
History* (New York: Penguin Random House, 2004), Used by permission of
Viking Books, an imprint of Penguin Publishing Group, a division of Penguin
Random House LLC. All rights reserved., p. 121.

10 *Ibid.*, p. 124.

11 *Sacramento Bee*, "Our Country First is Message Given at Flag Services,"
June 24, 1918, p. 3.

12 *Ibid.*

13 Spadier, M. G., SOMA-AC, Box 7, RG 1, 1.350.10, typescript memoir, p. 8.

14 Barry, *op. cit.*, p. 127.

15 *Sacramento Bee*, "Sisters Thanked for Patriotic Manuscript,"
July 11, 1918, p. 9.

16 Nolan, M. A., "Lafayette, We Are Here!" *Sacramento Bee,* Dec. 18, 1918, p. 18.

17 Kennelly, M. B., *Annals,* SOMA-AC, RG1, Box 7, 1.350.10, p. 31.

18 Bruce, A., "Watch Your Sneeze," *Sacramento Bee,* June 27, 1917, p. 15.

19 *Sacramento Union*, "Only La Grippe, Says Simmons," Oct. 17, 1918, p. 6.

20 *Sacramento Union*, "Several Churches to Hold Open Air Services Sunday,"
October 19, 1918, p. 5.

21 *Sacramento Bee*, "Horrors Exist in the Homes Where All Are Stricken with No
Nurse Attending," October 29, 1918, p. 1.

22 Kennelly, *op. cit.*, p. 31.

23 Jones, J. R., unpublished lecture notes on History of Mercy Hospital, p. 8.

24 *Sacramento Bee*, "Men Nurses Needed at County Hospital," Nov. 6, 1918,
p. 10

25 Kennelly, *op. cit.*, p. 32.

26 *Sacramento Bee,* "Sisters of Mercy Doing Big Part in Nursing Stricken," Nov. 5, 1918, p. 1.

27 *Sacramento Bee,* "Another Drop in Influenza Cases is Reported," Nov. 7, 1918, p. 1.

28 *Sacramento Bee,* "Influenza Cost City $8,227.09; County $16,454," May 27, 1919, p. 14.

29 Barry, *op. cit.*, pp. 234–236.

30 Nolan, M. A., *Annals of Mater Misericordiae Hospital*, SOMA-AC, Box 47, RG 1 3.400.2.14, p. 7.

31 *Sacramento Bee,* "Sisters of Mercy to Build New Hospital," May 21, 1921, p. 26.

32 An illuminating discussion of the tensions between sister administrators and physicians is found in *Unlikely Entrepreneurs* by Barbara Mann Wall. She traces the stories of multiple religious congregations and the patterns of autonomy witnessed through their healthcare ministries.

33 Nolan, *op. cit.*, p. 11.

34 *Ibid.*, p. 14.

35 *Ibid.*, p. 16.

36 Kennelly, *op. cit.*, p. 20.

37 Nolan, *op. cit.*, p. 17.

38 *Sacramento Bee,* untitled, Feb. 14, 1925, p. 50.

39 Nolan, *op. cit.*, p. 19.

40 Jones, *op. cit.*, p. 11.

41 *Ibid.* p. 12.

42 Nolan, *op. cit.*, p. 39.

43 Spadier, *op. cit.*, p. 8.

44 Letter to Sister Mary Teresita Durkin from Doris Donovan, SOMA-AC. RG1. Box 47, 3.400.2.6.

45 Typescript of Interview with Florence Bennetts, Radio Station KROY, 1947, SOMA-AC, RG I, Box 51, 3.400.3.49.

46 Spadier, *op. cit.*, p. 8.

Chapter 7

1 *Sacramento Bee,* "Last Rites For Bishop Grace Bring Honor To His Memory As Beloved Man," December 30, 1921, p. 1.

2 *Sacramento Bee,* "Thomas Grace, A Christian," December 27, 1921, p. 21.

3 *Sacramento Bee,* December 30, 1921, *op. cit.*, p. 15.

4 Avella, *The Diocese of Sacramento a Journey of Faith*, p. 44.

5 Deed to property, 1918, SOMA-AR.

6 *Sacramento Bee,* "Mother Mary Ligouri Noted For Charity," June 23, 1922, p. 16.

7 McClatchy here refers to the pioneer days of Sacramento.

8 *Catholic Herald*, "A Noble Woman and Ideal Religious," July 1, 1922, p. 4.

9 Nolan, M. A. handwritten notebook, SOMA-AC, RG 1, Box 7, 1.350.3.

10 *Ibid.*

11 Auburn Community Register, SOMA-AC.

12 Peters, E. N., *The 1917 Pio-Benedictine Code of Canon Law in English Translation* (San Francisco, CA: Ignatius Press, 2001), no. 604.

13 *Ibid.*

14 Written notes, Jean Lahey, May 15, 2020. SOMA-AR.

15 *Ibid.*

16 Bishop Patrick Manogue, typescript copy of letter to Cardinal G. Simeoni, Nov. 1881, Diocese of Sacramento, archives.

17 Sheridan, M. A., *And Some Fell on Good Ground, a History of the Sisters of Mercy of California and Arizona* (New York, N.Y.: Carlton Press, Inc., 1982), pp. 278–279.

18 *Ibid.* pp. 279–280.

19 Healy, K., *Sisters of Mercy Spirituality in America 1843–1900* (New York: Paulist Press, 1992), pp. 353–354.

20 Sabourin, M. J., *The Amalgamation* (St. Meinrad, Indiana: Abbey Press, 1976), p. 8.

21 Sheridan, *op. cit.*, pp. 168–69.

22 O'Brien, K., *Journeys A Pre-Amalgamation History of the Sisters of Mercy Omaha Province* (Omaha, NE: Omaha Province of the Sisters of Mercy, 1987), p. 215.

23 *Ibid.*, pp. 214–215.

24 *Ibid.*, p. 221.

25 Spadier, SOMA-AC, Box 7, RG 1, 1.350.10, typescript memoir, p. 7.

26 *Ibid.*

27 Sabourin, *op. cit.*, p. 16.

28 This is the same group, the American Protection Association, that earlier vandalized the fence at St. Joseph's Academy in Sacramento.

29 Sheridan, *op. cit.*, p. 172.

30 *Ibid.*, pp. 172–174.

31 *Ibid.*

32 Sabourin, *op. cit.*, pp. 16–23.

33 *Ibid.*, pp. 48–49.

34 *Ibid.*

35 *Ibid.*, p. 168.

36 Chapter minutes, Sisters of Mercy of Auburn, CA. June 21, 1921, SOMA-AC, RG III, Box 3, 1.1921, p. 101.

37 *Ibid.*, p. 102.

Chapter 8

1 McAuley, C., *Original Rule of the Sisters of Mercy*, Chapter II, #5 in Mary C. Sullivan, *Catherine McAuley and the Tradition of Mercy* (Notre Dame, Indiana: University of Notre Dame Press, 1995), p. 297.

2 Sullivan, M. C., *Path of Mercy* (Washington, D. C.: The Catholic University of America Press, 2012), pp. 25–26.

3 Dolphin, B. "Venerable Catherine McAuley: Aspects of her Life and Spirituality," www.mercyworld.org/library.

4 Kennelly, *Annals*, p. 4.

5 Doyle, *Like a Tree by Running Water*, pp. 332–333.

6 *Sacramento Bee*, "Play Drama at Commencement," July 1, 1910, p. 3.

7 *Sacramento Bee*, "St. Joseph's will honor graduates, Fourteen Students to Get Diplomas at Exercises at Academy To-Night," June 27, 1912, p. 18.

8 *Sacramento Union*, "St. Joseph Students to Hold Commencement Exercises June 13–14," June 8, 1922, p. 2.

9 *Sacramento Bee*, "Convent Alumnae to Equip Laboratories," October 1, 1917, p. 10.

10 *Sacramento Union*, January 17, p. 8; February 28, p. 6; March 7, 1922, p. 6.

11 Avella, *Sacramento and the Catholic Church Shaping a Capital City* (2008), p. 90.

12 *Ibid.*, p. 89.

13. Kennelly, *op. cit.* p. 7.

14 *Sacramento Bee*, "$932.70 Raised at Bazaar," March 7, 1914, p. 7.

15 Spadier, SOMA-AC, Box 7, RG 1, 1.350.10, typescript memoir, pp. 7–10.

16 Spadier, *op. cit.*, p. 9.

17 Doyle, *op. cit.*, pp. 216, 234

18 *Sacramento Bee*, "St. Joseph Students Visit Assembly," April 8, 1913, p. 10.

19 Avella 2008, *op. cit.*, p. 79.

20 *Chapter Book*, October 29, 1893. SOMA-AC, RG III, Box 3, 1.1887.

21 *Sacramento Bee*, "New Grammar Building for Catholic School," February 25, 1924, p. 12.

22 *Sacramento Bee*," St Joseph Academy to Have New High School Building," April 20, 1926, p. 21.

23 Sisters of Mercy of Auburn, *Chapter Book* 1887, *op. cit.*, p.108

24 *Superior California Register*, "New Auditorium to Be Dedicated on Saturday," June 28, 1931, p. 8

25 A Hooverville was a temporary shanty settlement often found outside cities during the depression years.

26 Avella 2008, *op. cit.*, p. 167.

27 Boll, J. E., Sacramento Diocesan Archives, Vol. 1, No 6, July 2012.

28 Handwritten note preserved in the Sacred Heart Community Annals, SOMA-AC, RG1, Box 21 2.100.2.51.

29 Avella 2008, *op. cit.*, pp. 174–175.

30 *Ibid.*

31 *Ibid.*

32 Riter, B., "Fire Escapes in Orphanage Bare Stairs of Wood," *Sacramento Bee*, March 26, 1931, p. 2.

33 *Sacramento Bee*, "Catholic Orphanage Work is Slated to Begin in July," April 18, 1931, p. 25

34 Avella 2008, *op. cit.*, p. 176.

35 Spadier, *op. cit.*, p. 10.

36 *Ibid.*

Chapter 9

1 *Superior California Register*, "Mercy Sisters Hope to Build New Mother House in the Sierra Foothills," Dec. 12, 1937 p. 3.

2 Morgan, M. E., draft of article for submission to local news outlets, undated, SOMA-AR.

3 *Sacramento Bee*, "Novitiate Is To Be Built Near Auburn," December 18, 1937, p. 4.

4 *Sacramento Bee*, "Campaign Is Resumed For Motherhouse," February 22, 1939, p. 27.

5 *Auburn Annals*, SOMA-AC, RG 1, Box 10, 2.109.3, p. 5.

6 *Auburn Annals*, SOMA-AC, RG 1,Box 10, 2.109.3, pp. 5–6.

7 *Ibid.*, p. 8.

8 *Ibid.*, pp. 46–47.

9 *Ibid.*, p. 40.

10 *Ibid.*, p. 37.

11 *Ibid.*, p. 31.

12 *Ibid.*, p. 8.

13 *The Sacramento Bee*, "Dr. Ferdinand Stabel, Redding Hospital Founder, Succumbs," December 9, 1943, p. 16.

14 *The Sacramento Bee*, "Redding Hospital Chief Appeals for Nurses," December 16, 1943, p. 13.

15 *The Sacramento Bee*, "Sisters of Mercy Inspect Hospital in Shasta County," June 5, 1944, p. 11.

16 *The Sacramento Bee*, "Shastans Act to Enable Nuns to Operate Hospital," July 18, 1944, p. 6.

17 *The Sacramento Bee*, "Hospital in Redding Will Change Owners," October 11, 1944, p. 8.

18 *Redding Annals*, SOMA-AC, RG 1, Box 30, 2.100.11.51, p. 3.

19 *Ibid.*, p, 16.

20 *Ibid.*, p. 10.

21 Dowd, M. L., The History of Abbeylands, unpublished manuscript, SOMA-AC, RG 1, Box 14, 211.4.

22 Private Correspondence from Monsignor Kirby, SOMA-AR, legal papers, 1948.

23 Interview with Sister Maureen Costelloe, April 14, 2021.

24 Interview with Sister Hannah Mary O'Donoghue, April 6, 2021.

25 Auburn Register of membership, SOMA-AR.

26 *Kerryman Newspaper*, June 1950.

27 Costelloe, *op. cit.*; O'Donoghue, *op. cit.*

28 McGuinness, M. M., *Called to Serve a History of Nuns in America* (New York: New York University Press, 2013), p. 69.

29 *Ibid.*, p. 74.

30 *Ibid.*, p. 156.

31 *Ibid.*, p. 82.

32 *Academy Hi-Lights*, 1941-43 SOMA-AR.

33 deCuir, D., *Academy Hi-Lights*, 1943, SOMA-AR.

34 McDonald, B., *Academy Hi-Lights*, 1943, SOMA-AR.

35 *Ibid.*

36 *Ibid.*

37 *Sacramento Bee*, "New Building is Considered for Catholic School," April 7, 1938, p. 3.

38 Spadier, SOMA-AC, Box 7, RG 1, 1.350.10, typescript memoir, p. 7.

Chapter 10

1 Jones, unpublished lecture notes on History of Mercy Hospital, pp. 14–15.

2 *Sacramento Bee*, "Modern Mercy Hospital Had Humble Start in 1895," July 26, 1941, p. 34.

3 *Mercy Progress*, SOMA-AR, RG 1, Box 37, 3.400.4, 1965/6, p. 6.

4 *Sacramento Bee*, "CC Board Gets Report on Plan of Expanding Hospitals," January 7, 1949, p. 3.

5 *Redding Annals*, SOMA-AC, RG 1, Box 30, 2.100.11.51, October 1945, p. 6.

6 *Ibid.*, May 1947, p. 14.

7 *Ibid.*, Sept. 1947, p. 15.

8 *Ibid.*, August 8, 1948, p. 21.

9 *Ibid.*, April 11, 1953, p. 72.

10 *Ibid.*, June 21, 1952, p. 5.

11 *Ibid.*, June 17, 1952, p. 56.

12 *Sacramento Bee*, "Public Drive for Hospital Funds May be Launched," April 21, 1948, p. 4.

13 *Ibid.*

14 *Superior California Catholic Herald*, "Community Organizes Campaign to Increase Hospital Facilities," March 9, 1951, p. 1.

15 *Ibid.*

16 *Ibid.*, p. 8.

17 *Sacramento Bee*, "Hospital Fund Appeal is to Stress Need," May 2, 1951, p. 25.

18 *Sacramento Bee*, "Inter-Racial Character of Mercy Hospital is Praised," May 25, 1951, p. 3.

19 *Superior California Catholic Herald*, "Parishes Assist in Drive to Aid Mercy Hospital Campaign," June 15, 1951, p. 1.

20 *Superior California Catholic Herald*, "Campaign to Aid Mercy Hospital is City's Most Successful Drive," July 6, 1951, p. 1.

21 *Superior California Catholic Herald*, "Sisters Express Gratitude," July 6, 1951, p. 1.

22 Lyons, A. E., "Knight Hails Mercy Nuns in Hospital Fete," *Sacramento Bee*, December 20, 1954, p. 21.

23 *Catholic Herald*, "Mercy Foundation to Provide for Future Growth," May 3, 1956, p. 1.

24 Redmond, M. B., *Mercy Memories, Golden Jubilee Book of Mercy College of Nursing*, pp. 8–9.

25 *Auburn Annals*, SOMA-AC, RG 1, Box 10, 2.109.3, May 8, 1950, p. 161.

26 *Mary Book*, SOMA-AR, Vol II:2, 1953, p. 4.

27 *Catholic Herald,* "Mercy College Accredited by Catholic U," November 20, 1952, p. 1.

28 *Mary Book*, SOMA-AR, Vol 1:1 1951, p. 10.

29 Elizabeth Marie Farrell RSM, Conversation with author, 1981.

30 Werntz, M.R., *Our Beloved Union A History of the Sisters of Mercy of the Union* (Westminster, MD: Christian Classics, Inc., 1989), p. 169.

31 *Over the Teacups*, summer, 1995, SOMA-AC, RG 1, Box 79, 3.500, 3.11, p. 4.

32 Avella, *Sacramento and the Catholic Church Shaping a Capital City*, p. 210.

Chapter 11

1 Avella, *The Diocese of Sacramento a Journey of Faith*, p. 189.

2 *Ibid.*, pp. 189–190.

3 Sisters of Mercy of Auburn, *Chapter minutes*, June 17, 1956, #4, SOMA-AR.

4 Rogers, R. C., "The First One Hundred Years of the Sacramento City Schools, 1854–1954," p. 9.

5 Avella, *Sacramento and the Catholic Church Shaping a Capital City,* p. 222.

6 *Ibid.*, p. 225.

7 *Ibid.*, p. 226.

8 *Ibid.*, p. 236.

9 *Ibid.*, p. 233.

10 *Ibid.*, p. 240.

11 Vatican II refers to a gathering of all the cardinals and bishops of the Catholic Church called by the Pope. This was the first Ecumenical Council in almost 100 years. Unlike other Councils that primarily dealt with doctrine, Vatican II focused on pastoral issues and the place of the Church in contemporary society.

12 Mary Mercy Longwich RSM, Conversation with author, 1970s.

13 1955 *Customs Book of the Sisters of Mercy of Auburn*, SOMA-AR, pp. 44–45.

14 *Ibid.*, p. 45.

15 *Ibid.*, p. 58.

16 *Ibid.*, p. 55.

17 Interview with Sr. Mary St. Michael Myles, January 20, 2021.

18 Interview with Sr. Eileen Mary O'Connor, January 20, 2021.

19 1955 *Customs Book, op. cit.*, p. 53.

20 *Ibid.*, p. 55.

21 Myles, *op. cit.*

22 *Ibid.*

23 O'Connor, *op. cit.*

24 Weakland, R., "Religious Life in the U.S.—Understanding the Moment." In *Living in the Meantime, Concerning the Transformation of Religious Life* (New York: Paulist Press, 1994), pp. 203–204.

25 Myles, *op. cit.*

26 Weakland, *op. cit.*, p. 203.

27 1955 *Customs Book, op. cit.*, pp. 80–82.

28 Durkin, Mary Teresita, letter to the community, March 28, 1971, SOMA, AR.

29 Draft Statement on the Religious Life, SOMA-AR.

30 O'Connor, *op. cit.*

31 These position papers are held in the SOMA heritage center in Belmont, NC. 2014.04, Box 4.

32 Interview with Sister Jeanette Noonan, April 24, 2021.

33 O'Connor and Myles, *op. cit.*

34 *Constitutions of the Sisters of Mercy, Auburn, CA.*, 1978, SOMA-AR, iv.

35 *Ibid.*, ii–iii.

Chapter 12

1 Interview with Sr. Eileen Mary O'Connor, January 20, 2021.

2 *Catholic Herald*, "New Mercy San Juan Plans Numerous Hospital First," May 16, 1963, section two, p. 1.

3 *Ibid.*

4 Minutes of the Superiors Meeting, September 18, 1964, SOMA-AC.

5 *Catholic Herald*, "Automation Will be King at New Mercy San Juan," May 2, 1966, p. 18.

6 *Catholic Herald*, May 16, 1963, *op. cit.*, p. 1.

7 Interview with Sr. Bridget McCarthy, April 8, 2021.

8 Interview with Sr. Mary St. Michael Myles, January 20, 2021.

9 O'Connor, *op. cit.*

10 Myles, *op. cit.*

11 Rendon, A., "Striving for Homelike Atmosphere," *Catholic Herald*, May 14, 1964, p. 13.

12 Interview with Sister Rosemarie Carvalho, April 12, 2021.

13 *Catholic Herald*, "Redding Bid Opening Sets Stage for Mercy Expansion," May 11, 1967, section two, p. 1B.

14 *Sacramento Bee*, "Mercy Hospitals Name Area Director, Controller," June 26, 1965, p. 7.

15 *Catholic Herald*, "Layman Will Head System," May 13, 1965, pp. 1, 3.

16 *Catholic Herald*, "New Buildings Match Old at Mercy College," July 27, 1967, p. 9.

17 Interview with Sister Maureen Costelloe, *op. cit.*

18 *Annals of Our Lady of Mercy, Auburn, CA.*, May 25, 1966, p. 19.

19 O'Connor, *op. cit.*

20 *Catholic Herald*, "Board of Regents is Inaugurated at Jesuit High," Feb. 13. 1969, p. 10.

21 General Council Minutes, SOMA-MHC, 2014.02, May 4, 1975, p. 4.

22 Interview with Sister Rita Irene Esparza, March 2, 2021.

23 *Catholic Herald*, "Mercy High to Close," July 26, 1982, p. 1.

24 Esparza, *op. cit.*

25 Interview with Sister Mary Philomene Gogarty, February 24, 2021.

26 *Redding Annals*, Oct. 12, 1966 SOMA-MHC, 2014.02, p. 285.

27 Esparza, *op. cit.*

28 This is a story from the author's own college experience.

29 Catherine McAuley, Letter to Sister M. deSales White, Dec. 20, 1840 in *The Correspondence of Catherine McAuley 1818–1841*, Ed. Mary C Sullivan (Baltimore, MD: The Catholic University of America Press, 2004), no. 220, p. 332.

30 *Constitutions of the Sisters of Mercy Auburn, California*, 1978, #3–4, 6 SOMA- AR.

31 Doyle, M. K., "Our First and All-Encompassing Love," *MAST*, Vol. 14, No. 1, pp. 14–19.

32 Sisters of Mercy of Auburn, California, *Proceedings of the Third General Chapter and Special Chapter of Renewal*, June 22-August 3, 1968, June 24-July 24, 1969, October 4, 1969, p. 2.

33 *Ibid.*, p. 30.

34 *Ibid.*

35 *Annals of the Sisters of Mercy of Auburn*, March 21, 1965 SOMA-MHC, RG1. 2014.02, Box 16.2.

36 *Catholic Herald*, "57% of Catholics Want Church Silent on Social Issues," April 18, 1968, p. 1.

37 *Catholic Herald*, "Christian Social Action Emphasis in Mercy Religion Program," school insert, Jan. 30, 1975, pp. 1, 4.

38 Gaskell, M., CSJ, "Hospitals Refuse Defense System," *Catholic Herald*, Feb. 4, 1982, p. 9.

39 *Ibid.*

Chapter 13

1 Catherine McAuley. Letter to Frances Warde #269, May 28, 1841 in Sullivan, *The Correspondence of Catherine McAuley 1818–1841*, p. 401.

2 The negotiation refers to the arrangements for the sale of property.
3 Alden J. Bell. Memorandum, March 28, 1977, SOMA-AR, St. Joseph Academy
4 A reredos is the screen or decorative background behind an altar.
5 *Sacramento Bee*, "Hospital Facelift," March 19, 1978, p. 79.
6 *Updater, Mercy General Hospital*, June 12, 1978, p. 4.
7 *Ibid.*, p. 2.
8 *Ibid.*, p. 6.
9 Interview with Sister Marilee Howard, April 10, 2021.
10 Divoky, D., "Mercy Addition Previewed," *Sacramento Bee*, April 3, 1981, p. 39
11 Interview with Sister Mary Virginia Sullivan, January 20, 2021.
12 Christiansen, Valeria, "New $17 Million Wing at Mercy," *Catholic Herald*, April 9, 1981, pp. 1–2.
13 Interview with Sister Rosemarie Carvalho, April 12, 2021.
14 *Ibid.*
15 O'Donoghue, *op. cit.*
16 Carvalho, *op. cit.*
17 Sisters of Mercy of Auburn, *Chapter Minutes*, June 23, 1982, p. 9, SOMA-AC, RC III, 2014.02. Chapter 1982.
18 *Ibid.*
19 Summary of Task Force Interviews, Pastor Royal Blue, SOMA-AC,2014.2, RG3-26.7.101.3.
20 *Ibid.*
21 Sisters of Mercy of Auburn, Congregational Apostolic Plan, 1983-1993, SOMA-AC,2014.2, RG3-26.7.101.3, p. 41.
22 *Catholic Herald*, "Mercy sisters opt for future expansion," February 20, 1984, p. 5
23 Summary Report, Apostolic Study Task Force, *op. cit.*, p. 5
24 Interview with Sister Kathleen Horgan, April 7, 2021.
25 Sisters of Mercy of Auburn, Chapter Minutes, July 10, 1982, SOMA-AC,2014.2, Chapter 1982.
26 Interview with John Diepenbrock, April 28, 2021.
27 Interview with Larry Garcia, April 27, 2021.
28 Interview with Michael Genovese, April 16, 2021.
29 Kauffman, C. J. and Pamela Schaeffer, *A Passionate Voice for Compassionate Care celebrating 100 years of the Catholic Health Association of the United States* (St. Louis, Missouri, The Catholic Health Association of the United States, 2015), p. 72.
30 *Ibid.*
31 Interview with Sister Maura Power, March 31, 2021.
32 Sisters of Mercy of Auburn, *Chapter Minutes*, July 5, 1972, p. 83 SOMA-AC, RC III, 2014.02. Chapter 1982.
33 Garcia, *op. cit.*
34 Interview with Sister Terese Marie Perry, April 13, 2021.
35 *Catholic Herald,* "Health Care Systems to Merge," March 17, 1986, p. 8.
36 Perry, *op. cit.*
37 Interview with Sister Eileen Enright, April 19, 2021.
38 *Catholic Herald,* "Mercy sisters opt for future expansion," February 20, 1984, p. 5.
39 Mercy Education Board Minutes, May, 1985, SOMA-AR.
40 Enright, *op. cit.*
41 Carvalho, *op. cit.*

42   Memoir of Sister Mary Dolores Wagner, December 2020.
43   Parent (name withheld), Conversation with the author, January 1981.

Chapter 14

1   Sisters of Mercy of Auburn, Council Minutes, August 12, 1981, SOMA-AC, RG3 2104.02 Council 1981, p. 3.
2   Colgan, D. and Gottemoeller, D., *Union and Charity: The Story of the Sisters of Mercy of the Americas* (Silver Spring, Maryland: Institute of the Sisters of Mercy of the Americas, 2017), p. 4.
3   *Ibid.*, p. 5.
4   Interview with Sister Susan McCarthy, May 3, 2021.
5   O'Connor, Interview with Sr. Eileen Mary O'Connor, January 20, 2021.
6   *Ibid.*
7   Colgan and Gottemoeller, *op. cit.*, pp. 10–11.
8   Power, *op. cit.*
9   Interview with Sister Sheila Browne, May 6, 2021.
10   Founding Document of the Institute of the Sisters of Mercy of the Americas in *Constitutions and Directory of the Sisters of Mercy*. p. 102.
11   McCarthy, S., *op. cit.*
12   *Ibid.*
13   This particular commitment was added at the Dayton Chapter of 1995.
14   Colgan and Gottemoeller, *op. cit.*, p. 21.
15   Sister of Mercy, Auburn Regional Community, *Mercy Scenes*, March/April 1992, p. 2.
16   McCarthy, S., *op. cit.*
17   sacloaves.org.
18   Interview with Sister Libby Fernandez, April 23, 2021.
19   Sisters of Mercy, Auburn Regional Community, *Mercy Scenes*, February 1992, p. 4.
20   Interview with Dorothy Smith, April 22, 2021.
21   *Ibid.*
22   Sisters of Mercy, Auburn Regional Community, *Mercy Scenes*, October 1993, p. 6.
23   Interview with Sister Cora Salazar April 21, 2021.
24   Westlund, N., "Nun's Program Helps Empower Immigrants," *Catholic Herald*, December 4, 1999, pp. 8–9.
25   Silva, B., "Sewing and Reaping," *Sacramento Bee*, November 24, 1998, pp. D1,4.
26   Interview with Sister Maria Campos, April 29, 2021.
27   Sister Anne Chester, written memoir, May 9, 2021.
28   Westlund, N., "Mercy Care Team Tackles Students' Learning Disabilities," *Catholic Herald*, January 25, 1997, p. 6.
29   *Ibid.*
30   Weigand, W., "Cristo Rey—A New High School that Works," *Catholic Herald*, August 19, 2006, p. 6.
31   Interview with Sister Michelle Gorman, May 12, 2021.
32   Browne, *op. cit.*
33   Cox, W., "How to Sustain Catholic Hospitals as Church Ministries," *Catholic Herald*, January 22, 2005, pp. 6–7.

34 Interview with Sister Bridget McCarthy, April 8, 2021.

35 Sly, J., "Union Reject Proposed Accord with Catholic Hospitals," *Catholic Herald*, August 14. 1999, pp. 19–20.

36 Fisher, J. P., "Clash of principles, profits at Mercy?" *Sacramento Bee*, December 15, 1999, pp. E1, 3.

37 *Ibid.*

38 Sly, J., "Mercy Healthcare's workers turn down union," *Catholic Herald*, February 5, 2000, pp. 1, 13.

39 Browne, *op. cit.*

40 Westlund, N., "Mercy expansion project approved," *Catholic Herald*, December 15, 2007, p. 4.

Chapter 15

1 Interview with Stan Atkinson, April 30, 2021.

2 Interview with Walt Gray, April 9, 2021.

3 Interview with Sharon Margetts, April 10, 2021.

4 *Catholic Herald*, "Golf Classic New to Mercy All-Star Week," August 11, 2001, p. 26.

5 *Catholic Herald*, "Diocesan Agencies Receive Mercy Healthcare Grants," December 16, 2000, p. 4.

6 Sly, J., "St. Francis Terrace addressing need for Affordable housing," *Catholic Herald*, March 24, 1995, pp. 1, 3, 13.

7 Interview with Jane Graf, April 28, 2021.

8 Interview with Dorothy Smith, April 22, 2021.

9 Graf, *op. cit.*

10 Interview with Sister Libby Fernandez, April 23, 2021.

11 Sly, *op. cit.*, p. 3.

12 Smith, *op. cit.*

13 Westlund, N., "Mercy Charities Housing builds lives for Folsom residents," *Catholic Herald*, August 28, 1999, p. 8.

14 Smith, *op. cit.*

15 Doriot, J., "Mercy McMahon Terrace: a new place to call home," *Catholic Herald*, January 3, 1990, p. 4.

16 Rall, L., *The Golden Umbrella A History of Sharing and Caring* (Redding, CA: Shasta Historical Society, 1980), p. 1.

17 *Catholic Herald*, "Golden Umbrella Campaign in Redding launched with major donation," January 9, 1999, p .3

18 *Catholic Herald*, "Seniors in Shasta Country will benefit from expanded services," February 21, 1998, p. 6

19 Creamer, A., "Convent Tends to Aging Nuns—Many return to Sisters of Mercy facility in Auburn to retire," *Sacramento Bee*, October 27, 2012, p. 1.

20 *Catholic Herald*, "Chapel renovated at Mercy motherhouse," November 3, 2001, p. 5.

21 Westlund, N., "Remodel set for Sisters of Mercy Convent in Auburn," *Catholic Herald,* July 3, 2004, p. 1.

22 Interview with Sister Sheila Browne, May 6, 2021.

23 Creamer, *op. cit.*

24 Murphy, J., "Quiet Revolution at Auburn". In *Catholic Herald*, April 7, 1977, p. 1.

25 *Catholic Herald.* "Marian Retreat Center offers prayerful climate," May 6, 1992, p. 11.
26 *Catholic Herald.* "Marian Retreat Center plans special ways to celebrate Jubilee Year," January 8, 2000, p. 8.
27 *Mercy Scenes*, January 2003, p. 8.
28 Interview with Sister Juliana Clancy, May 18, 2021.
29 Sisters of Mercy of the Americas, Direction Statement, Fourth Institute Chapter, 2005.
30 *Catholic Herald*, "Blessing ceremony for new parish steward in Siskiyou area," November 20, 1999, p. 3.
31 Vovakes, C., "Parish stewards find challenges in parishes," *Catholic Herald*, April 10, 2004, pp. 1, 12.

Chapter 16

1   Gorman, M., "Eight is Enough" in *Mercy Scenes*, April, 1996, p. 3.
2   "Entire Institute invited into Pathways process," in *Vita*, May 1997, pp. 1, 3.
3   *Ibid.* p. 3
4   Colgan and Gottemoeller, *Union and Charity*, p. 31.
5   Interview with Sister Sheila Browne, May 6, 2021.
6   *Ibid.*
7   Quinio, C. "Provisional Areas Move to Intentional," in *Vita*, September 2004, p. 1.
8   Westlund, N. "Sisters of Mercy donate $1 million for affordable housing," *Catholic Herald*, March 27, 2004, p. 9.
9   Interview with Sharon Margetts, April 10, 2021.
10 Westlund, N., "Events to Celebrate 150 years of life, service of Sisters of Mercy," *Catholic Herald*, August 18, 2007, pp. 3, 4.
11 Interview with Kerry Wood, May 10, 2020.
12 Sly, J. "Sisters of Mercy Celebrate 150 Years in State," *Catholic Herald*, October 6, 2007, p. 11.
13 Wood, *op. cit.*

Chapter 17

1   Interview with Sister Susan McCarthy, May 3, 2021.
2   Interview with Jane Graf, April 28, 2021.
3   Interview with Kerry Wood, May 10, 2020.
4   *Annals of the Sisters of Mercy,* SOMB, p. 15.
5   Interview with Sister Bridget McCarthy, April 8, 2021.
6   *San Francisco Call Bulletin*, August 4, 1856.
7   *Morning and Evening Prayer of the Sisters of Mercy*, p. 916.
8   Avella, *Sacramento and the Catholic Church Shaping a Capital City*, pp. 73–74.
9   *Constitutions of the Sisters of Mercy*, no. 18.
10 *Constitutions of the Sisters of Mercy*, no. 19.
11 Interview with Larry Garcia, April 27, 2021.
12 *Ibid.*
13 *Ibid.*

14 Weigand, W., "The Sisters of Mercy: 150 years in Sacramento," in *Catholic Herald*, October 20, 2007.
15 Sullivan, *The Correspondence of Catherine McAuley 1818–1841*, p. 332, # 220
16 Interview with Michael Genovese, April 16, 2021.
17 Matt. 6:25-34
18 Interview with Walt Gray, April 9, 2021.
19 Wood, *op. cit.*
20 Interview with Sharon Margetts, April 10, 2021.
21 Sly, J., "Sisters of Mercy Celebrate 150 Years in State," *Catholic Herald*, October 6, 2007, p. 11.

Bibliography

Prime Documents on Mercy History-Spirituality held at Mercy Archives and
   Heritage Center, Belmont, North Carolina

Annals of the Sisters of Mercy, Sisters of Mercy, Burlingame Regional Community,
   1854–1898
Chapter Book 1886–1945, *Sisters of Mercy of Auburn*
Kennelly, M. B., *Annals of the Sisters of Mercy, 1857–1932*
King, M. G., *Annals of the Sacramento Foundation, 1857–1905*
McArdle, M. A., Collection of talks on early founders
Morning and Evening Prayer of the Sisters of Mercy (Chicago: Institute of the Sisters of
Mercy of the Americas, 1998)
Nolan, M. A., *Annals of Mater Misericordiae Hospital*
Original Rule of the Sisters of Mercy, in *Catherine McAuley and the Tradition
   of Mercy* (Notre Dame, IN: Notre Dame University Press, 1995) by Mary C.
   Sullivan RSM)
Sisters of Mercy of Auburn, *Chapter Minutes,* 1974–2008
Sisters of Mercy of Auburn, Council Minutes, 1974–2008
Spadier, M. G., *Memoir*
Sullivan, M. C., *The Correspondence of Catherine McAuley 1818–1841* (Baltimore,
   MD: Catholic University Press, 2004)

Secondary Mercy Sources

Carroll, Mother M. A., *Leaves from the Annals of the Sisters of Mercy* (New York:
   The Catholic Publication Society, 1889), Vol. III and Vol. IV
Colgan, D., RSM, and Gottemoeller, D., RSM, *Union and Charity: The Story of
   the Sisters of Mercy of the Americas* (Silver Spring, MD: Sisters of Mercy of the
   Americas, 2017)
Doyle, M. K., RSM, *Like a Tree by Running Water The Story of Mary Baptist
   Russell, California's First Sister of Mercy* (Nevada City, CA: Blue Dolphin
   Publishers, 2004)

Healy, K., RSM, *Sisters of Mercy Spirituality in America 1843–1900* (New York: Paulist Press, 1992)

McArdle, Sister M. A., RSM, *California's Pioneer Sister of Mercy* (Fresno, CA: Academy Guild, 1954)

Morgan, Sister M. E., RSM, *Mercy Generation to Generation History of the First Century of the Sisters of Mercy in Sacramento* (San Francisco, CA: Fearon Publishers, 1957)

O'Brien, Sister K., RSM, *Journeys A Pre-Amalgamation History of the Sisters of Mercy Omaha Province* (Omaha, NE: Omaha Province of the Sisters of Mercy, 1987)

Sheridan, Sister M. A., ... *And Some Fell on Good Ground, a History of the Sisters of Mercy of California and Arizona* (New York, N.Y.: Carlton Press, Inc., 1982)

Sabourin, Sister M. J., RSM, *The Amalgamation* (St. Meinrad, Indiana: Abbey Press, 1976)

Sullivan, M. C. RSM, "Catherine McAuley and the Care of the Sick," *The MAST Journal*, Vol. 6, No. 2 (Spring, 1996); *Path of Mercy* (Washington, D. C.: The Catholic University of America Press, 2012)

Werntz, M. R., RSM, *Our Beloved Union, A History of the Sisters of Mercy of the Union* (Westminster, MD: Christian Classics, 1989)

General Bibliography

Avella, S. M., *Sacramento and the Catholic Church: Shaping a Capital City* (Reno, Nv., University of Nevada Press, 2008)

Avella, S. M., *The Diocese of Sacramento: A Journey of Faith.* (Ireland: Booklink, 2006)

Avella, S. M., *Sacramento Indomitable City* (Charleston S.C.: Arcadia Publishing, 2003)

Barry, J. M., *The Great Influenza: the Story of the Deadliest Pandemic in History* (New York: Penguin Random House, 2018)

Butler, A. M., *Across God's Frontier: Catholic Sisters in the American West, 1850–1920* (Chapel Hill, NC: University of North Carolina Press, 2012)

Coburn, C. K. and Smith, M., *Spirited Lives: How Nuns Shaped Catholic Culture and American Life, 1836–1929* (Chapel Hill, N.C.: University of North Carolina Press, 1999)

Connolly, E. and Self, D., *Capital Women: An Interpretive History of Women in Sacramento, 1850–1920* (Sacramento, CA: Capital Women's History Project, 1995)

Delgado, J. P., *To California by Sea: A Maritime History of the California Gold Rush* (Columbia, SC: University of South Carolina Press, 1990)

Holden, W. M., *Sacramento* (Fair Oaks, CA: Two Rivers Publishing Co., 1988.)

Jones, R., *Memories, Men and Medicine: A History of Medicine in Sacramento, California* (Sacramento, CA: Sacramento Society for Medical Improvement, 1950)

Kauffman, C. J. and Schaeffer, P., *A Passionate Voice for Compassionate Care Celebrating 100 Years of the Catholic Health Association of the United States* (St. Louis, MO: The Catholic Health Association of the United States, 2015)

Lord, M. S., *A Sacramento Saga* (Sacramento, CA: Sacramento Chamber of Commerce, 1946).

McGloin, J. B., *California's First Archbishop: The Life of Joseph Sadoc Alemany, O.P. 1814–1888* (New York: Herder and Herder, 1966)

McGloin, J. B., *San Francisco: The Story of a City* (San Rafael, CA: Presidio Press, 1978)

McGuinness, M. M., *Called to Serve: A History of Nuns in America* (New York: New York University Press, 2013)

Stapp, C. A., *Disaster & Triumphant: Sacramento Women, Gold Rush through the Civil War* (Sacramento, California: Cheryl Anne Stapp, 2012);

Stapp, C. A., *Sacramento Chronicles: A Golden Past* (Charleston, S.C.: The History Press, 2013)

Starr, K., *Americans and the California Dream 1850–1915* (New York: Oxford University Press, 1973)

Wall, B. M., *Unlikely Entrepreneurs Catholic Sisters and the Hospital Marketplace, 1865–1925* (Columbus, Ohio: The Ohio State University Press, 2005)

Weakland, R. G., O.S. B., "Religious Life in the U.S.—Understanding the Moment" in Philibert, P. J. (ed.), *Living in the Meantime Concerning the Transformation of Religious Life* (New York: Paulist Press, 1994), pp. 197–213

Newspaper Holdings

Sacramento Bee (1857–2008)

NBSPL: All citations from the *Sacramento Bee* may be accessed through: *NewsBank: Sacramento Bee—Historical and Current, 0-infoweb*-newsbankcom.www. saclibrarycatalog.org/apps/news/document-view

Sacramento Union (1857–1980)

All citations from the *Sacramento Union* may be accessed through CDNC (California Digital Newspaper Collection), Center for Bibliographic Studies and Research, University of California, Riverside, cdnc.ucr.edu

Catholic Herald (1908, 1922 to present)

Index